THE GREAT DEMOCRACY

ALSO BY GANESH SITARAMAN

The Public Option:
How to Expand Freedom, Increase Opportunity,
and Promote Equality (with Anne L. Alstott)

The Crisis of the Middle-Class Constitution:
Why Economic Inequality Threatens Our Republic

The Counterinsurgent's Constitution:
Law in the Age of Small Wars

Invisible Citizens: Youth Politics after September 11
(ed., with Previn Warren)

THE GREAT DEMOCRACY

HOW TO FIX OUR POLITICS,
UNRIG THE ECONOMY,
AND UNITE AMERICA

GANESH SITARAMAN

BASIC BOOKS
New York

Basic Books
Hachette Book Group
1290 Avenue of the Americas, New York, NY 10104
www.basicbooks.com

Printed in the United States of America

First Edition: December 2019

Published by Basic Books, an imprint of Perseus Books, LLC, a subsidiary of Hachette Book Group, Inc. The Basic Books name and logo is a trademark of the Hachette Book Group.

The Hachette Speakers Bureau provides a wide range of authors for speaking events. To find out more, go to www.hachettespeakersbureau.com or call (866) 376-6591.

The publisher is not responsible for websites (or their content) that are not owned by the publisher.

Print book interior design by Amnet Systems.

Library of Congress Control Number: 2019948649

ISBNs: 978-1-5416-1811-4 (hardcover), 978-1-5416-1810-7 (ebook)

LSC-C
10 9 8 7 6 5 4 3 2 1

CONTENTS

INTRODUCTION
THE EDGE OF A NEW ERA

This is not an ordinary political moment. Everywhere around us, the old order is collapsing. The golden age of postwar economic growth is over, replaced by a new Gilded Age of inequality and stagnation. The long march toward justice and equality now faces intolerant resistance storming the streets. People once united by common culture and information are now fractured into social media echo chambers. The liberal international order is cracking as nationalism grows in strength and global institutions decay. The United States' role as a global superpower is challenged by the rising strength of China and a new era of Russian assertiveness. Optimists hope that generational and demographic change will restore inexorable progress. Pessimists interpret the current moment as the decline and fall of democracy.

Moments of extraordinary political change, moments like this one, have long fascinated political observers. Since the time of the Greeks and Romans, political observers believed that history was cyclical. Monarchies, aristocracies, and republics would degrade into tyrannies, oligarchies, and mob rule, leading ultimately to revolution and the creation of a new regime. In the United States, Henry Adams—the grandson and great-grandson of presidents and a distinguished historian—thought history was like a pendulum, oscillating between unity and complexity. Arthur Schlesinger Jr. argued that history moved in phases, periods in which one approach to politics dominated only to be replaced by another. The idea came from his father, who had once written that politics moved like the tides, ebbing and flowing between periods of public purpose and private interest.[1]

Nor has this way of thinking been limited to historians. The economist Joseph Schumpeter understood capitalism through the business cycle, emphasizing entrepreneurs and creative destruction rather than stability and equilibrium. Thomas Kuhn described the march of science as a series of revolutionary paradigm shifts. One framework would dominate for a time, but exceptions would eventually undermine the paradigm, and another would take its place.[2]

The premise and argument of this book is that we are currently in the midst of one of these epochal transitions. We live on the edge of a new era in politics—the third since the Great Depression and World War II. The first era is probably best described as liberal. *Liberal* is a complicated word, with almost as many meanings as there are individuals who use it. But from the 1940s through the 1970s, a version of political liberalism provided the paradigm for politics. Charting a path between the state control of communists and fascists and the laissez-faire market that dominated before the Great Depression, liberals adopted a form of regulated capitalism. Government set the rules of the road for the economy, regulated finance, invested to create jobs and spark consumer demand, policed the bad behavior of businesses, and provided a social safety net for Americans. Big institutions—big government, big corporations, big labor—cooperated to balance the needs of stakeholders in society. In the United States, it was called New Deal Liberalism. In Europe, social democracy. There were differences across countries, of course, but the general approach was similar.

The best proof that this was a liberal era is that even the conservatives of the time were liberal. Republican president Dwight Eisenhower championed the national highway system and warned of the military-industrial complex. President Richard Nixon said, "I am now a Keynesian in economics." His administration created the EPA and expanded Social Security by indexing benefits to inflation. The Tory prime minister Harold Macmillan in Britain didn't undo the National Health Service; he passed the 1956 Clean Air

Act and supported full employment. On the international stage, economic policy was a form of embedded liberalism, markets wrapped in the political and social needs of states and individuals, empowering national welfare states while facilitating international economic cooperation. Containment—which involved accepting the existence of the Soviet Union—was the North Star of foreign policy across the political spectrum.[3]

In the United States, the liberal era reached its end with Democratic president Jimmy Carter. In control of the House, Senate, and presidency, Democrats could only pass a watered-down Full Employment Act that abandoned their long-held goals, and they failed to pass modest labor law reforms altogether. Their coalition seemed increasingly fractured between more conservative Democrats like Carter and old liberals like Senator Ted Kennedy (who challenged Carter for the presidency in 1980). An increasing number of people worried that liberalism's solutions were unsuited to the challenges of the time.[4]

Since the 1980s, we have lived in a second era—that of neoliberalism. In economic and social policy, neoliberalism's tenets are simple: deregulation, privatization, liberalization, and austerity. Under neoliberalism, individuals are on their own and should be responsible for themselves. Instead of governments, corporations, and unions balancing the interests of all stakeholders, the primary regulator of social interests should be the marketplace. Neoliberals opposed unions and unionization, they wanted to pursue vouchers instead of public provision of services, and they sought to shrink the size and functioning of government, even if it meant a less effective government. Markets worked like magic, and market logic would be applied to all aspects of life. Around the world, the neoliberal era came with an aggressive emphasis on expanding democracy and human rights, even by military force. Expanding trade and commerce came with little regard for who the winners and losers were—or what the political fallout might be.

Although many of them chafe at this label, even the liberals were neoliberal during this era. It was President Bill Clinton who said that the "era of big government is over" and who celebrated legislation deregulating Wall Street. Prime Minister Tony Blair pioneered the Third Way in Britain, transforming Labour into New Labour and embracing market principles. After the Great Recession, the United States and Europe toyed with Keynesian spending but soon opted for austerity. Even core aspects of the Affordable Care Act—the signature achievement of President Barack Obama—were originally developed by the Heritage Foundation, a conservative think tank. Obamacare's central feature is not public provision of health insurance; it is a system of private markets with targeted subsidies. Around the world, the Washington Consensus united liberals and conservatives who pushed liberalization policies on developing countries through economic diplomacy and the International Monetary Fund. Both parties also adopted aggressive foreign policies to expand democracy and human rights abroad; the main difference was that neoconservatives were willing to go it alone while liberal internationalists preferred to operate through the United Nations.[5]

With the election of Donald Trump, the neoliberal era has reached its end. While in control of the House, Senate, and presidency, Republicans neither repealed the Affordable Care Act nor privatized Social Security and Medicare. Their party is increasingly fractured between Trumpist conservatives, who are far more nationalist, and the never-Trump old-line conservatives like Bill Kristol or Jeb Bush. An increasing number of people recognize that neoliberalism's solutions are unsuited to the challenges of our time.[6]

Liberalism and neoliberalism each rose to power in response to specific problems. Each grew dominant, overextended, and, unable to adapt to new realities, ultimately collapsed. Liberalism lost its force as the crisis of the 1970s brought economic challenges—oil shocks, unemployment and inflation, competition from rising economies, personal anxieties, and family insecurity. Neoliberalism lost its force with the economic crisis and the Great Recession; with deregulation, privatization, and liberalization proving a failure at maintaining economic stability and security for all; and with increasing social fracturing. In the wake of both crises, people floundered for years before a new paradigm took hold. They were, as Matthew Arnold once wrote, "wandering between two worlds, one dead, the other powerless to be born."[7]

The central question of our time is what comes next. The transition between eras is never sharp, and the collapse of the old regime often contains within it the seeds of the new. Neoliberalism has left us with a social crisis, a breakdown of community values and solidarity. And it has left us with a political and economic crisis in which both arenas are rigged to work for the wealthy and well connected rather than the general public.

Four possible responses to these crises could define the next era of politics. The first possibility is reformed neoliberalism, keeping the system essentially intact while sanding off some of the rough and inhumane edges. This approach, with its nostalgic wish to get things back to "normal," simply threatens more of the same: persistent disaffection, further erosions of trust and social solidarity, and demagogues waiting in the wings.

The second possibility is nationalist populism, which combines ethnic, religious, or cultural nationalism with economic populism. This approach, most associated with Steve Bannon, might be compelling to significant swaths of the population. But it seems unlikely, as political and economic elites oppose both tenets of the framework. Indeed, Candidate Trump campaigned in 2016 on this agenda only to abandon it as president.

The third possibility, which many refer to as authoritarianism, has gotten the most attention. Scholars and commentators have argued that there is a global rise in autocracy. Political insurgents around the world are channeling popular unrest to win surprising victories. Strongman regimes are breaking constitutional constraints and norms. Meanwhile, constitutional democracies are on the ropes. There is a proliferation of books and pamphlets with titles such as *How Democracies Die*, *Fascism: A Warning*, and *On Tyranny*, all seeking to awaken Americans to the looming threat. They argue that electoral rules, political institutions, the free press, and

constitutional norms are critical to the functioning of democracy—
and that their erosion comes with a creeping authoritarianism.[8]

These accounts are alarming, but they misdiagnose the problem. Getting the diagnosis right is critical because an inaccurate
description of this ascendant form of government will lead to a
flawed response. The rise-of-authoritarianism story focuses almost
exclusively on political and constitutional constraints. These commentators worry about the breaking of constitutional and political
norms, assaults on the independent media, and the politicization
of the judiciary. Each is hugely important. But they largely ignore
the economic and social aspects of these so-called authoritarian
countries. They rarely discuss that these nations are run by a small
number of oligarchs who rely on crony capitalism and political
corruption to get rich and then use divide-and-conquer nationalist
tactics to mobilize the people and stay in power.

The better term for this third future is nationalist oligarchy. This
form of government feeds nationalism to the people but delivers
oligarchy—special privileges to the rich and well connected. Its economic approach is a corrupt outgrowth of neoliberalism. Its social
policy is nationalist backlash. Its political program involves rigging
the rules so popular majorities cannot overthrow the powerful.
Nationalist oligarchy is undesirable, to say the least—but it could
easily define the next era of politics.

The final possibility is that a new era of democracy will follow the age of neoliberalism. Just as it is a mistake to reduce
nationalist oligarchy to authoritarian politics, it is wrong to think
that preserving elections, voting, the free press, and constitutional
norms will be sufficient for democracy. Democracy has always
demanded much more of societies and individuals. For thousands
of years, since at least the ancient Greeks, political leaders and
philosophers have recognized that democracies could not succeed
in the presence of extreme economic inequality. In an unequal
society, either the rich would oppress the poor and democracy
would descend slowly into oligarchy, or the masses would overthrow the rich, with a demagogue leading the way to tyranny.

Economic democracy is therefore critical to the persistence of democracy.

Similarly, when a society is deeply divided by race, religion, clan, tribe, or ideology, democracy becomes difficult to sustain. Democracy requires us to determine our own destiny. But when the people are so divided that we aim toward diametrically opposed futures, politics increasingly becomes a zero-sum conflict, the equivalent of warfare rather than the exercise of freedom. "A house divided against itself," Lincoln famously noted, "cannot stand." A measure of social solidarity, a united democracy, is thus essential to the functioning of democracy.

An economic and united democracy cannot be achieved or sustained without a political process that is responsive to the people. Political democracy means more than just the right to vote. It requires that elections capture the popular will rather than the will of interest groups and wealthy individuals, that elected officials act in the public interest rather than doing the bidding of lobbyists, and that civil servants and judges do not stray from their popular mandates. As important as constitutional restraints and protections of minorities are, majoritarianism is critical to democracy. A system of government that is mostly unresponsive to the people is not a democracy at all.

The core problem with our democracy today is that we have never truly achieved what democracy requires. Democracy in America was severely restricted before the liberal era. But the people of that era reined in economic power during the New Deal, expanded economic opportunity through the GI Bill and investments in the New Frontier, and fought a war on poverty to promote economic equality and build a Great Society. And in the midst of these reforms, they struggled fiercely to end Jim Crow, integrate the nation racially, and promote equal rights for women and minorities—because they knew that segregation could never mean equality, let alone solidarity. Their efforts caused massive upheaval, and democracy—real democracy—was visible on the horizon.

But the late 1960s and early 1970s also brought warfare and economic, social, and political crises—and with them, the exhaustion of the liberal era and the ultimate emergence of the neoliberal era. The neoliberal era's individualistic and market-focused ideology then prevented the realization of democracy. It put economic growth above a strong middle class, leading to century-high levels of inequality. It emphasized individuals over communities and divided us by race, class, and culture. And because it preferred markets to democracy, it looked away as the wealthiest people and corporations rigged the government to serve their own interests, even at the expense of everyone else.

If a new era of democracy is to take hold, we will need an agenda commensurate with the scope of our challenges. We must become a united democracy by creating opportunities for civic engagement across our differences and by refusing to fall prey to divide-and-conquer tactics that perpetuate rule by the rich and powerful. We must create an economic democracy by breaking up economic power and expanding opportunity for people of all races and from all geographies. We must reclaim political democracy from lobbyists, interest groups, and wealthy donors while ensuring that everyone can participate. And we must defend democracy from national oligarchies abroad. This agenda does not look backward to a bygone era with promises to make America great again. Instead, it looks forward to the future. As Theodore Roosevelt once said, "A great democracy has got to be progressive, or it will soon cease to be either great or a democracy."[9]

The neoliberal era has put us in this moment of crisis, and the central battle of our time is now between nationalist oligarchy and democracy. The fight for a great democracy will require boldness and creativity, courage and resolve. It cannot be nostalgic because at the very moment democracy was last within reach, it eluded our grasp. If we want to save democracy, we will need to achieve democracy.

1
THE ORIGINS AND MEANING
OF NEOLIBERALISM

The day after Ronald Reagan won the presidency in 1980, the PBS television show *The MacNeil/Lehrer Report* convened a panel of experts for the usual election postmortem. Pat Buchanan, former Nixon aide and future presidential candidate, called the election a "rejection of the Carter administration," but more importantly, a "repudiation of the liberal philosophy, because by and large the liberals were defeated." If Reagan could continue stealing blue-collar Democrats, Buchanan foresaw the creation of a "grand coalition . . . realigning the parties."

Anthony Lewis, columnist at the *New York Times*, largely agreed with Buchanan and thought the election was a "conservative revolution" not directed solely at Jimmy Carter. But his analysis was slightly broader even than Buchanan's: this was a "conservative time," he said, in which traditional liberals were never going to win—and that partly explained the loss of twelve Senate Democrats in addition to Carter. In this new era, the Democrats were a "party without an idea."

But the most interesting comments came later in the program, from Morton Kondracke, the executive editor of the *New Republic*. The magazine had historically been a bastion of progressive and liberal thought, but it had endorsed Republican-turned-Independent John Anderson for president that year. Anderson, of course, never had a chance and ultimately won zero states and received zero electoral votes.

Representing the rogue liberal magazine, Kondracke argued that the entire worldview of the Democratic Party had failed and that the election was a repudiation not just of Carter but of President Lyndon Johnson's Great Society. Far from being an armchair critic, Kondracke also came with a solution: "It seems to me that what the Democratic Party has to adopt is some sort of a—what might be called a neoliberal ideology."

Jim Lehrer had clearly never heard the phrase. "What in the world is that, Mort?"

Kondracke had an answer. He said it meant embracing the traditional Democratic values of compassion for the downtrodden, but without government action through things like bureaucratic programs. He cited Senators Gary Hart and Paul Tsongas as exemplars of this new liberal ideology. At the time both were young members of Congress; with neoliberalism on the ascent, they would each run for the presidency in the years to come.

Pat Buchanan chimed in and rejected Kondracke's position. He didn't think Democrats needed to repudiate the New Deal or the Great Society and certainly not President John F. Kennedy's muscular, patriotic New Frontier. If Democrats adopted Kondracke's neoliberal approach, Buchanan warned, they would cease to offer voters a choice. They would become "what the Republican Party used to be—a 'me too' party" that stood for nothing more than "let's split the difference on this proposal."[1]

This one exchange, at the dawn of the Reagan administration, captured many of the core features and controversies of politics in the neoliberal era: the ideological dominance of conservatives, the strategy of liberals adopting conservative tactics, and the risks of liberals becoming a pale imitation of conservatives.

But before going further, it is necessary to go back to Jim Lehrer's question: What in the world is neoliberalism?

Forty years after Reagan's election, the term is becoming more and more prominent—from newspapers and magazine articles to scores of academic studies. To some, it is nothing more than a slur, an insult socialists hurl against conservatives, centrists, liberals, and

even progressives. To others, it is synonymous with global capitalism. Still others think of it as a totalizing ideology that touches not
just public policy but all aspects of life. Of course, historians are
quick to note that its meaning has shifted over the eighty-year period in which it has been in use.

For the most part, the various uses of neoliberalism relate closely
to the common understanding of the term in public policy—or at
least derive from its worldview. Neoliberalism is an approach to
public policy that relies on individuals operating through private
markets as much as possible. The role of the state is to provide a
minimal framework for markets, and to the extent that government
acts, it should do so in ways that maximize market strategies.[2]

The intellectual origins of neoliberalism go back to conservative economists and intellectuals of the 1920s. But its most famous
proponents were Friedrich Hayek, organizer of the Mont Pelerin
Society, and his junior-partner-turned-popularizer, Milton Friedman. Hayek was an Austrian economist who spent most of the
1930s as a professor at the London School of Economics. Ever
a skeptic of government action, he dissented from John Maynard
Keynes's approach to economic policy during the Great Depression
and even debated the giant in a series of journal articles. In 1938,
Hayek helped bring together a colloquium to celebrate Walter Lippmann's book *The Good Society*, which argued for a renewed form
of liberalism—one that critics and supporters alike characterized
as neoliberalism. The goal of neoliberalism was largely economic:
ensure free enterprise and prevent price regulation. Hayek's group
met again in 1947 at Mont Pèlerin, Switzerland. The first meeting
of the newly christened Mont Pelerin Society included a variety
of past and future luminaries who would work over the years to
advance the cause of neoliberalism. Hayek's efforts at institution
building didn't stop there. Over time, he orchestrated the creation
of a cohort of like-minded intellectuals at the University of Chicago, including Milton Friedman. The Chicago School, as it was
called, would come to outline neoliberalism in economics, law, and
public policy.[3]

Hayek's intellectual arguments also paved the way for the emergence of neoliberalism as a force in the late twentieth century. Although his 1944 book, *The Road to Serfdom*, was often balanced in supporting a role for government in the economy, from the title on down, the book's rhetoric frequently boiled down to a slippery slope argument. Government action anywhere risked tyranny and fascism everywhere. The conclusion of many slippery slope arguments is not to articulate and defend a sensible, balanced policy but to reject it in favor of something more radical. And this is what made *The Road to Serfdom* so politically potent in the postwar fights over public policy. Hayek's ideas offered an ideological counterpoint to the extremes of authoritarianism and communism—one that conservative activists used to argue against even moderate liberal policies. Anti-communist critic Max Eastman and *Reader's Digest* editor DeWitt Wallace took it upon themselves to reprint *The Road to Serfdom* in the popular magazine. Their edition, in the words of one historian, was "less an abridgement than a re-creation." Sentences were "reordered and reconnected," "new sentences were written," and "qualifications were lost." The real *Road to Serfdom* sold forty thousand copies. The *Reader's Digest* edition sold a million copies. Corporations like General Motors and New Jersey Power and Light gave reprints of the revised edition to their employees. The National Association of Manufacturers sent copies to its fourteen thousand members. The partisan success of *The Road to Serfdom* made Hayek a celebrity and public intellectual, though this newfound status cost him legitimacy within the economics profession. Years later, Hayek would comment, "I discredited myself by publishing *The Road to Serfdom*."[4]

Milton Friedman had no such misgivings about his role as a popularizer of ideas. For all their similarities, Hayek and Friedman were fundamentally different. Hayek was a senior figure when he created the Mont Pelerin Society. Friedman was a junior economist who said the Swiss conference was what "got me started in policy and what led to *Capitalism and Freedom*," his popular bestseller. Hayek didn't have organizations to help him navigate public affairs.

By the time Friedman was writing for the public, he benefited from a variety of organizations that had emerged to support neoliberal ideas, including those Hayek had helped create. And importantly, Hayek and the other founders of the Mont Pelerin Society were writing during and in response to the Great Depression, when the ideologies of the future were an open question. Friedman's context was the Cold War, an era of existential conflict between two ideological adversaries.[5]

Friedman's 1962 book, *Capitalism and Freedom*, articulated a far more radical and minimalistic vision of government. Friedman thought that unregulated monopolies were unlikely to be threatening to society. He was skeptical of government action to alleviate poverty. He called for abolishing the minimum wage, public housing, and even national parks. He wanted to get rid of the Federal Communications Commission and, later, the Food and Drug Administration. Over time, Friedman would also register opposition to the Marshall Plan and promote privatization of education through school vouchers. After supporting Senator Barry Goldwater's failed presidential run in 1964, Friedman continued his advocacy. "Ideas have little chance of making much headway against a strong tide," Friedman once wrote. "Their opportunity comes when the tide has ceased running strong but has not yet turned."[6]

By the 1970s, the tide of liberalism had ceased running strong. Economically, the decade ushered in wave after wave of anxiety and insecurity. The 1973 Arab oil embargo and resulting energy shortage hit consumers hard. That same year, the US stock market plummeted, losing half its value and leaving the economy in a recession until 1975. Inflation and a stagnant economy pushed Americans from saving to borrowing. Competition from abroad was also on the rise. At the end of World War II, most of the countries in the world with significant industrial potential were either lying in smoldering ruins or still under the thumb of colonialism. By the 1970s, these countries had bounced back, were industrializing, and were offering goods on the global market. Commentators worried about a "crisis of industrial society." From 1967 to 1977,

Boston, Philadelphia, Pittsburgh, and Chicago saw manufacturing down by a third.[7]

Economic shocks were not limited to the United States. Fixed exchange rates were abandoned in 1971, fundamentally changing the Bretton Woods monetary system that had existed since the end of World War II. The IMF had to bail out Great Britain in 1976, demoralizing the Labour Party and imposing greater spending cuts than was necessary. Declaring the end of Keynesian economic policy, Prime Minister James Callaghan remarked to the Labour Party conference, "We used to think you could spend your way out of a recession and increase employment by cutting taxes and boosting government spending. I tell you in all candor that option no longer exists." In the winter of 1978–1979, when Callaghan called for a limited pay increase for union workers, the unions protested. During the "winter of discontent," schools were closed, mountains of trash filled the streets, and the dead were left unburied. "It was not a revolution, or an attempt to overthrow a government," BBC reporter Andrew Marr writes in his history of modern Britain. "Yet that is the effect it had."[8]

The social conditions that helped build the postwar liberal era were also increasingly under stress. In this era, a rising middle class and growing economy meant that the expansion of civil rights, economic rights, and social opportunities posed comparatively little threat to economic security. The 1950s and 1960s brought progress along all these lines—from *Brown v. Board of Education* to the Civil Rights, Voting Rights, and Immigration Acts of the Johnson years. But in the new, anxious world of the 1970s, working-class whites began to fear that scarcity, not abundance, would define the future. As society became more inclusive, offering greater opportunities to women and minorities than ever before in history, people began to fear that the result would be a zero-sum economic game.[9]

Big business contributed to this anxiety as well. Since the end of World War II, big business had cooperated with government and unions to establish a form of regulated capitalism in which the benefits of economic growth were broadly shared. Regulations blocked the most egregious and speculative practices, particularly in the financial sector. Taxes were extremely high: top marginal tax rates were 90 percent during the postwar years and remained at 70 percent after the Kennedy tax cut. Perhaps most importantly, business and labor worked together to share their success. Under the Treaty of Detroit, manufacturers agreed to provide significant social welfare benefits to employees—health insurance, pensions—in addition to regular wage increases. The result was that workers, managers, and shareholders alike benefited from growth.

The 1970s brought the end of the business-labor-government partnership. Big business terminated the Treaty of Detroit, ending the era of cooperation. The Chamber of Commerce, the Business Roundtable, the National Association of Manufacturers, and other groups now fiercely opposed even moderate labor law reforms proposed during the Carter administration and increasingly targeted unions, wage increases, and benefits provision in order to cut costs and increase profits. George Meany, the head of the AFL-CIO, asked businesses in the *Wall Street Journal*: "Do you secretly seek a death sentence for the collective bargaining system you so often hail in public forums?" Republican senator Orrin Hatch said the late 1970s was the "starting point for a new era of assertiveness by big business in Washington."[10]

With the crisis of the 1970s, as John Kenneth Galbraith once remarked, "the age of John Maynard Keynes gave way to the age of Milton Friedman." A new type of politician came to power, pushing neoliberalism against the reigning liberal consensus. In his first inaugural address, Ronald Reagan famously announced, "Government is not the solution to our problem; government is the problem." Once in office, Reaganomics had four pillars: cut government spending, cut taxes, deregulate, and fight inflation through monetary policy. Prime Minister Margaret Thatcher's agenda wasn't so different: reduce taxes and spending, break the power of unions, privatize government services, and shift monetary policy away from a focus on unemployment.[11]

The spread of these ideas was not limited to the United States and Britain. Neoliberalism was global from the start: Malcolm Fraser in Australia in 1975, Deng Xiaoping in China in 1979, Brian Mulroney in Canada in 1984. Although contexts were different in every country, neoliberalism's core came to be associated with four elements: deregulation, liberalization, privatization, and austerity, or DLPA.[12]

Deregulation

Deregulation really involves two things: not issuing new regulations and rolling back existing regulations. Neoliberals generally have a rosy view of markets and profit seekers. As a result, they think that the marketplace will generally do a fine job of policing fraud and bad behavior and that most regulations are unnecessary. Of course, regulation of some kind is essential for neoliberals: private property rules and contract laws, for example, are critical for markets to function. But the goal is to minimize the rules.

Reagan's deregulation agenda, for example, began immediately. The president banned the promulgation of any new regulations, appointed deregulatory heads of agencies, and tasked the vice president with leading a task force on regulatory relief. Within six months, some 180 regulations had been "withdrawn, modified, or delayed." Reagan's Department of Transportation quickly rescinded a rule requiring auto manufacturers to install seat belts or airbags in cars, claiming there would be virtually no safety benefits from those technologies. The administration also "eased or eliminated price controls on oil and natural gas, cable TV, long-distance telephone service, interstate bus service, and ocean shipping."[13]

In 1982, the administration supported deregulation of the saving and loans sector, which allowed the S&Ls to take on broader— and riskier—lending practices. Instead of placing limits on these risky behaviors, the neoliberal approach instead suggested more deregulation—now for S&L bookkeeping rules. The ultimate result was the S&L crisis in the late 1980s, which cost taxpayers $124 billion in bailouts and interest.[14]

Environmental inaction was also particularly notable. During Reagan's first term, enforcement of strip-mining laws was down 62 percent, and enforcement of hazardous waste was down 50 percent. Exposure levels to chemicals were increased. In 1982 alone, the government approved 97 percent of business petitions for an "emergency" ability to use otherwise banned pesticides. In the mid-1980s, more than 375,000 hazardous waste sites needed reform, mostly because they threatened to pollute groundwater. During Reagan's first four years, his EPA cleaned only six of these sites, and in 1985, the administration proposed zero funding for groundwater programs and suggested ending the Superfund program for toxic waste cleanup altogether.[15]

Democrats were on board with deregulation too. During the Clinton era, the Telecommunications Act of 1996 deregulated the sector, allowing the consolidation of television stations and radio stations, increased cross-ownership of cable and broadcast networks, and higher cable prices. The Gramm-Leach-Bliley Act of 1999 deregulated the financial sector, repealing parts of the New Deal–Era Glass-Steagall regime, which barred investment banks, depository banks, and insurance companies from consolidating. Regulators had watered down the Glass-Steagall regime over the years, but the 1999 law ended a system that had worked since the 1930s. A year later, big banks succeeded in pushing Congress to exempt complex financial products called over-the-counter derivatives from regulation—which would play an important role in the 2008 financial crash.

Labor also serves as a regulator in the economy—and it, too, came under attack. In Britain, coal miners went on strike in 1984 and gained considerable sympathy across the country. Had the head of the union not made a series of tactical errors, the strike might have brought down Thatcher's government. But the prime minister had prepared for precisely this occasion—and she refused to cave to the union's demands. Thatcher's commitment to fight unions was so strong that she would prevent her government from settling with public sector workers, even if cutting a deal would be financially better for British taxpayers.[16]

Although Reagan had been a member of the Screen Actors Guild, he, too, contributed to labor's decline. Appointees at the National Labor Relations Board and the Department of Labor were part of the strategy, but the marquee event was breaking the air traffic controllers strike. The Professional Air Traffic Controllers Organization (PATCO) sought higher pay given rapidly rising inflation. When they went on strike, Reagan fired eleven thousand air traffic controllers. No one thought Reagan would do it, and the consequences were significant. Strikes had long been one of the most effective tools for labor unions to get managers to bargain. But with a hostile federal government willing to declare war on workers, the number of strikes per year collapsed—and with it the power of the working class.[17]

The British Labour Party had worker power built into its DNA, but even that changed with the rise of neoliberalism. From the time of its founding in 1918, the party had advocated for common—rather than private—ownership as a way to ensure a broad distribution of wealth in society and prevent the accumulation of private power. This commitment was codified as Clause IV in the party's manifesto. In 1995, Tony Blair took perhaps the boldest symbolic step he could in reforming the Labour Party. He pushed for Labour to drop Clause IV from its manifesto. Blair argued that the means and ends of politics were different. Economic equality as an end did not require common ownership as a means. When Blair won the fight, New Labour was born.[18]

Liberalization

Liberalization is the global counterpart to deregulation. The goal is to unleash the free flow of goods, capital, people, and services across borders. Neoliberalism thus champions globalization and mandates that foreign countries deregulate internally. But although this approach might sometimes seem inescapable today, the global economic system was not always designed with these goals in mind.

From the end of World War II until the end of the 1970s, the international economic system was best characterized as what

John Ruggie once called embedded liberalism. The foundational idea, inspired by the work of economist Karl Polanyi, was that markets are embedded in society and cannot be disentangled from broader social and political considerations. As a result, the architects of the postwar system balanced two separate concerns. First, they wanted to establish a freer international trade system than the one that immediately preceded the war. Second, they wanted to ensure that countries had the freedom to encourage full employment and establish social safety nets and welfare programs. The Bretton Woods system, adopted in a 1944 agreement, thus placed restrictions on capital controls, pegged currencies to gold, and created the IMF and World Bank. The system was neither laissez-faire nor radically protectionist. Rather, it balanced the interests of different stakeholders within and across countries.[19]

In the 1970s, embedded liberalism came to an end. Richard Nixon unpegged the US dollar from gold, making it a fiat currency and effectively terminating the Bretton Woods system. Over the decade, countries began to unwind capital controls. The two aims of embedded liberalism were eventually both under assault: neoliberals pushed increasingly for international agreements that guaranteed laissez-faire trade and, starting in the 1980s, advocated for abolishing the safety net and deemphasizing government action on unemployment.

Historically, trade policy had always focused on two goals: domestic economics and foreign policy. The domestic economic goals of trade are sometimes seen as protectionist—incubating infant industries, raising revenues, protecting workers, maintaining a middle class—and they dominated trade policy in the United States from the eighteenth century to the mid-twentieth century. Foreign policy goals are purely geopolitical—the use of trade agreements and sanctions to win friends and punish enemies—and they were central at the height of the Cold War.

Neoliberalism abandoned both in search of global economic growth and efficiency. It brought a shift from merely dismantling the pre–World War II era restrictions on trade to a new age of hyperglobalization. The general argument was that dropping trade barriers would enlarge the economic pie, and under conventional economic theory, the benefits from liberalizing trade would be more than enough to compensate the losers. But in reality, neoliberals never compensated the losers adequately. Labor and environmental standards are touted as protections but almost never enforced. Trade Adjustment Assistance—money for workers to retrain— is minimal, ineffective, and time limited. Corporate profits and reduced costs, on the other hand, are gigantic and, like diamonds, seem to last forever.[20]

In the United States, trade law and policy followed this course. From the 1930s until 1974, the trade regime gave significant power to the president to lower tariffs. Successive presidents did so, but they emphasized the geopolitical benefits of particular trade agreements, and Congress retained considerable power over nontariff barriers—basically any regulation or other government action because they all can be interpreted as a barrier to trade. Increasingly in the 1970s and 1980s, Congress gave the president even more power, including fast-track authority and power to negotiate changes in nontariff barriers. This delegation of power further unhooked trade from domestic economic goals (which Congress polices more carefully than the president does). In addition, as the president and his trade negotiators embraced neoliberalism, they began to see trade as an end in itself, always to be expanded.[21]

The contemporary view that neoliberalism is coextensive with global capitalism is a function of the World Bank, IMF, and many Western countries that promoted the DLPA agenda abroad during the 1980s, 1990s, and 2000s. This approach was called the Washington Consensus, and it included a ten-point program of fiscal discipline, reduced public spending, tax reform, financial liberalization, competitive exchange rates, trade liberalization, foreign direct investment, privatization, deregulation, and property rights. The program was designed for Latin America in the

1980s, but the IMF and the World Bank became "missionary institutions" and used this framework to proselytize the world. *Proselytize* might be too weak of a word. In reality, the Washington Consensus was imposed at the barrel of a checkbook; if a country wanted or needed international loans, it was locked into the IMF's draconian conditions. So strong were the IMF and World Bank's ideological convictions that staff for the global institutions would write reports advising countries prior to visiting the country for fact-finding missions.[22]

Most famously, Washington Consensus economists pushed for Russia to embrace "shock therapy" after the collapse of the Soviet Union. This meant rapid economic liberalization (especially on price controls and currency), privatization of public institutions, and trade liberalization. Neoliberalism's DLPA agenda was thus not just a matter of domestic policy; it became an objective of foreign policy as well. With the supposed end of history after the Cold War, the theory went even a step further, as policy makers came to believe that spreading neoliberal capitalism would also lead countries to more open and pluralistic political systems. China's admission to the World Trade Organization in 2000 represents the pinnacle of this idea. The theory was that entry into the global trade system would push the state-capitalist country to reform internally, becoming at once more liberal and more democratic.

The project for European integration also pushed forward the cause of liberalization. In 1985 and 1986, Thatcher began to realign Great Britain toward Europe, championing the Single European Act. The act boosted European integration and promised to advance four liberties: the free movement of goods, services, capital, and people. The plan was, in the words of one commentator, "a crash programme of Euro-Thatcherism" that would involve deregulation, privatization, and liberalization across the continent. The act also created momentum for a single monetary and political union. Decades later, Tony Blair would take up Thatcher's mantle of further European integration. So committed was Blair to European integration along these lines that he was commonly proposed as the future president of a fully integrated Europe.[23]

Privatization

Privatization is shorthand for the view that democratic governments should not, by and large, provide public services to their citizens. The private sector should instead offer these services. To the extent that government is already providing such services, those services should be turned over to the private sector. And if people want services and cannot afford them, the government should subsidize the private system through vouchers and tax credits rather than offer a public option.

Privatization of public services had not been a major part of the Tory manifesto in 1979—they thought it would frighten off voters—but it was central to Thatcher's governing agenda. At the end of the 1970s, the British government owned or operated a variety of public services and industries: "It ran railways, shipbuilding, car making, coal mining, ports and harbours, airlines and airports, gas, electricity, nuclear energy and arms manufacture. It owned the nation's hospitals, schools, prisons and old people's homes, and ran a national pension scheme." Privatization took British Telecom and British Gas out of the public realm. And Thatcher moved public housing (called council houses) into private hands, in the process creating a new generation of homeowners. But with privatization afoot, local governments stopped building new public housing, meaning the central government now had to provide subsidies to unaccountable, undemocratic nonprofits to accomplish the same goals. In effect, the first era of privatization in Britain replaced local government provision with central government subsidies.[24]

Privatization moved a little more slowly during the Reagan years. During his first term, the administration made some privatization proposals: private prisons, the sale of federal lands, the use of housing vouchers instead of building public housing. But it wasn't until 1987 that the Reagan administration thought of privatization as a "general, unified strategy for reducing the size and scope of the federal government." In remarks announcing the creation of a Privatization Commission, Reagan tasked the group with "propos[ing] how we can return appropriate Federal activities to the private sector through the sale of government operations and assets, the use of private enterprise to provide services for government agencies, or the use of vouchers to provide services to the public through the private sector." Selling, outsourcing, and vouchers—these were the key tools of the neoliberal era's privatization agenda.[25]

Democrats also joined the privatization bandwagon—and early on. At a 1981 dinner hosted by *Esquire* magazine, Congressman Richard Gephardt of Missouri declared, "I would get rid of government in health care. I would get rid of government in education to a much greater extent than we have. I would discharge those responsibilities either to the private sector or to the states." Few conservatives could have put it better.[26]

During the Clinton administration, Vice President Al Gore was tasked with reinventing government, an initiative that also included privatization. Over time, the Seafood Inspection Service was privatized; mine safety accreditation, privatized; background checks for government contractors, privatized; petroleum reserves, the United States Enrichment Corporation, electromagnetic spectrum, airport control towers, the list goes on—all privatized. Reagan's head of privatization said that the Clinton administration had "the boldest privatization agenda put forth by any American president to date."[27]

Blair claimed that he did not support privatization on anti-government grounds. "Privatization," Blair said in 1999, "should have a role to play not out of dogmatism but out of pragmatism." But whether it was dogmatism or pragmatism, the consequence was the same. Blair and Chancellor of the Exchequer Gordon Brown sought to privatize air traffic control, the Royal Mint, and the Commonwealth Development Corporation. Even the Royal

Mail and National Rail, which the Iron Lady had forbid as a bridge much too far, were on the list. She was right. The privatization of rail ended up costing British taxpayers five times as much as nationalized rail.[28]

Austerity

When most people think of austerity, they think of fiscal policy, but here the term is shorthand for broader macroeconomic policy—both fiscal and monetary. Neoliberals have a few policy goals when it comes to austerity. First is that monetary policy should focus primarily on inflation and not on both inflation and unemployment, as the Keynesian liberal position holds. The second is that tax cuts for the wealthy can spark economic growth. The final aim is for smaller government generally, which means less government spending—and occasionally has meant a tactical choice to focus on the rhetoric of balanced budgets. The idea is that because tax increases are off the table (because neoliberals simultaneously seek tax cuts), balanced budgets require spending cuts.

Thatcher navigated these aims due to good luck more than political skill. When Thatcher took office, her efforts at combatting inflation, rather than unemployment, met with so much resistance that they were dubbed "sado-monetarism." Had it not been for a rally-around-the-flag effect during and after the Falklands War, Thatcher would have faced a full-fledged civil war within the Tory Party over monetary policy. Fiscally, Thatcher's government pursued tax cuts on high incomes and increased the value-added tax (VAT), a consumption tax that falls disproportionately on the poor and working class. Trickle-down economics was British, not just American.[29]

Reagan's first term economic recovery plan proposed to cut education, the arts, economic development, and Trade Adjustment Assistance. It would restrict food stamps, tighten welfare requirements, means-test school breakfasts and lunches, cap Medicaid payments to the states, and tighten the belt of the space program.

Reagan knew it would be a political disaster to attempt to cut Social Security or Medicare right out of the gate, and he wanted to increase spending on defense. With those three categories excluded, cuts fell to social programs that disproportionately hurt the working class and poor.[30]

At the same time, Reaganomics offered tax cuts, particularly for the wealthy. The theory was called supply-side economics. The idea was that large tax cuts for the wealthy and for corporations would lead to economic growth. This was directly contrary to the liberal-era Keynesian approach of demand-side economics. Under that theory, the economy works because middle-class people have money to spend. An additional dollar to the middle class is likely to get spent—not so with the additional dollar to the wealthy, who already have more than they want to spend. But the Keynesians also showed that capitalism was unstable and prone to boom and bust cycles. So in a downturn, government needed to step in and jump-start the demand that middle-class consumers would ordinarily provide. The supply-siders disagreed. They rejected the boom-bust problem, holding that recessions and depressions were a function of government action, not capitalist speculation. And they held firm to the belief that more money in the hands of the wealthy would lead to economic growth.[31]

Although supply-side economics had the patina of economic theory to it, even members of the Reagan administration thought it made little sense. Vice President Bush had called it "voodoo economics" in his primary campaign against Reagan. OMB director David Stockman told a reporter at the *Atlantic* that it was a "Trojan horse to bring down the top rate." There was no science behind it. "The whole thing is premised on faith." Because people would never support "trickle-down" economics, they simply reframed it as supply-side economics. The Reagan tax cut slashed the top marginal income tax rate from 70 to 50 percent. Capital gains rates went from 28 to 20 percent. Tax cuts came before spending cuts, throwing a balanced budget out the window. The plan was for tax cuts to force future spending cuts. The reality was ballooning federal deficits and widening inequality.[32]

*　　*　　*

So there it is: deregulation, liberalization, privatization, austerity. The basic policy agenda of neoliberalism—simple and straightforward. But neoliberalism was not just a collection of policies that came to the forefront of politics in the 1980s. Hayek, Friedman, and their fellow travelers were serious thinkers, intellectuals who had built neoliberal ideas on philosophical foundations. And whether or not it ultimately resembled what those intellectuals had first intended, neoliberalism soon took hold—not just as a set of policies but as an ideology.

2
THE NEOLIBERAL IDEOLOGY

The founders of the neoliberal era wanted it to be a totalizing ideology, a worldview that would grow so dominant that the ideas
of "competitiveness, self-interest, and decentralization" would
rewire people's brains to think differently about every aspect of
life. In 1981, for example, Margaret Thatcher stated her ambitions
in plain terms: "What's irritated me about the whole direction of
politics in the last 30 years is that it's always been towards the
collective society. . . . And therefore, it isn't that I set out on economic policies; it's that I set out really to change the approach, and
changing the economics is the means of changing that approach. If
you change the approach you really are after the heart and soul of
the nation. Economics are the method; the object is to change the
heart and soul."[1]

Thatcher's grand ambitions have been realized. Today, people
often speak in the language of markets, not the language of politics or morality. We talk more about consumers or taxpayers than
about citizens. We expect government to work like a business. We
think civil servants are motivated by money or invidious ideology
rather than patriotism. We expect schools to prepare children for
jobs, not participation in a democracy. And because the logic of the
market is our new default for how any human interaction works,
why not apply it to every aspect of our society? Proposals abound to
pay students to attend elementary school and replace organ donations to the needy with markets for kidneys and lungs. Maybe we
should allow people to shoot and kill endangered rhinos for a fee

or allow prisoners to pay to upgrade to cleaner cells. The fact that these examples don't seem outrageous shows just how dominant neoliberalism has become. People didn't used to think of schools as job-training grounds, government agencies as businesses, citizens as consumers, or body parts as commodities. Now we do.[2]

The heart and soul of neoliberal economics is the individual, and so neoliberal ideology emphasizes individual works, efforts, and responsibility. This might seem unproblematic at first glance. But neoliberalism gives us a particularly radical form of individualism in which all successes and failures fall to the individual. During the 2012 election season, as the neoliberal era was waning, President Barack Obama clunkily suggested that successful people owed some of their success to those who helped along the way. Mitt Romney viciously attacked him afterward, celebrating the heroic industrialist who built his own business without any help from anyone. This story had no mention of the public school teacher who helped our heroic industrialist learn to read and write, no mention of the coaches and mentors who helped our heroic industrialist make it through school and get that first job, no mention of the police officers and firefighters who fostered safe neighborhoods, no mention of the city governments that brought electricity and water to the workplace, and of course no mention of the federal government that ensured the rule of law. The heroic industrialist did everything alone with no help from anyone else or from society. After all, as Margaret Thatcher once said, "There is no such thing as society."[3]

Of course, the corollary is that individuals are solely to blame for all of their failures. If we are all perfectly free in this competitive, individualistic Hunger Games, the losers deserve to lose. Luck plays no role in success or failure, though we all know that it does. Context doesn't matter—who your parents were, if you had an inheritance, what kind of community you grew up in—though we all know that it does. But perhaps the most troubling feature is that because neoliberalism rejects the "collective society," as Thatcher called it, it also rejects the possibility that broader trends or social structures restrict freedom and conspire against individual success.

Economic crises, corporate fraud, deliberately racist laws, crony-ism, the absence of regulation—none of these things matter. Except that they do.

Neoliberalism thus promises a specific kind of freedom: Peo-ple are autonomous. Government is minimized. Markets structure choices. But after four decades of neoliberal hegemony, people seem to be lashing out and protesting all around the world. On the left and right, the one thing people seem to agree on is that the system is rigged against them. The sociologist Zygmunt Bauman puts it nicely: "Never have we been so free. Never have we felt so powerless."[4]

Part of the reason for our powerlessness is neoliberal ideolo-gy's approach to freedom. Political philosophers have long distin-guished between two kinds of liberty. The first is sometimes called the liberty of the ancients, positive liberty, or public freedom. Posi-tive liberty is the freedom to participate actively in self-government. The paradigmatic case is ancient Athens, where democracy meant that citizens gathered to make decisions and govern themselves. And in the mid-twentieth century, some political leaders and philosophers argued that the exercise of freedom required basic minimum social rights and conditions—housing, health care, income. Without them, positive liberty wasn't achievable.

The second type of liberty is called the liberty of the moderns, negative liberty, or private liberty. Negative liberty is the freedom *from* constraints. It emphasizes things like the free choice of a per-sonal religion and no restrictions on speech, but it is not focused on the exercise of self-government. Neoliberal freedom is framed within this philosophically liberal tradition. But it takes it to an extreme because neoliberal freedom is almost single-minded in its obsession with government regulation. Fear of government so dominates the neoliberal worldview that it crowds out virtually everything else, even if neoliberals on occasion acknowledge other threats to freedom. The explanation for this odd position might be historical. Neoliberalism emerged in response to authoritarianism during the Great Depression and World War II and was worked out during the Cold War struggle with communism. Because the challenge of the time was total government control with a collectivist economic valence, neoliberalism overcorrected—condemning government as the source of all problems and championing the supposed utopia of markets. Then with the end of the Cold War and the declaration of the end of history, neoliberals felt further emboldened.

But there is another way to look at negative liberty, and it is essential for understanding why neoliberalism failed. We can call it the freedom of the republicans, meaning those who believe in having a republic as a form of government. We could also perhaps call it the freedom of the progressives, after conservatives like Teddy Roosevelt and liberals like Louis Brandeis, who lived during the Progressive Era of the early twentieth century. Republicans and progressives alike feared power in any place and in any form, public or private, and they thought that power of any kind threatened freedom.

This broader approach shows the limitations of neoliberal ideology's preoccupation with freedom from government. First, neoliberals pay too little attention to the fact that private parties can oppress individuals—and that this undermines freedom as well. When Wells Fargo opens millions of fraudulent checking accounts for consumers who don't ask for them and then charges those consumers fees and torches their credit scores—that is a form of private oppression that undermines the freedom of those consumers. When an industrial company dumps toxic waste into a lake, destroying a space for fishing and swimming, that is a form of private oppression that undermines the freedom of swimmers and fishers. Many large employers now control virtually every aspect of their employees' lives. They insert noncompete and no-poach clauses into contracts so the employees cannot work anywhere else. And on top of that, they pay low wages. These workers are not free. This is private tyranny, modern serfdom. Government is how we would normally prevent private actors from using force and fraud against us; government action can enhance freedom. Yet the strategies of maximal privatization and minimal regulation mean that neoliberals offer virtually no protection from these kinds of harms.[5]

The second problem is that neoliberal freedom undervalues the fact that private parties can use government to oppress people. When the rich and powerful can use money to elect and lobby officials or when they themselves roll in and out of government, they can skew the laws to serve their own interests. Some neoliberals are very concerned with this problem, but they think the solution is to reduce the scope of government action altogether: no government, no private capture of government. Senator Ted Cruz of Texas, for example, commented in a 2017 debate with Vermont senator Bernie Sanders, "If the problem is government is corrupt, why on earth would you want more power in Washington?" But this solution collapses us back into the first problem, leaving us facing the issue of private tyranny.[6]

Part of the issue is that neoliberals often make a cardinal error in comparing corrupt government to utopian markets instead of comparing either utopian government to utopian markets or corrupt government to corrupt markets. Because they assume that markets are utopian and that government is corrupt, they are willing to leave our fates to the marketplace. The problem is that humans are not always kindhearted, and markets are filled with predators hunting for their prey.

A third problem is what scholars call structural domination. The structure of the social and economic system itself can be oppressive and restrict freedom. Markets are a good example of this problem. As Professor Sabeel Rahman explains, in a market, it might be that "no single actor intends to create such an unequal social structure. Rather, each party is simply seeking its own advantage established by background laws. Yet the aggregate effect is to create situations like low wages, unemployment, or other market failures." One of Hayek's great contributions was to argue, following Adam Smith, for the value of the invisible hand. Hayek thought that because knowledge is diffused in the general public, the many millions of unconnected actions individuals take would lead to favorable outcomes, particularly when compared with government policy-making. But it also might be that the aggregation of thousands of self-interested actions leads to a selfish and predatory dystopia, not a free and fair utopia.[7]

The problem of structural domination is more challenging than the problems of private power and money capturing government. Structural domination appears to us to be natural, and naturalizing the system can lead to hopelessness. People resign themselves to private oppression and personal poverty. But the system isn't natural. We are the ones engaging in thousands of decisions each day. And we created the laws of the marketplace that structure each of those decisions.

Finally, neoliberalism's understanding of freedom leaves no room for the freedom to reject neoliberalism. If society is free to chart its own course, then it might choose public libraries and national health care. People might choose to regulate Wall Street speculation and toxic chemicals in food. Freedom means that people might choose *not* to be neoliberal. This is a problem for neoliberals, and it explains why, for all its anti-government rhetoric and ideology, neoliberalism often leads to a strong state. Thatcherism, for example, actually stripped power away from local governments and expanded the power of the central government at Westminster. It took a strong government to reverse decades of entrenched social democracy. As one historian of Thatcherism comments, "The citizens have to be forced to be free and enterprising, otherwise there is no guarantee they will be so." A free economy *requires* a strong state.[8]

Indeed, neoliberalism has frequently been opposed to democracy because in a democracy, people might not choose neoliberalism. Historian Quinn Slobodian has shown in his book *Globalists* that the intellectuals behind neoliberalism strongly supported building international institutions "to inoculate capitalism against the threat of democracy." The idea was that if international laws and institutions were designed in a way that systematically favored neoliberal goals, then democratic populations within nation-states would be constrained from regulating markets.[9]

Many prominent neoliberals were also fainthearted at best in their support for political freedom. Consider some of the responses to apartheid in South Africa from members of the Mont Pelerin Society. German economist Wilhelm Röpke argued that uncivilized peoples would not support capitalism, and so he supported apartheid outright. English economist William H. Hutt opposed apartheid—but also democracy. Instead of one-person, one-vote, he advocated for weighting votes by wealth so the economically powerful would determine policy. Hayek opposed apartheid as well, but he also opposed economic sanctions designed to pressure the South African government to change its racist policies. Why? Hayek thought sanctions would "destroy the international economic order."[10]

The preference for neoliberalism over democracy was so strong that some neoliberals have even been willing to jump into bed with authoritarians to accomplish their goals. In the early 1970s, for example, the United States supported a military coup in Chile, overthrowing the democratically elected Salvador Allende and replacing him with General Augusto Pinochet. Thousands "disappeared," thousands more were imprisoned and tortured, and all others were left in an authoritarian state of terror. But upon Pinochet's seizing power, a set of economists trained at the University of Chicago worked with the government to implement a neoliberal economic agenda. Milton Friedman visited and offered advice, as did Hayek. Budgets were slashed, state enterprises privatized, regulations abolished, trade liberalized. The Mont Pelerin Society even met in Chile in 1981. At that session, economist James Buchanan argued in his paper "Limited or Unlimited Democracy" that if democracy was opposed to the neoliberal marketplace, then the only option was to curtail democracy. In an interview with *El Mercurio*, Hayek shared this sentiment, commenting that "a dictatorship . . . can be more liberal in its policies than a democratic assembly."[11]

Neoliberalism by fiat might have been necessary at first, but the heart and soul would eventually change as Thatcher predicted. And when that happened, neoliberalism would appear to be normal, natural, invisible—and inevitable. This is why it was so important that New Labour and the New Democrats embraced the spirit of neoliberalism. Even though they often pursued neoliberal policies out of pragmatism instead of dogmatism, as Blair said, the consequence was to entrench neoliberal ideology into our social and political fabric.

Many left-of-center American commentators are often frustrated when they are characterized as neoliberals. They agree that neoliberalism refers, in most of the world, to "the Thatcher-Reagan revival of the political right based on dogmatic market capitalism." But they argue that in the United States, it referred to a small handful of forward-looking Democrats in the early 1980s and that this group was not the same as the Reaganites. They are partly right about this—this is what Mort Kondracke was talking about the morning after Reagan's victory. But they're also partly wrong. The left and right neoliberals of the 1980s (and onward) are far more similar to each other than partisan identification might suggest.[12]

On policy issues, the center-left neoliberals' core principles were strikingly similar to those of their right-wing antagonists: a focus on economic growth rather than the distribution of wealth in society, a skepticism of government, and reliance on economic theory and market solutions. In 1982, the historian Arthur Schlesinger Jr. observed that the center-left neoliberals had "joined in the clamor against 'big government,' found great merit in the unregulated marketplace, opposed structural change in the economy and gone along with swollen military budgets and the nuclear arms race. Far from rejecting the Reagan frameworks," he said, "they would at most rejigger priorities here and there." When neoliberal (Democrat) Paul Tsongas penned *The Road from Here*, even Mort Kondracke's *New Republic* understood where he stood on the political spectrum. It titled its 1981 review, "Reaganism with a Human Face."[13]

One of the important puzzles of neoliberalism is why anyone on the left embraced it. There are, I think, three answers. First, some people truly believed in neoliberalism. They thought deregulation, liberalization, privatization, and austerity were the best policy tools for the moment. The second explanation is financial: needing campaign cash, those on the left turned to corporate political action committees and wealthy individuals, and over time, their policies migrated to follow the money. The third answer is political. Center-left neoliberals first embraced the tools and rhetoric of their opponents for short-term gain. But the hangover of political constraints lasted long after those constraints had subsided. Over time, liberals would continue to trim their sails, offering an echo rather than a choice, perhaps more from habit and timidity than from reasoned conviction.

In the United States, the rise of the New Democrats was tied to successive losses in the 1980, 1984, and 1988 presidential elections. Businesses and trade associations had expanded their political involvement starting in the 1970s, but largely on the side of Republicans. Some New Democrats, like Congressman Tony Coelho of California, who ran the Democratic Congressional Campaign Committee, saw an opportunity to rebalance those financial flows by appealing to these corporate interests. Indeed, as early as 1985, *Washington Post* reporter Tom Edsall noted Coelho's "ability to meld legislation and campaign contributions." By their Cleveland convention in 1991, the emergent New Democrat coalition had broken with the old liberal approach in a variety of areas: it celebrated markets as an alternative to environmental regulation, pushed for vouchers to help the poor, and embraced protrade policies to the ire of labor unions.[14]

With the election of Bill Clinton, the New Democrats now had the White House and a bully pulpit from which to reshape Democratic politics. But in his first few years in office, Clinton didn't fully embrace the mantle of New Democrat. In part, his early years were defined by missteps and by liberal policy proposals on gays in the military and national health care. In part, the New Democrats did not have enough support among insiders. As Bruce Reed observed, "We didn't have enough followers in enough places, and the Old Democrats, they ran the town." Clinton's popularity dropped, and the result was the election of 1994, in which the Republicans gained control of the House of Representatives and the Senate for the first time in decades. It was divided government that saved center-left neoliberalism, pushing Clinton back to his New Democratic roots. As Al From, founder of the New Democrat Democratic Leadership Council, noted in a memo to Clinton after the midterm elections, "The increased polarization in Congress is an opportunity for you to seize the vital center of the political spectrum." Clinton's recaptured centrism would come to be known as the Third Way.[15]

There were actually three different strands of Third Way politics. One strand, the one most often remembered, was the political tactic of triangulation. Because liberal ideals were unachievable in a conservative era, a savvy politician could make progress by co-opting conservative agenda items and putting a liberal spin on them or by taking liberal goals and using conservative means to achieve them. Perhaps the classic, though crude, example is tax cuts. Liberals are for helping the poor; conservatives are for tax cuts. Triangulation suggests tax cuts for the poor. Was that a conservative policy or a liberal policy? The truth is, to paraphrase a Clinton phrase, it was both and it was different. Another example of triangulation was co-opting traditionally conservative agenda items—balanced budgets, deficit reduction, crime, welfare reform, parental controls for television—with the result of gaining bipartisan victories. Triangulation thus offered ways of gaining policy victories in a time of conservative hegemony and divided government.

The second strand of the Third Way was minimalism. Instead of seeking bold changes that would reshape the nature of state, society, and the world, policy minimalism embraced small changes—tweaks—that could be implemented relatively easily and justified preferably as technocratic changes. The paramount tool was the tax credit, and Clinton passed the child tax credit and lifetime learning tax credit. Over time, it seemed almost as if tax credits were the only tool policy makers knew how to use: there was the saver's credit and the credit for the elderly or disabled; the American opportunity tax credit and the residential energy efficient property credit; the non-business energy property credit and the health coverage tax credit. The list goes on and on and on. Instead of giving people money directly or building public institutions, tax credits enable people, at tax time, to benefit from activities they undertook during the year. But policymaking through the tax code is comparatively ineffective and exceedingly complicated. It means people have to know to take advantage of the credit at tax time, they actually have to take the credit, and in the process, it makes filing taxes more complicated and frustrating (which, in turn, doesn't inspire a fondness for government). But with simple and direct public programs out of favor, policymaking through the tax code became the new normal.

The third strand of the Third Way was fundamentally transformative. Starting in the early 1980s, center-left neoliberals recognized that technology and globalization were fundamentally reshaping the American economy. Instead of fearing these changes, the "Atari Democrats" welcomed them and wanted to design policy to adapt to them. The best-known thinker in this vein was economist Robert Reich. In a series of books, Reich embraced a vision of modernizing the United States to adapt to a global society in which the nature of education and work had to be dynamic to keep up with the rapid changes in society, technology, and industry. This intuition led Reich to argue for investment in human capital, such as education and retraining, to embrace industrial policy so the economy would lever up into the high-tech sector, and, more generally, to shift the conversation to address the consequences of globalization and rapid innovation in technology, transportation, communication, and other sectors.[16]

But the ambitious vision of a transformative third way was never realized. As secretary of labor during the Clinton administration, Reich clashed with other economic policy makers who were more concerned with lowering the interest rate (to coax capital out of the bond market) and with balanced budgets and deficits.

As James Carville famously remarked, "I used to think that if there was reincarnation, I wanted to come back as the president or the pope or as a .400 baseball hitter. But now I want to come back as the bond market. You can intimidate everybody." Reich advocated for an investment budget that would place America on the cutting edge—but without success. When he shifted gears and pushed for the administration to emphasize corporate responsibility and to confront corporate welfare, he was told these ideas were "inflammatory."[17]

The fundamental problem was that the transformative third way conflicted with the tactics of triangulation and the straitjacket of minimalism. A far-reaching agenda to reform the economy and equip workers and employees with new skills and opportunities would require government action and money—and both were disfavored, at least on the scale necessary to meet the enormity of the challenge. The true-believer neoliberals and the financiers disagreed with the Reich faction. And tacticians suggested bold ideas weren't possible within the political constraints of the time. The transformative third way was accordingly subordinated to the deregulation and consolidation of industry, tax cuts and shrinking budgets, privatization's anti-government agenda, and the liberalization of trade. It was the neoliberal era's biggest missed opportunity, the path not taken.

As those in the center-left also adopted neoliberal policies, the interests that benefited had greater and greater power to capture government and push for further neoliberal reforms. Political scientists have shown that the more time staffers in Congress spend with corporate interest groups, the less accurate they are at identifying what policies their constituents want. Members of Congress, executive branch officials, and junior staff may also pursue policies with one eye to a lucrative exit option in the private sector, and they might not want to regulate their friends from industry. The consequence is to further entrench neoliberal policies.[18]

There is also a longer-term problem that emerges when political constraints lead to policy choices. Over time, people develop habits. They start to believe the policies they embraced for tactical reasons are actually desirable on their own terms. But people are also susceptible to believing they are politically constrained even when the underlying political context changes. They fail to update their views fast enough and thus end up fighting wars that have already ended. Years after the Clinton administration, when Democrats once again wielded power, the hangover of Third Way neoliberalism continued to suggest that ambitious solutions were impossible and ill-advised.

Whether it was from conviction, capture, or custom, when neoliberalism took hold on the left as well as the right, it became the ideology that defined the era. This shared worldview engulfed virtually every area—and not just in domestic policy. International economic policy, as we have seen, pursued an aggressive liberalization agenda under both Republicans and Democrats. But the 1970s also brought a transformation in foreign policy and national security thinking. Since the end of World War II, the Soviet Union and the West had achieved an uneasy equilibrium best defined by the grand strategy of containment. The United States would not seek to roll back Soviet authority but simply contain it from spreading. As John Lewis Gaddis has written, "What was required was not to remake the world in the image of the United States, but rather to preserve its diversity against attempts to remake it in the image of others." There were proxy wars and major moments of crisis, but even when it went wrong (as in Vietnam), American foreign policy was premised on maintaining the status quo—not on global transformation. Over time, containment migrated to détente, an attempt to ease the tensions of the Cold War even further.[19]

By the late 1970s, the status quo was no longer acceptable. Foreign policy advocates on the right and left moved against Henry Kissinger's realism and toward incorporating moral values into foreign policy. Democratic senator Henry "Scoop" Jackson attacked détente, as did Ronald Reagan and a new generation of foreign policy neoconservatives. The neoconservatives were also scarred by Vietnam, but unlike liberals who sought refuge in disarmament and peace, they came to believe "that America should not suffer any similar defeats in the future, that it should more vigorously promote American values overseas and that it should not be so willing to compromise with Communist regimes." The Iranian revolution confirmed these intuitions. The United States could not rely on other countries to guarantee the safety of core US interests—in that case, oil—so it had to be able to police the world itself. The result was a more hawkish, unilateral, and aggressive foreign policy. It championed rolling back the power of the Soviet Union, as when Reagan demanded that Gorbachev "tear down this wall." It promoted new armaments and technologies—like the Star Wars missile defense program. And it was grounded rhetorically and practically in the moral values of expanding democracy, free markets, and human rights.[20]

As Yale professor Samuel Moyn has shown, human rights did not become a major topic of international concern or activism until the 1970s, after decolonization. Like neoliberalism, the human rights movement is fiercely individualistic, and it is skeptical of nationalism, majoritarian democracy, and other group-oriented political movements. And although human rights was a companion to social democracy in the middle of the twentieth century— the United Nations' Universal Declaration of Human Rights was meant to be achieved *within* countries and through their welfare states—by the 1980s, the human rights movement had come to an accommodation with neoliberalism. Activist groups emphasized naming and shaming dictators. To the extent that they engaged economic issues (largely after the Cold War), they focused on alleviating poverty rather than creating equitable societies. Human rights was thus perfectly compatible with the aggressive foreign policy approach of the neoconservatives, and after the Cold War, it was largely unthreatening to the economic neoliberalism of the Washington Consensus.[21]

When the Cold War ended, the neoconservatives were again critical in shaping the future of American foreign policy. The then chairman of the Joint Chiefs, Colin Powell, said in 1991, "What we plan for is that we're a superpower." Zalmay Khalilzad, then a Defense Department aide and later ambassador to Afghanistan, Iraq, and the United Nations under George W. Bush, penned a famous memo suggesting that in the post–Cold War era, the United States' goal should be to ensure that no other power can challenge US leadership.[22]

Many people think of the end of the Cold War as the major break in American foreign policy, but as James Mann astutely points out in his book *Rise of the Vulcans*, this perspective misses an important continuity. Think about the cohort of foreign policy professionals that ran American foreign policy in the neoliberal era. Many of the neoconservatives—Rumsfeld, Cheney, Wolfowitz, Powell, Armitage—were significant figures both before and after the Cold War. They were the key players in shifting the United States away from détente to a more aggressive foreign policy in the 1970s, crafting its role as the post–Cold War superpower, and executing the Iraq War during the George W. Bush presidency.[23]

At the same time that neocons wanted to maintain defense budgets after the Cold War, many liberals at the time hoped instead for a peace dividend—one that would reduce defense budgets and allow for greater focus on domestic economic priorities. They also hoped that the future would bring a reemphasis on the UN Security Council as a forum and vehicle for global cooperation. But what is striking is how little Democrats diverged from the neoconservative vision. The usual categorization of foreign policy camps during this era is that there were neoconservatives on the right and liberal internationalists on the left. Although both would certainly chafe at the suggestion, the two sides were actually far more alike than they would want to admit. Both had a similar view on expanding neoliberal free market capitalism, with liberal internationalists emphasizing it perhaps even more aggressively than the neoconservatives. Both emphasized the importance of spreading democracy and human rights around the world, in addition to rooting this activist foreign policy in American values. And both were willing to use force in support of those goals. The central difference was that neoconservatives stressed their willingness to take unilateral action, while liberal internationalists emphasized the need for UN involvement. Secretary of State Madeleine Albright frequently celebrated that the United States was the indispensable nation, without whom nothing in the world could be accomplished. The Clinton administration fought wars to prevent atrocities, spread human rights, and promote democracy. And in 1999, the Clinton administration even engaged NATO in a war in Kosovo *without* authorization from the UN Security Council. Defenders said that conflict was "illegal but legitimate." A few years later, Kosovo would serve as a precedent for "going it alone" in Iraq.[24]

The Iraq War is still a festering wound in Democratic politics. But we shouldn't move past it so quickly because it shows how much consensus there was during this era, even on the most significant question of the day. Future presidential candidates John Kerry, Hillary Clinton, and Joe Biden all voted for the Iraq War. Liberal commentators Peter Beinart and Michael Ignatieff championed it. Indeed, even some of the skeptics of the Bush administration appeared at times uncomfortably optimistic. For example, although human rights advocate Samantha Power (and later ambassador to the United Nations) refused to call the Iraq War a just war and worried openly about the lawlessness of unilateralism, she also said that "an intervention in Iraq, even a unilateral one, is undoubtedly going to make Iraq a more humane place."[25]

The neocons and liberal internationalists blur together even further when we compare them with what came before. American foreign policy from the 1930s to the 1970s wasn't aggressively promoting democracy or human rights, using force to spread those values, or exporting laissez-faire capitalism. The foreign policy establishment first allied with Stalin to defeat Hitler in the 1930s, then decided to accept the existence of the Soviet Union and its sphere of influence through containment. Ultimately, in the throes of Kissingerian realism, they even established relations with communist China and facilitated détente with the Soviets. This is a far cry from the morally infused policies on the right and left that would define the following generation.

President Obama was, in some ways, the exception that proves the rule. Obama famously opposed the war in Iraq, saying it was a "dumb" war. And as president, his personal views appeared to have diverged from many of his advisors'. He advocated leading from behind, thought revolutions had to bubble up from below, worried about getting further bogged down in Afghanistan, and was hesitant about airstrikes in Libya (but ordered them) and Syria (and didn't order them). Critics on the right and left assailed him for inaction, taking a back seat on global leadership, and not having an organizing principle (as his former secretary of state Hillary Clinton said). On foreign and security policy, Obama's advisors largely pushed for the conventional liberal internationalist approach— Susan Rice, Hillary Clinton, and Samantha Power especially—but Barack Obama himself was the outlier.[26]

The fact that the president was the exception is indicative of the degree to which there was a shared worldview in the foreign policy community. Some commentators and participants decried groupthink among foreign policy makers, referring to them as "the Blob." This moniker showed just how similar both sides in foreign policy had become as the neoliberal era progressed. In both foreign and domestic affairs, the neoliberal ideology was not just prevalent—it defined the era.

3
THE LAST DAYS OF
NEOLIBERALISM

With the 2008 financial crash and the Great Recession, the neoliberal ideology lost its force. The approach that defined an era led not to never-ending prosperity but utter disaster. "Laissez-faire is finished," declared French president Nicolas Sarkozy. Federal Reserve chairman Alan Greenspan admitted in testimony before Congress that his ideology was flawed. In an extraordinary statement, Australian prime minister Kevin Rudd declared that the crash "called into question the prevailing neoliberal economic orthodoxy of the past 30 years—the orthodoxy that has underpinned the national and global regulatory frameworks that have so spectacularly failed to prevent the economic mayhem which has been visited upon us."[1]

For some, and especially for those in the millennial generation, the Great Recession and the wars in Iraq and Afghanistan started a process of reflection on what the neoliberal era had delivered. Disappointment would be an understatement. The complete wreckage of economic, social, and political life would be more accurate. In each of these arenas, looking at the outcomes that neoliberalism delivered increasingly called into question the worldview itself.

Start with the economy. Over the course of the neoliberal era, economies around the world have become more and more unequal. In the United States, the wealthiest 1 percent took home about 8.5 percent of the national income in 1976. After a generation of neoliberal policies, in 2014, they captured more than 20 percent of national income. In Britain, the top 1 percent captured more than 14 percent of national income—more than double the amount they took home in the late 1970s. The story is the same in Australia. The top 1 percent took about 5 percent of national income in the 1970s and doubled that to 10 percent by the late 2000s. As the rich get richer, wages have been stagnant for workers since the late 1970s. Between 1979 and 2008, 100 percent of the United States' income growth went to the top 10 percent of Americans. The bottom 90 percent actually saw a decline in their income.[2]

Over the course of the neoliberal era, the racial wealth gap did not fare much better. In 1979, the average hourly wage for a black man in the United States was 22 percent lower than for a white man. By 2015, the wage gap had grown to 31 percent. For black women, the wage gap in 1979 was only 6 percent; by 2015, it had jumped to 19 percent. Homeownership is one of the central ways that families build wealth over time, yet homeownership rates among African Americans in 2017 were as low as they were before the civil rights revolution, when racial discrimination was legal.[3]

It is also worth putting the 2008 economic crash into perspective—both historical and global. Between 1943 and the middle of the 1970s, the number of bank failures in the country was minimal—never getting above single digits in any given year. Deregulation of the S&Ls brought widespread failures and bailouts in less than a decade. Deregulation of Wall Street brought the epic crash of 2008 in less than a decade.[4]

This shouldn't have been too much of a surprise, as neoliberal policies had already wreaked havoc around the world. Looking back at the 1997 Asian financial crisis, Joseph Stiglitz comments that "excessively rapid financial and capital market liberalization was probably the single most important cause of the crisis," and after the crisis, the IMF's policies "exacerbated the downturns." Neoliberals pushed swift privatization in Russia after the Cold War, alongside a restrictive monetary policy. The result was a growing barter economy, low exports, and asset stripping as burgeoning oligarchs bought up state enterprises and then moved their money out of the country.[5]

Despite its alleged commitment to market competition, the neoliberal economic agenda instead brought the decline of competition and the rise of close to monopoly power in vast swaths of the economy: pharmaceuticals, telecom, airlines, agriculture, banking, industrials, retail, utilities, and even breweries. A study by the *Economist* found that between 1997 and 2012, two-thirds of industries became more concentrated. Even centrist think tanks like the Brookings Institution have recognized the dangerous rise of monopolies and argued that the concentration of economic power brings with it higher prices for consumers, increased economic inequality, and a less dynamic economy.[6]

Rising economic inequality and the creation of monopolistic megacorporations also threaten democracy. In study after study, political scientists have shown that the US government is highly responsive to the policy preferences of the wealthiest people, corporations, and trade associations—and that it is largely unresponsive to the views of ordinary people. The wealthiest people, corporations, and their interest groups participate more in politics, spend more on politics, and lobby governments more. Leading political scientists have declared that the United States is no longer best characterized as a democracy or a republic but as an oligarchy—a government of the rich, by the rich, and for the rich.[7]

Neoliberal embrace of individualism and opposition to "the collective society," as Thatcher put it, also had perverse consequences for social and political life. Humans are social animals. But neoliberalism rejects both the medieval approach of having fixed social classes based on wealth and power *and* the modern approach of having a single, shared civic identity based on participation in a democratic community. The problem is that amid neoliberalism's individualistic rat race, people still need to find meaning somewhere in their lives. And so there has been a retreat to tribalism and identity groups, with civic associations replaced by religious, ethnic, or other cultural affiliations. To be sure, race, gender, culture, and other aspects of social life have always been important to politics. But neoliberalism's radical individualism has increasingly raised two interlocking problems.

First, when taken to an extreme, social fracturing into identity groups can be used to divide people and prevent the creation of a shared civic identity. Self-government requires uniting through our commonalities and aspiring to achieve a shared future. When individuals fall back onto clans, tribes, and us-versus-them identities, the political community gets fragmented. It becomes harder for people to see each other as part of that same shared future. Demagogues rely on this fracturing to inflame racial, nationalist, and religious antagonism, which only further fuels the divisions within society. Neoliberalism's war on "society," by pushing toward the privatization and marketization of everything, thus indirectly facilitates a retreat into tribalism that further undermines the preconditions for a free and democratic society.

The second problem is that neoliberals on right and left sometimes use identity as a shield to protect neoliberal policies. As one commentator has argued, "Without the bedrock of class politics, identity politics has become an agenda of inclusionary neoliberalism in which individuals can be accommodated but addressing structural inequalities cannot." What this means is that some neoliberals hold high the banner of inclusiveness on gender and race and thus claim to be progressive reformers, but they then turn a blind eye to systemic changes in politics and the economy. Critics argue that this is "neoliberal identity politics," and it gives its proponents the space to perpetuate the policies of deregulation, privatization, liberalization, and austerity. Of course, the result is to leave in place a political and economic system that disproportionately harms the very groups that inclusionary neoliberals purport to support. On the left, this tactic usually focuses on racial and gender inclusion; on the right, it emphasizes nationalism of one sort or another. But in either case, this variant on identity politics can turn into a way to reinforce neoliberal policies.[8]

The foreign policy adventures of the neoconservatives and liberal internationalists haven't fared much better than economic policy or cultural politics. The United States and its coalition partners have been bogged down in the war in Afghanistan for eighteen years and counting. Neither it nor Iraq is a liberal democracy, nor did the attempt to establish democracy in Iraq lead to a domino effect that swept the Middle East and reformed its governments for the better. Instead, power in Iraq has shifted from American occupiers, to sectarian militias, to the Iraqi government, to ISIS terrorists, and back to the Iraqi government. Far from being humanitarian, more than a hundred thousand Iraqis are dead. Or take the liberal internationalist 2011 intervention in Libya. The result was not a peaceful transition to stable democracy but instead civil war and instability, with thousands dead as the country splintered and portions were overrun by terrorist groups. On the grounds of democracy promotion, it is hard to say these interventions were a success. And for those motivated to expand human rights around the world, on the civilian death count alone, it is hard to justify these wars as humanitarian victories.[9]

Indeed, the central anchoring assumptions of the American foreign policy establishment have been proven wrong. Foreign policy makers largely assumed that all good things would go together—democracy, markets, and human rights—and so they thought opening China to trade would inexorably lead to it becoming a liberal democracy. They were wrong. They thought Russia would become liberal through swift democratization and privatization. They were wrong. They thought globalization was inevitable and that ever-expanding trade liberalization was desirable even if the political system never corrected for trade's winners and losers. They were wrong. These aren't minor mistakes. And to be clear, Donald Trump had nothing to do with them. All of these failures were evident prior to the 2016 election.[10]

In spite of these failures, most policy makers did not have a new ideology or different worldview through which to view the problems of this time. So, by and large, the collective response was not to abandon neoliberalism. After the Great Crash of 2008, neoliberals chafed at attempts to push forward aggressive Keynesian spending programs to spark demand. President Barack Obama's advisors shrank the size of the postcrash stimulus package for fear it would seem too large to the neoliberal consensus of the era, and on top of that, they compromised on its content. About one-third of the stimulus ended up being tax cuts, which have a less stimulative effect than direct spending. After Republicans took back the Congress in 2010, Obama was forced into sequestration, a multiyear austerity program that slashed budgets across government, even as the country was only beginning to emerge from the Great Recession. The British Labour Party's Chancellor of the Exchequer said after the 2008 crash that Labour's planned cuts to public spending would be "deeper and tougher" than Margaret Thatcher's.[11]

When it came to affirmative, forward-looking policy, the neoliberal framework also remained dominant. Take the Obamacare health care legislation. Democrats had wanted to pass a national health care program since at least Harry Truman's presidency. But with Clinton's failed attempt in the early 1990s, when Democrats took charge of the House, Senate, and presidency in 2009, they took a different approach. Obamacare was built on a market-based model that the conservative Heritage Foundation helped develop and that Mitt Romney, the Republican governor of Massachusetts, had adopted. It is worth emphasizing that Obamacare's central feature is a private marketplace in which people can buy their own health care, with subsidies for individuals who are near the poverty line. There was no nationalization of health care through a single-payer system, and centrist Democrats like Senator Joe Lieberman blocked the creation of a public option that might coexist and compete with private options on the marketplaces. Fearful of losing their seats, centrists extracted these concessions from progressives. Little good it did them. The president's party almost always loses seats in midterm elections, and this time was no different. For their caution, centrists both lost their seats and gave Americans fewer and worse health care choices. Perhaps the bigger shock was that courageous progressive politicians who also lost in their red-leaning districts, like Virginia's Tom Perriello, actually did better than their cautious colleagues.[12]

On the right, the response to the crash went beyond ostrich-like blindness to doubling down on the failed approaches of the past. The Republican Party platform in 2012, for example, called for weaker Wall Street, environmental, and worker safety regulations; lower taxes for corporations and wealthy individuals; and further liberalization of trade. It called for abolishing federal student loans, in addition to privatizing rail, western lands, airport security, and the post office. Republicans also continued their support for cutting health care and retirement security. After forty years moving in this direction—and with it failing at every turn—you might think they would change their views. But Republicans didn't, and some still haven't.[13]

Although neoliberalism had little to offer, in the absence of a new ideological framework, it hung over the Obama presidency—but now in a new form. Many on the center-left adopted what we might call *the technocratic ideology*, a rebranded version of the policy minimalism of the 1990s that replaced minimalism's tactical and pragmatic foundations with scientific ones. The term itself is somewhat oxymoronic, as technocrats seem like the opposite of ideologues. But an ideology is simply a system of ideas and beliefs, like liberalism, neoliberalism, or socialism, that shapes how people view their role in the world, society, and politics. As an ideology, technocracy holds that the problems in the world are technical problems that require technical solutions. It is worth pointing out what this implies: First, it means that the structure of the current system isn't broken or flawed. Any problems are relatively minor and can be fixed by making small tweaks in the system. Second, the problems are not a function of deep moral conflicts that require persuading people on a religious, emotional, or moral level. Instead, they are problems of science and fact, in which we can know "right" answers and figure out what works because there is consensus about what the end goals are. The result is that the technocratic ideology largely accepts the status quo as acceptable.

The technocratic ideology preserves the status quo with a variety of tactics. We might call the first the *complexity canard*. Technocrats like to say that entire sectors of public policy are very complicated and therefore no one can propose reforms or even understand the sector without entry into the priesthood of the technocracy. The most frequent uses of this tactic are in sectors that economists have come to dominate—international trade, antitrust, and financial regulation, for example. The result of this mindset is that bold, structural reforms are pushed aside and highly technical changes adopted instead. Financial regulation provides a particularly good case, given the 2008 crash and the Great Recession. When it came time to establish a new regulatory regime for the financial sector, there wasn't a massive restructuring, despite the biggest crash in seventy years.

Instead, for the most part, the Dodd-Frank Act was classically technocratic. It kept the sector basically the same, with a few tweaks here and there. There was no attempt to restructure the financial sector completely. Efforts to break up the banks went nowhere. No senior executives went to jail. With the exception of creating the Consumer Financial Protection Bureau, most reforms were relatively minor: greater capital requirements for banks, more reporting requirements. Where proponents claimed they were doing something bold, Dodd-Frank still fell prey to the technocratic ideology. The Volcker Rule, for example, sought to ban banks from proprietary trading. But instead of doing that through a simple, clean breakup rule (like the old Glass-Steagall regime), the Volcker Rule was subject to exceptions and carve outs—which federal regulators were required to explain and implement with hundreds of pages of technical regulations.[14]

Dodd-Frank also illustrates a second tenet of the technocratic ideology: *the failures of technocracy can be solved by more technocracy.* Whenever technocratic solutions fail, the answer is rarely to question the structure of the system as a whole. Instead it is to demand more and better technocrats. Those who acknowledge that voting for the Iraq War was a mistake regretted not having better intelligence and postwar planning. Rare was the person who questioned the endeavor of policing vast regions of the world simultaneously with little knowledge of the local people, customs, or culture. All that was needed was better postwar planning. It was a technical, bureaucratic problem. Dodd-Frank created the Financial Stability Oversight Council, a government body tasked with what is called macroprudential regulation. What this means is that government regulators are supposed to monitor the entire economy and turn the dials of regulation up and down a little bit to keep the economy from another crash. But ask yourself this: Why would we ever believe they could do such a thing? We know those very same regulators failed to identify, warn about, or act on the 2008 crisis. We know markets are dynamic and diverse and that regulators can't have full information about them. And we know regulators are just as likely as anyone else to be caught up in irrational exuberance or captured by industry. Instead of establishing structural rules for permissible financial activities, even if they are a little bit overbroad or underinclusive, Dodd-Frank, once again, put its faith and our fates in the hands of technocrats.

Perhaps the most prominent and celebrated technocratic approach to liberal public policy in recent years is nudging. If there was a court intellectual in the Obama administration, it was surely Cass Sunstein—one of the most prolific, brilliant, and influential legal scholars of his generation and the leading proponent of nudging. Behavioral psychologists have shown that small changes in how choices are framed can have meaningful effects. For example, whether desserts or fruit are served first or last in a school cafeteria can radically change what students will eat. In their book *Nudge*, Richard Thaler and Sunstein argue that it makes sense to design the structure of choices in a way that helps people become healthier, wealthier, and happier. Nudges have become so popular that the Obama administration created a Social and Behavioral Sciences Team to apply the lessons of nudging across the federal government, and UK prime minister David Cameron created a Behavioural Insights Team, nicknamed the Nudge Unit.[15]

Nudges assume that policy makers should work within the existing structures and frameworks of public policy. Many proponents of the behavioral approach to public policy see this as a feature, not a bug. As the heirs to the minimalism of the 1990s, Thaler and Sunstein declare that in an age of political polarization and partisan gridlock, nudging is the "real third way." But as with minimalism more generally, the result is a comparatively unambitious approach to public policy. The dominance of nudges has severely limited our ability to see the full range of policy options and to tackle some of the biggest problems facing our society.[16]

Consider retirement security as an example. Nudgers suggest that employers adopt automatic enrollment in retirement plans for their employees at a relatively low rate of 3 percent. The policy, however, has had a variety of problems. First, it only changes the behavior of people who have employers that offer retirement plans—and who make enough money that they can put away savings on a regular basis. It does nothing for those who either don't have access to an employer-based retirement plan or those who are too poor to save. Indeed, one recent study suggests that not having enough money to make ends meet—not psychological biases—is why people fail to save. If you can't afford to save, nudging isn't going to help.[17]

A second problem is that nudgers often don't think about the broader trade-offs between the programs that they try to improve and other policy options. In their critique of behavioral policy, professors Ryan Bubb and Richard Pildes point out that the United States spends billions on tax incentives for people to save through private retirement plans, like 401(k)s and IRAs. But studies suggest that for every dollar spent on these tax incentives, there is an increase in savings of only one penny—a single penny. As a result, they argue that we are spending billions of dollars on policies that have almost no impact. And yet, instead of arguing for fixing *that* problem or the broader retirement savings crisis, nudgers have put their efforts into making minor changes to the existing regime. Why not, instead, spend that money to expand Social Security?[18]

Economist George Loewenstein has said that "the single biggest contribution of behavioral economics to public policy is taking this flawed approach to retirement savings and making it a little bit more viable." To be fair, the leading proponents of nudging do not claim that their approach can solve every policy problem or that it is an all-encompassing vision for the future. But the fact that this is considered one of the cutting-edge and most celebrated paradigms for public policy shows that technocracy cannot possibly rise to meet the challenges of today. And the fact that the biggest brains and brightest minds spend their time on tweaking the system shows how limited the ambitions of policymakers had become in the late neoliberal era.[19]

We should not be surprised by these dynamics. The arc of neoliberalism followed a pattern common in history. In the first stage, neoliberalism gained traction in response to the crises of the 1970s. It is easy to think of Thatcherism and Reaganism as emerging fully formed, springing from Zeus's head like the goddess Athena. But it is worth remembering that Thatcher was a gradualist. Rhetorically, she would champion the causes of the right wing. But practically, her policies would often fall short of the grand vision. For example, she refused to allow any attempt to privatize the Royal Mail and the railways. She even preferred to use the phrase *denationalization* to *privatization*, thinking the latter unpatriotic and far too radical. The central problem, as she noted in her memoirs, was that "there was a revolution still to be made, but too few revolutionaries."[20]

A similar story can be told of Ronald Reagan. Partly because he faced a Democratic House of Representatives, conservative radicals were occasionally disappointed with the extent the Reagan administration pushed its goals. Under Ronald Reagan, William Niskanen writes, "no major federal programs . . . and no agencies were abolished." The Intergovernmental Panel on Climate Change (IPCC) was created during the Reagan administration, and President Reagan signed a variety of environmental laws. Early leaders were not as ideologically bold as later mythmakers think.[21]

In the second stage, neoliberalism became normalized. It persisted beyond the founding personalities and, partly because of its longevity in power, grew so dominant that the other side adopted it. Thus, when the Tories ousted Thatcher and replaced her with John Major, they unwittingly made Thatcher*ism* possible. Major objected to the term *Majorism* because he wanted to be Thatcher's heir, "to dust himself with the gold of greatness, to render Thatcherism safe for perpetuity." Major wasn't the bare-knuckled fighter that Thatcher was; he was a lower-key prime minister. He wanted to offer Britain "Thatcherism with a human face," and he set himself to smoothing out the rough edges. The result was to consolidate and advance the neoliberal project in Britain. When Major was elected in his own right in 1992, he got more votes than Thatcher ever had—and more than Tony Blair received in 1997. As Major himself noted, "1992 killed socialism in Britain . . . Our win meant that between 1992 and 1997 Labour had to change."[22]

The American story is similar. Reagan passed the torch to George H. W. Bush. Although Bush was not from Reagan's political camp within the Republican Party (he had challenged Reagan for the presidency in 1980 and was viewed with skepticism by the true believers), Bush moved to embrace Reaganism in his campaign commitments. At the same time, with the losses of Carter in 1980, Walter Mondale in 1984, and Michael Dukakis in 1988, Democrats began to think they *had* to embrace neoliberalism as a path out of the political wilderness.

Eventually, however, what started as a reform agenda attempting to correct the excesses of the previous era transformed into an ideology that extended its tentacles into every area of policy and even social life. Having lost any sense of balance, in its third stage, neoliberalism overextended. The result in economic policy was the Great Crash of 2008, economic stagnation, and inequality at century-high levels. In foreign policy, it was the disastrous Iraq War and ongoing chaos and uncertainty in the Middle East.

The fourth and final stage is collapse, irrelevance, and a wandering search for the future. With the world in crisis, neoliberalism no longer has even plausible solutions to today's problems. As an answer to the problems of deregulation, privatization, liberalization, and austerity, it offers more of the same or, at best, technocratic nudges. The solutions of the neoliberal era offer no serious ideas for how to confront the collapse of the middle class and widespread economic insecurity. The solutions of the neoliberal era offer no serious ideas for how to address the corruption of politics and the influence of moneyed interests in every aspect of civic life—from news media to education to politics and regulation. The solutions of the neoliberal era offer no serious ideas for how to restitch the fraying social fabric, in which people are increasingly tribal, divided, and disconnected from civic community. And the solutions of the neoliberal era offer no serious ideas for how to confront the fusion of oligarchic capitalism and nationalist authoritarianism that has now captured major governments around the world—and that seeks to invade and undermine democracy from within.

In 1982, as the neoliberal curtain was rising, Colorado governor Richard Lamm remarked that "the cutting edge of the Democratic Party is to recognize that the world of the 1930s has changed and that a new set of public policy responses is appropriate." Today, people around the world have recognized that the world of the 1980s has changed and that it is time for a new approach to politics. The central question of our time is what comes next. What comes after neoliberalism?[23]

4
AFTER NEOLIBERALISM

The central failures of neoliberalism were twofold. Neoliberalism sapped society of community and solidarity, leaving people lonely and isolated and pushing us to retreat into tribal identities. And neoliberalism's preference for private action had few limits—it created gaping inequality and, with it, unleashed the economically powerful to reshape politics, markets, and even society to serve their interests.

These two crises—neoliberalism's social crisis and its crisis in political economy—lead to four main possibilities for the future along, two dimensions: inclusive or exclusive communities and economic populism or concentration. *Reformed neoliberalism* seeks to fix the biggest failures of neoliberalism; it preserves the old ideology's individualism and cosmopolitan sensibilities while seeking to mitigate some of the worst errors of its upwardly redistributionist economics. *Nationalist populism* rejects neoliberalism on both grounds, organizing a community around ethnic, racial, or otherwise nationalist sentiments while delivering economically populist policies. *Nationalist oligarchy* combines cultural nationalism with economic oligarchy. *Great democracy* is at once socially inclusive and economically democratic.

Although there are examples of each of these approaches in the world today, they are necessarily ideal types—paradigms for what politics might bring. As a result, no person or even political theorist is likely to fit any one of these approaches perfectly. Each of these responses to the neoliberal era is evident in contemporary politics, but not all of them appear to be equally viable. At the moment, reformed neoliberalism and nationalist populism both suffer from serious deficiencies that make them unlikely to succeed as models for reform in the next few decades. The battle is more likely between nationalist oligarchy and great democracy. Both are complete worldviews, both could be stable systems of politics, and both are therefore viable contenders for defining the next era of politics.

Reformed Neoliberalism

Neoliberalism promised a system of individual freedom and competitive markets. It delivered a system in which political and economic power are concentrated in the hands of a small number of corporations and individuals. If neoliberalism went wrong, one possibility is to make it right, to curb its greatest excesses and mitigate its worst consequences. In a sense, we could adopt a measured, promising neoliberalism instead of the steroid-enhanced version that emerged in the 1990s and 2000s. Although they don't identify this way, a variety of thinkers have, in effect, advanced elements of what we can think of as a reformed neoliberalism.

The most prominent and sophisticated strand is *liberaltarianism*, a portmanteau that reflects a desire to bridge the divide between liberals and libertarians. Although they rarely discuss it, liberaltarians embrace a libertarian attitude toward equality—support for racial, religious, gender, and sexual tolerance. But their real contribution to rethinking public policy is economic. Liberaltarians like Brink Lindsey and Steven Teles are concerned about rising economic inequality, and they argue that government contributed to inequality due to private actors capturing government and skewing public policy. They call this the "captured economy" and focus on four areas of policy: Wall Street subsidies, intellectual property, occupational licensing, and neighborhood zoning. In each of these areas, they argue that interest groups—banks, companies, licensed professionals, and homeowners—have skewed policy to benefit themselves at the expense of market competition and efficiency. Without capture, Wall Street wouldn't get subsidies, companies wouldn't own the intellectual property in drugs or music for generations, hairdressers and dentists wouldn't be able to restrict entry into their profession, and neighborhood density would increase as builders put up more housing.[1]

Liberaltarians Will Wilkinson and Samuel Hammond argue that the next era should be one defined by the "free market welfare state." Their key insight is that Republicans who opposed big government were grouping regulations and social services together when the two are actually distinct. Unbundling these components, they argue for a society with few regulations (the free market part) and significant public benefits, like Social Security and Medicare (the welfare state part). They claim that this approach is superior to other regimes because it will unleash dynamism in the economy while simultaneously protecting those who are on the losing end of change.[2]

All four of these thinkers must be applauded for grappling seriously with real problems and for creative, insightful thinking to find solutions. But as a defining paradigm for the next era of politics, both endeavors suffer from some problems. Start with the liberaltarian approach. First, it is unclear that liberaltarianism will accomplish its goals. For example, Lindsey and Teles argue that inequality is partly a function of upward redistribution—wealthy people and interests capturing government and using it to serve themselves. This seems right in the case of Wall Street subsidies and intellectual property. But consider their example of occupational licensing. There is a significant income difference between most licensed hairdressers on the one hand and most doctors and lawyers on the other. Are hairdressers really the wealthy elites who are contributing to rising inequality in America? It seems unlikely. This is a problem because people are more likely to agree to deregulate hairdressers than doctors or lawyers, which means that in practice, reforming occupational licensing rules is likely to hit lower-income professions disproportionally hard. Lindsey and Teles also argue that there is real harm to consumers: licensing means there are fewer hairdressers, which increases prices for poorer consumers. This might be true. But licensing also raises the wages of hairdressers, creating jobs with better wages. It isn't obvious that society would be better off with slightly cheaper haircuts, compared with better-paying jobs that can't be outsourced—and which, in turn, would help families pay for slightly more expensive haircuts.

Wilkinson and Hammond face a similar problem. They argue that the free market welfare state will unleash economic dynamism and innovation due to lower regulatory burdens. It is certainly possible that regulations—and especially badly designed regulations—can frustrate economic innovation. But at present, the evidence suggests this focus is misplaced. Alex Tabarrok, a libertarian economist, conducted a study that shows that government regulations are not the cause of the lack of dynamism in the economy. The study is particularly notable because Tabarrok undertook the research seeking to prove the opposite. Regardless of how he broke down the numbers, he was unable to find any burdensome effect of regulations on dynamism.[3]

The second problem with liberaltarianism is that its deregulatory policies might harm freedom and increase inequality because they could unleash and concentrate private power. Liberaltarians, like neoliberals, are more concerned with government action than inaction. And although they recognize that private actors can capture government, they don't confront how unregulated private actors can oppress people in the marketplace. Without regulations, companies would be free to dump toxic waste into rivers, remove safety protocols from mines and oil rigs, and use lead paint in children's toys. Some liberaltarian thinkers tend to focus on a narrow set of areas—licensing and zoning are the primary areas—and many make claims about regulation. But they pay less attention to all the benefits of regulations—clean air, clean water, safe workplaces, and safe toys. Nor do they attend as much to government regulations that preserve market competition and prevent fraud. Whether the goal is combatting the concentration of wealth or increasing economic dynamism, it isn't clear why liberaltarians do not focus more on reinvigorating antitrust enforcement to break up tech companies or airlines. For some reason, one of the greatest threats to the economy is hairdressers getting paid a few extra dollars, not price-gouging telecom companies, Amazon taking over the lion's share of online retail sales, or consolidation in the defense sector.

It may be that they are a bit reticent to abandon neoliberalism. In his article coining *liberaltarianism* as a term, Lindsey suggests that liberals and libertarians might find common cause if libertarians abandon their goal of ending Social Security and Medicare and liberals, in turn, agree to cut these programs. Nothing about this proposal seems any different from the conventional neoliberal position on those programs. Coming to liberaltarianism as a self-described liberal, Teles acknowledges that his intellectual journey began with the *Washington Monthly* (run by Charles Peters, who was an intellectual leader of the center-left neoliberals in the early 1980s) and the Clinton-era Democratic Leadership Council. Left liberaltarianism's origins, in other words, are an outgrowth of neoliberalism.[4]

Another strand of reformed neoliberalism makes bold claims but with a single specific policy. In recent years, many people have become interested in the transformative possibility of a universal basic income (UBI), a policy by which everyone would get a cash income from the government every month. The advocates for this policy are wide ranging: philosophers, former labor union leaders, tech company CEOs—even Milton Friedman was for it. Some are interested in UBI as a way to alleviate poverty. Others are fearful that technology, artificial intelligence, and automation will lead to the widespread destruction of jobs, and they see UBI as a way to guarantee an income to those whose livelihoods will be wiped out by technology.[5]

As a policy matter, much depends on how the UBI is designed. Some people see it as a supplement to the social safety net. But others argue that it should replace the social safety net—just give people cash and let them buy, for example, health care on the private market. There's also the question of how much the UBI would pay, with some of the leading proponents suggesting $1,000 per month. Economically, the UBI suffers from serious challenges. Twelve thousand dollars a year falls just south of the federal poverty level for a single person in the United States. And if the UBI is a replacement for the social safety net, rather than a supplement, poor people won't have access to Medicaid for health care. Imagine trying to pay for housing, food, transportation, and other expenses—plus health care costs on the private market—on $12,000 a year. To make things worse, the existence of a UBI might also depress wages: businesses could decide to drop wages to minimum wage because they know people have a supplementary income of $1,000 per month. For those who want to adopt a UBI because they fear that technology will eliminate most jobs in the future, the challenge is perhaps even greater: if the UBI is set too low, people will still need jobs to survive. The challenge is that raising the amount of the UBI to a livable dollar figure gets extremely costly extremely quickly. As Luke Martinelli has put it, "An affordable UBI would be inadequate, and an adequate UBI would be unaffordable."[6]

The central problem with the UBI is that its supporters—even on the left—frequently assume that there is no alternative to a neoliberal economy that distributes wealth to a small number of very wealthy people and leaves everyone else impoverished. Even those motivated by fears of automation and technology assume both that there won't be jobs that require humans and that a small number of oligarchs will own all the robots. Whether consciously or not, they have resigned themselves to living within the structure of the neoliberal economy, seeking only to mitigate its worst excesses. But it isn't clear why we have to accept such a fate. Instead of accepting the distribution of wealth and then slightly redistributing wealth through a limited UBI, we could instead embrace what Jacob Hacker has called "predistribution," the idea of reshaping the rules of the market so the distribution of wealth isn't so skewed in the first place. Such a policy, however, requires thinking about regulation, antitrust, and corporate ownership. But such policies are rarely on the lips of the UBI proponents.[7]

None of this is to say that addressing licensing rules, creating a UBI, or other liberaltarian proposals might not each be desirable as a matter of policy to solve some more narrowly tailored problems. These are creative ideas, and well-designed versions of them certainly have merit. The problem is that, on their own, they don't do enough to address the magnitude of contemporary political, economic, and social challenges.

Indeed, while the theorists of reformed neoliberalism have been dreaming up policies to address the excesses of the last era, the ground of capitalism has shifted, initiating what Shoshona Zuboff has called "the age of surveillance capitalism." Technological developments have fundamentally reformed industrial capitalism, Zuboff argues, into a system built on constant, widespread surveillance of the population. Tech companies such as Google and Facebook have a business model based on collecting data on every aspect of a person's life—where you are at any moment, what you eat, how well you sleep, what temperature your house is, what you listen to. This information, along with everything else they collect, can be used for increasingly narrowly targeted advertising. But it can also be used to modify behavior and to control actions. With so much data, for example, big tech companies have the power to steer users to particular restaurants, political candidates, and even emotions. When this is coupled with psychological research on how to manipulate people's actions, free choice is reduced to little more than a fig leaf.[8]

In China, the fusion of state and market takes these dynamics to their logical extension, which some commentators call "digital authoritarianism." China's tech companies are transforming personal data into social credit scores that rise and fall as people engage in prosocial or antisocial behavior. And because any individual's score is impacted by the scores of people in his or her social network, there is a strong incentive for people to pressure their friends into prosocial behaviors. The result is an authoritarian society without the degree of violence and oppression that has accompanied these governments in the past. The Chinese approach,

Zuboff argues, leads to "guaranteed political and social outcomes: certainty without terror."[9]

Some of the proponents of reformed neoliberalism recognize that their policy solutions are partial, and they see their proposals as complementary to other reforms. But when thought of as a comprehensive vision, reformed neoliberalism falls short. In return for amassing great wealth in the lightly regulated marketplace, the titans of industry will agree to pay higher taxes to fund a slightly better welfare state that keeps ordinary people just above water. It should be no surprise, therefore, that some of the leading UBI proponents are extremely well-off technology entrepreneurs. Instead of ending surveillance capitalism, they would only alleviate its worst consequences. Reformed neoliberalism, it turns out, is little more than a social contract for oligarchy. This is not desirable, and it is unlikely to be stable. It is hard to imagine that deregulating hairdressers and paying individuals $12,000 a year will stop demagogues from stirring up nationalist hatreds and mobilizing people to overthrow self-indulgent wealthy elites. And if reformed neoliberalism helps legitimize digital authoritarianism instead, is that any better? Constant surveillance and behavior control are hard to square with any modern idea of a free society.

Still, reformed neoliberalism is a plausible path forward—and for many, a tempting one. It requires less political courage to make minor changes to the current trajectory of society than it does to push for big reforms. Powerful elites are willing to trade minor tax increases and redistribution for maintenance of a system that benefits them. And nostalgia and the desire for a return to normalcy have a natural pull, particularly in times of uncertainty and flux. For many who oppose President Trump and remember the Obama era, reformed neoliberalism may seem like the best path because incremental reforms appear to be a way to recapture the past. The problem is that history only goes in one direction. Reforming neoliberalism is not only the least ambitious path we could take going forward and not only unlikely to clean up the wreckage of the neoliberal era. It is also unlikely to address the fundamental transformations taking place today.

Nationalist Populism

It has become commonplace to think of populism as nationalist and racist, as speaking for the supposed real people of a country. In his book *What Is Populism?*, for example, Jan-Werner Müller takes this approach. But this tenet of right-wing populism is not coextensive with populism itself. The Populist Party in the United States during the late nineteenth century placed their greatest emphasis on issues of economic power and distribution and had an important strand that sought to build bridges across racial lines. Indeed, left-wing populists today follow this alternative tradition. The populism of the self-described democratic socialist Bernie Sanders condemned how the "billionaire class" was rigging the system, even as he supported racial justice efforts. Nationalist populism combines the ethnic, religious, racial, or cultural nationalism of right-wing populism with the economics of left-wing populists. In contemporary politics, the latter agenda includes breaking up the banks and regulating the financial industry, redistributing wealth, expanding jobs through federal programs, and protecting and expanding universal public programs.[10]

Perhaps the best examples of nationalist populism are Donald Trump, when he was in campaign mode in 2016, and his erstwhile strategist Steve Bannon. During his campaign for the presidency, Donald Trump offered a mix of right-wing nationalism—from his Make America Great Again slogan to his thinly veiled support for white nationalists—and left-wing economic populism. Trump repeatedly promised not to cut Social Security, Medicare, and Medicaid—and even attacked his fellow Republican candidates for wanting to cut those programs. He argued for Medicare to directly negotiate drug prices with pharma companies—a position long held by liberal Democrats. He argued that Wall Street was "getting away with murder" and that elites had "bled our country dry." He even suggested raising taxes on hedge fund managers. Trump's administration has not pursued this course, but his campaign combined left and right populism, often to cheers from gigantic crowds.[11]

Bannon has called his similar approach "economic nationalism." Bannon supports increased taxes on the rich and a trillion-dollar infrastructure plan to create working-class jobs, and he thinks tech companies like Facebook and Google should be regulated as public utilities. He has argued that over the last few decades, "the globalists gutted the American working class and created a middle class in Asia." In response, he has advocated for "economic war" with China, starting with a far more aggressive trade policy. For Bannon, economic populism is also a sound political strategy. In a conversation with liberal journalist Robert Kuttner, Bannon said that "the longer [the Democrats] talk about identity politics, I got 'em. I want them to talk about racism every day. If the left is focused on race and identity, and we go with economic nationalism, we can crush the Democrats."[12]

Despite being the best example of a national populist, Bannon has been fainthearted in his commitment. His call for the "deconstruction of the administrative state," for example, was explicitly made in response to businesses asking for fewer and less stringent regulations. It is unclear why Bannon thinks this is good for working-class people as part of his economic nationalism agenda. A trillion-dollar infrastructure plan requires an administrative state to administer the plan. An economic war with China requires a Commerce Department and US trade representative with the power to engage in investigations and tariff setting. And regulating tech platforms as public utilities requires, unsurprisingly, regulation. When playing to the traditional Republican base of big corporate interests, Bannon's economic nationalism goes into retreat.[13]

Taken as an ideal type, however, nationalist populism builds off of the backlash to neoliberalism. Its nationalism rejects neoliberalism's individualistic tendencies and replaces them with communal identity. Its economic populism rejects neoliberalism's oligarchic policies and replaces them with redistributionist policies.

Nationalist populism also has the potential to be popular. Scholars have shown that a sizable population is culturally conservative but supports active government. Political scientist Lee Drutman, for example, broke down the 2016 electorate along two dimensions: social/identity issues and economic issues. He found that there were a large number of Americans who are liberal or conservative on both metrics. An extremely small number of people are economically conservative and socially liberal, what we might think of as libertarian, but an enormous number of Americans are economically liberal and socially conservative. Another political scientist, Larry Bartels, found similar dynamics when looking at political attitudes in 2017. Bartels also investigated internal party divisions, and he found that nationalist populists split the parties: "Rank and file Democrats are relatively united in their enthusiasm for an active government, but less united on cultural issues, where a sizable minority cling to the traditional values downplayed or even rejected by most party leaders." In contrast, he notes, "rank and file Republicans seem to be relatively united and energized by 'hard-edge nationalism,' but less united on the role of government, with a sizeable minority expressing rather un-Republican enthusiasm for a strong welfare state."[14]

What this means is that both parties are competing to retain and win over Americans who are economically liberal and socially conservative—in other words, national populists. Although this approach might be popular with a significant chunk of the electorate, we should not hold our breath in anticipation of nationalist populism flooding politics like a tidal wave. Nationalist populism simply does not have the support of political elites. Liberal leaders do not agree with the right-wing populist positions on race, gender, and sexual orientation and would not run a government that pursued such policies. Conservative leaders do not support an economically populist agenda, in spite of Trump's successful 2016 campaign or Bannon's quotable turns of phrase, and cannot run a government along those lines. This is partly why President Trump has betrayed these voters and shifted away from national populism since he has been in office. Because neither side will embrace nationalist populism wholeheartedly, voters with these intuitions are, for the time being at least, one of the battlegrounds of politics.

Nationalist Oligarchy

Across the political spectrum, a variety of commentators fear the global rise of autocracies and authoritarian governments. They cite Russia, Hungary, the Philippines, and Turkey as examples. And they fear that the United States is next. Former secretary of state Madeleine Albright published a book called *Fascism: A Warning*. Cass Sunstein gathered a variety of scholars for a collection titled *Can It Happen Here? Authoritarianism in America*. After the election of Donald Trump, Yale professor Timothy Snyder's pamphlet *On Tyranny* was a bestseller for more than a year.[15]

The authoritarian lens is familiar from the heroic narrative of democracy defeating autocracies in the twentieth century. But as a framework for interpreting—and predicting—the future, it is far too narrow. The rise-of-authoritarianism narrative has little, if anything, to say about economics. Its emphasis is almost exclusively political and constitutional—free speech, an independent judiciary, voting rights, equal treatment for minorities, and the like. In some ways, it makes sense that so many commentators raised in the neoliberal era frame the problem in these terms: neoliberalism seeks to separate politics from economics, to see each as an autonomous sphere. But politics and economics cannot be dissociated from each other. Both have to be considered together. This approach has long been called political economy. Political economy looks at economic and political relationships together, and it is attentive to how power is exercised in both sectors. If authoritarianism is the future, there must be a story of its political economy—how it uses politics and economics to gain and hold power. Yet the rise-of-authoritarianism theorists have less to say about these dynamics.[16]

The better label for this third possible future is *nationalist oligarchy*. Oligarchy means rule by a small number of rich people. In an oligarchy, wealthy elites seek to preserve and extend their wealth and power. In his definitive book *Oligarchy*, Jeffrey Winters calls this "wealth defense." Elites engage in "property defense," protecting what they already have, and "income defense," preserving and extending their ability to hoard more. In the old days, castles and walls were forms of property defense; force and violence could guarantee income defense. Modern oligarchs instead rely on cronyism, corruption, and manipulating legal rules (such as tax rates, property rules, and regulations). Importantly, oligarchy as a governing strategy accounts for both politics and economics. Oligarchs use economic power for political purposes and, in turn, use politics to expand their economic power.[17]

In even a nominally democratic society, as most countries around the world are today, it should be possible for the majority to overthrow the oligarchic minority with either the ballot or the bullet. So how can oligarchy persist? This is where both populism and authoritarianism come in. Oligarchies remain in power through two strategies: first, by using divide-and-conquer tactics to ensure that a majority doesn't come into being, and second, by rigging the political system to make it harder for any emerging majority to overthrow them.[18]

The divide-and-conquer strategy is an old one, and it works through a combination of coercion and co-optation. Nationalism—whether ethnic, religious, or racial—serves both functions. It aligns a portion of ordinary people with the ruling oligarchy, mobilizing them to support the regime. At the same time, it divides society, ensuring that inspired by nationalism will not join forces with everyone else to overthrow the oligarchs. We therefore see fearmongering about minorities and immigrants and claims that a country belongs only to its so-called true people. Activating these emotional, cultural, and political identities makes it harder for people to unite across these divides to challenge the regime. Rigging the system is, in some ways, more obvious as a tactic. It means changing the legal rules of the game or shaping the political marketplace to preserve power. Voting restrictions, gerrymandering, manipulation of the media—each makes fundamental reform more difficult.

Nationalist oligarchies thus use the politics of nationalism to mobilize (and sometimes divide) the people while delivering oligarchic economic policies to benefit the wealthy and well connected. Not all regimes of this type operate in precisely the same way. Just as there are many variants of liberal democracy—the Swedish model, the French model, the American model—there are many types of nationalist oligarchy. Each country's approach is unique, but there is a family resemblance that is readily identifiable.

Perhaps the most obvious example is Vladimir Putin's Russia. For example, the Russian constitution allowed a president to serve for no more than two *consecutive* terms. Putin dutifully followed the constitutional provision, serving two four-year terms as president, from 2000 to 2008, before turning over the office to his ally Dmitry Medvedev and taking the post of prime minister. During Medvedev's single four-year term, the government put forward a constitutional amendment to extend the presidential term to six years. The amendment passed through the Duma and the Federation Council in less than two months. Putin then retook the presidency in 2012 and was reelected in 2018. When his term finishes in 2024, he will have run Russia for virtually a quarter century. Over time, Putin's government has also passed new laws that have "increased penalties for participation in unauthorized protests, broadened the definition of treason, [and] required that NGOs receiving foreign money . . . register as 'foreign agents.'" The arrest and imprisonment of the band Pussy Riot was perhaps the most famous example of illiberalism in Russia.[19]

But to focus solely on these political changes misses that Russian politics is also intertwined with economics. As Brian Taylor writes in his book *The Code of Putinism*, "Putin is both president of the formal political system and boss of the informal clan network system." Putinomics mixes state capitalism, market capitalism, and informal networks of friends. The origins of this system were the infamous privatization campaigns of the 1990s, in which major state-owned enterprises from the Soviet era were "sold off" to oligarchs for highly "favorable prices." Taylor argues that Putin understood that he needed to control these new oligarchs rather than let them develop independent power centers. So he pushed media tycoons Boris Berezovsky and Vladimir Gusinsky out of the country, forcing them eventually to divest their media holdings. In their place, and at the helm of virtually all of the major companies in the country, are now Putin allies. Take, for example, the Bank of Russia, whose central figures are a physicist, a dentist, a former KGB agent, and an electrical engineer. Their common connection is that they were all close to Putin in the early 1990s. Taylor notes that the "prime minister, presidential chief of staff, secretary of the Security Council, speakers of the two houses of parliament, and the heads of three of the most important companies in the economy—Gazprom, Rusneft, and Russian Railways—as well as other key economic actors, such as the defense industry conglomerate Rostec and the media giant National Media Group" are all friends of Putin's. The result of this system is that Russian corporations are intertwined with the state.[20]

As another example, consider Viktor Orbán's Hungary. While in office, Orbán and his Fidesz party have embraced nationalist oligarchy, combining ethnic nationalist rhetoric, crony capitalism, and the systematic rigging of the political system to preserve power even when his party falters at the ballot box—and all while cozying up to Vladimir Putin's government in Russia.

Well before taking office, Orbán commented, "We have only to win once, but then properly." In 2010, Orbán's Fidesz party won just over 50 percent of the popular vote but a two-thirds majority of the seats in parliament. Once in office, Fidesz used its power to ensure it would keep it. In 2012, Fidesz used expedited procedures to draft and pass a new constitution in two months, with only nine days of parliamentary consideration. Among other things, the new constitution expanded the size of the constitutional court (so Fidesz could gain a majority) and extended the terms of the justices. Fidesz also expanded the electorate to ethnic Hungarians living abroad (with different voting rules for those in countries adjacent to Hungary compared with expats far away), engaged in gerrymandering, reduced the number of members of parliament, and abolished the two-round system of voting—all of which helped his party stay in power. As a result, the 2014 elections, one observer said, were "free but not fair."[21]

Immediately after the 2010 election victory, Orbán announced that June 4 would be deemed a Day of National Solidarity. On that day in 1920, Hungary signed the Treaty of Trianon, giving up its empire as part of the resolution to World War I. Fidesz frames this moment as the Trianon Trauma, blaming the West for stripping Hungary of two-thirds of its territory. Orbán has declared that Hungary should be an "illiberal democracy" and that non-Hungarians, and particularly refugees, are unwelcome. "We do not want to see in our midst any minorities whose cultural background differs from our own," he said in 2015. "We want to keep Hungary for the Hungarians."[22]

But like other nationalist oligarchies, ethnic nationalism has not been coupled with economic populism. Instead, according to Bálint Magyar, the former Hungarian minister of education, Orbán has created a "privatized form of a parasite state, an economic undertaking run by the family of the Godfather exploiting the political and public instruments of power." Paul Lendvai, former *Financial Times* reporter and author of a book on Orbán, reports that "leases of state-owned land" and licenses for national tobacco shops are doled out to supporters. The government has used the export-import bank (meant to help businesses exporting goods) to prop up a domestic media company that supports the government and attacks its critics. Orbán's friends and family also benefit. Orbán's childhood friend Lorinc Meszaros, for example, went from being a gas fitter to the fifth-richest Hungarian, all because he won a variety of state-building contracts. Worse still, the European Union funds Hungary's oligarchy, as Orbán draws on EU money to fund about 60 percent of the state projects that support "the new Fidesz-linked business elite." Nor do Orbán and his allies do much to hide the country's crony capitalist model. András Lánczi, president of a Fidesz-affiliated think tank, has said that "if something is done in the national interest, then it is not corruption." "The new capitalist ruling class," one Hungarian banker comments, "make their money from the government."[23]

Jan-Werner Müller captures Orbán's Hungary this way: "Power is secured through wide-ranging control of the judiciary and the media; behind much talk of protecting hard-pressed families from multinational corporations, there is crony capitalism, in which one has to be on the right side politically to get ahead economically."[24]

Crony capitalism, coupled with resurgent nationalism and central government control, is also an issue in China. Although some commentators have focused on state capitalism—when government has a significant ownership stake in companies—this phenomenon is not the same as crony capitalism. Some countries with state capitalism, like Norway, are seen as extremely noncorrupt and indeed are often held up as models of democracy. State capitalism also rejects the neoliberal myth that markets are somehow disconnected from politics: it acknowledges the interplay between the two. Crony capitalism, in contrast, is an "instrumental union between capitalists and politicians designed to allow the former to acquire wealth, legally or otherwise, and the latter to seek and retain power." In essence, it is a form of oligarchy.[25]

China expert Minxin Pei argues that neoliberal reforms from the Deng Xiaoping era are the root of the country's growing problem with corruption and oligarchy. Just as in the former states of the Soviet Union, China engaged in privatization and decentralization in the 1990s. But frequently, Chinese privatization—particularly of lucrative state assets like mining and lands—only extended to use rights rather than complete ownership rights. Combined with decentralization of administrative power to lower levels of government, the opportunity for collusion became evident: local government officials had the power to grant private actors use rights over land, and private actors, in turn, made it worthwhile for officials to give them the contracts.[26]

The result was widespread corruption. Consider the example of Zhou Yongkang, who was on the Politburo Standing Committee (one of the most powerful bodies in China) and received a life sentence for corruption in 2015. During Zhou Yongkang's sentencing, the court said that his wife and son had taken 129 million yuan in bribes and the family had 2.1 billion yuan in illegal earnings. This isn't an isolated incident. In a bombshell story, the *New York Times* reported in 2012 that Prime Minister Wen Jiabao's family had amassed $2.7 billion during his rise through the ranks of government. So significant is corruption in China that even Xi Jinping has condemned it and made fighting it a central part of his agenda. But what remains unclear is whether Xi's anti-corruption efforts are bona fide attempts at public integrity or maneuvers designed to solidify and expand his power.[27]

The Chinese government has also responded to the realities of an oligarchic economy with greater nationalism and centralization. As Zhang Yunling, director of international studies at the Chinese Academy of Social Sciences in Beijing, put it, "Patriotism is very important for a rising power." For his part, Xi has recognized that reinvigorating national ideology is critical for preserving the regime: "The disintegration of a regime often starts from the ideological area, political unrest and regime change may perhaps occur in a night, but ideological evolution is a long-term process. If the ideological defenses are breached, other defenses become very difficult to hold." Carl Minzner, a scholar of Chinese law, observes that "playing the populist card has gone hand in hand with reinforcing hardline policies." The government has identified "Seven Nos," including universal values, a free press, civil society, and an independent judiciary. Meanwhile, Xi has gained more and more control over all aspects of the government, with the government abolishing limits on a third term in office.[28]

Russia, Hungary, and China present three different and notable trajectories of the trend toward nationalist oligarchy, but they aren't the only cases. After the coup in 2016, Turkey's president engaged in widespread purges of the government, crackdowns on opponents, and constitutional reforms to centralize and strengthen his power—all while emphasizing religious nationalism. Right-wing nationalist parties are also on the rise in other countries in Europe, Asia, and Latin America.

With all of these examples in mind, it is hard not to see the United States as marching in a similar direction. Although this trend has been growing throughout the late neoliberal era, the Trump administration encapsulates the rise of nationalist oligarchy. The president's nationalist tendencies are well known. He began his presidency with the swift declaration of a travel ban on persons from Muslim countries and the unleashing of immigration officials to engage in raids across the country. These policies were challenged in court almost immediately, but their substantive, symbolic, and rhetorical value persisted, showing his core supporters that he would protect so-called real America from foreigners who he claimed threatened the security or culture of the country. President Trump has also normalized white nationalism. After the KKK, neo-Nazis, and other white supremacists marched through the streets in Charlottesville, Virginia, leading to the death of one woman, President Trump remained neutral for days before making a statement formally condemning racism, the KKK, and neo-Nazis. The president went on to say that both sides were blameworthy and "very violent." Few saw the combination of these statements as anything less than an indication of support for the white nationalist groups. For their part, white supremacists didn't take his statements as a rebuke. David Duke, a former leader of the KKK, tweeted, "Thank you President Trump for your honesty & courage to tell the truth about #Charlottesville." This type of nationalism was also part of Trump's campaign for the presidency in 2016. He announced his campaign by claiming that Mexican immigrants were rapists and murderers, attacked a federal judge of Mexican descent, and attacked a Muslim gold star family.[29]

Trump's nationalism, however, has not extended to economic populism—despite his campaign promises to drain the swamp and fight for working people. Instead, President Trump's administration has deepened the emerging American oligarchy. The signature legislative efforts of the Trump presidency have been an effort to repeal Obamacare and a massive tax cut. Some analysts showed that the full Obamacare repeal would mean that up to thirty million people would lose their health insurance. Although the overall repeal failed, the repeal of just the individual mandate was pushed through as part of a tax bill—and according to the Congressional Budget Office, that change would leave thirteen million uninsured. The people affected by the repeal, of course, aren't the wealthy. They are the very working people that a populist claims to support.[30]

The Trump and Republican tax plan provides an even better example of expanding oligarchy. The tax bill included the largest corporate tax cut in American history, totaling $1 trillion over a decade. It cut the tax rate on the wealthiest people in the country while increasing the income level where that rate takes effect. It shrunk the estate tax—the tax wealthy people pay to pass wealth on to their heirs and heiresses—so that there's no tax on the first $22 million that married couples pass down to their children. Each of these policies alone is an example of income and wealth defense for the richest people and corporations in the country, but together, they are truly radical. Instead of spending $1.46 trillion (the total cost of the bill) on rebuilding infrastructure or improving education or expanding Social Security, the Trump administration chose to expand corporate profits, with benefits for wealthy executives and shareholders, then cut those people's taxes, and then allow them to build a hereditary aristocracy by passing tens of millions of that wealth on to their children.[31]

The Trump administration has also delayed and rolled back regulations that will ultimately benefit big corporations while harming ordinary people. The administration delayed regulations designed to decrease the amount of silica and beryllium that people inhale and delayed highway safety rules to prevent sleepy truckers from getting behind the wheel. It has opened up national monuments for natural resource extraction. Regulations on access to courts, net neutrality, clean power, and fuel efficiency are under attack. These policies all favor large corporate interests over consumer interests. But this is unsurprising, given that the president who once promised to drain the swamp has instead filled his administration with lobbyists for industries opposed to those regulations and to the agencies where they now work. A March 2018 report found that the Trump administration had appointed 187 lobbyists to government positions.[32]

As public policies are being skewed to benefit oligarchic interests, the president himself has been engaged in self-enrichment of the kind that is more befitting a petty dictatorship rather than the world's most powerful democracy. The president hosts events at the Trump Hotel, down the street from the White House. He continues to visit Mar-a-Lago, his Florida getaway/resort, where members hobnob with him—for a (now increased) fee. Foreign governments seek to curry favor with the administration by hosting events at his properties. And to put a cherry on top, taxpayers are footing the bill, covering the costs of travel and security when the president visits these properties. If a multibillionaire president in a foreign country didn't cover the costs of a lavish lifestyle, we would certainly condemn that political leader for corruption and graft.[33]

At the same time, the Trump administration and the Republicans aspire to rig the political system to preserve their own power, even in the face of majority opposition to an oligarchic agenda. Gerrymandering is the most obvious example. Our constitutional system gerrymanders the Senate and electoral college, which is why presidential candidates like Al Gore and Hillary Clinton can win the popular vote and lose the presidency. But gerrymandering for the House of Representatives or state legislatures is not constitutionally required. And yet many partisans use the tactic to benefit their party in elections.

Trump and Republicans, however, have gone much further than gerrymandering. They have claimed widespread voter fraud when there is no evidence of such practices (except perhaps by Republicans who tampered with ballots in North Carolina) and have used those claims to impose restrictions on voting. The Trump administration created a presidential commission to investigate voter fraud and make recommendations on how to address the fake issue (the commission disbanded amid extensive litigation). It even attempted to ask census questions in a manner that experts showed would depress cooperation with census officials and lead to undercounting minority populations.[34]

In Georgia, Secretary of State Brian Kemp has been compared to Viktor Orbán for his tactics: purging more than one hundred thousand voters from the rolls because they chose not to vote in a recent election, delaying voter registrations for minor issues, accusing opponents of hacking without evidence, and refusing help from the Department of Homeland Security. Dodge City, Kansas, which has seen an increase in its Latinx population, moved its only polling place—for twenty-seven thousand residents—from the civic center to a location one mile from the nearest bus stop and outside the city limits. When Republicans lost statewide elections in Wisconsin and Michigan in 2018, they did not go quietly into the minority but instead passed laws stripping power from incoming Democratic officials. Their corporate contributors and allies, unsurprisingly, remained silent in the face of these antidemocratic actions.[35]

It's not just politicians who are undermining democratic institutions. The decline of local news media, critical for democratic engagement, is often thought of as a byproduct of the rise of the internet. Although there is truth to this story, the collapse of local media wasn't inevitable or solely due to technology. In communities around the country, local papers like the *Bastrop Daily Enterprise* (Louisiana) and *Fayetteville Observer* (North Carolina) were thriving until they were bought out by private equity firms, which then gutted their newsrooms, outsourced operations to regional or national centers, and raised prices. For the firms, the result is profits. For the paper, lower circulation. For the communities, a loss of quality information about public affairs.[36]

At the same time, big media companies are on the rise, some of which have an ideological agenda designed to support the rich and powerful. In the spring of 2018, the Sinclair Media Group, a pro-Trump media company, gained infamy for forcing local news reporters across the country to read an antimedia statement.

At the time, Sinclair operated in 193 stations in 89 media markets, reaching 39 percent of Americans. It also wanted to purchase Tribune Media, which would give it 235 stations in 108 markets—and the ability to reach 72 percent of Americans. If the Trump administration approves the merger, it would mean a propagandistic outlet broadcasting to most Americans through the guise of local news.[37]

Nationalist oligarchy may not be a desirable future, but it is a plausible one. Looking back, it is easy to see how nationalist oligarchy emerged from the late stages of the neoliberal era. The neoliberal strategy of deregulation, liberalization, privatization, and austerity has the consequence of concentrating wealth and power in private hands. This was coupled with a theory of politics that ignores the power of wealth. The view that money is speech under the First Amendment first emerged only in the 1970s, and over time, it unleashed wealthy individuals and corporations to spend as much as they wanted to influence politics. The "doom loop of oligarchy," as Ezra Klein has called it, is an obvious consequence: the wealthy use their money to influence politics and rig policy to increase their wealth, which only increases their capacity to influence politics. Crony capitalism, self-enrichment, and other kinds of corruption are but variations on the theme.[38]

The authoritarian and antidemocratic tendencies of nationalist oligarchies are also an outgrowth of neoliberal failures. The neoliberals preached that all good things would go together. They argued that the swift adoption of democracy would mean a growing economy. They imposed the Washington Consensus, proclaiming that liberalization would create booming economies. But this didn't happen. Peoples around the world, as Joshua Kurlantzick has observed, "soured on the notion of democracy itself" when it failed to bring growth. The result was "decreased public participation in politics; nostalgia for previous authoritarian eras; the rise of elected autocrats; increasingly poisoned, violent election campaigns; and sometimes an outright return to autocracy, whether through a coup or some other extra-constitutional means." The United States has not been immune to these changes in attitudes. A study published in 2016 found that only 30 percent of millennials thought it was essential to live in a democracy. And between 1995 and 2010, the percentage of wealthy Americans who supported authoritarianism jumped from 20 percent to nearly 35 percent.[39]

More broadly, the rise of nationalism can also be interpreted as a response, or backlash, to neoliberalism. Neoliberalism's atomistic individualism and its marketization of everything leaves people with little by way of community, tradition, or social bonds. Nationalists—whether ethnic, religious, cultural, racial—thus find a hungry constituency, yearning for connections to each other and to something bigger than themselves.

* * *

The central question today is whether nationalist oligarchy will come to dominate the next era of politics. Conservatives can support an oligarchic economic system, rig the political system to stay in power, and use nationalism to divide and conquer. In those moments when liberals win elections, they would be forced to operate largely within the constraints of the era—most likely by advancing reformed neoliberal policies that further entrench economic power, albeit with a human face. But there is another path forward, a path that is politically, economically, and socially inclusive—a path toward a great democracy.

5

TOWARD A GREAT DEMOCRACY

Nationalist oligarchy, nationalist populism, and reformed neoliberalism are all undesirable futures. Nationalist oligarchy and nationalist populism exclude major segments of the population, stirring fear and hatred in order to mobilize a political coalition. Nationalist oligarchy and reformed neoliberalism concentrate wealth and power in the hands of the few, undermining equality, opportunity, and freedom. What we should want is a path forward that is inclusive politically and economically—offering opportunity and community to every member of society. This fourth option for the future of politics requires an agenda to achieve a *great democracy*.

Democracy, of course, causes confusion. Right-wing trolls like to point out that the United States is a republic, not a democracy. They ignore that James Madison himself defined a *republic* in *The Federalist* as a government based on representation and that no one using the term *democracy* today means a direct democracy along the lines of ancient Athens or the New England town meeting. Democracy today means representative democracy—a republic.[1]

When many others think of democracy, they think primarily about voting and elections. Countries in transition from dictatorships are celebrated when their first elections take place. Photos abound of proud voters with inky fingers. And yet, in many countries around the world, elections aren't competitive, and they aren't free or fair. They instead ratify the power of authoritarian leaders. North Korea's official name, for example, is the Democratic People's Republic of Korea, and its leader, Kim Jong-un, was elected with 100 percent of the vote in 2014. But no one thinks of North Korea as a democracy.[2]

In recent years, when scholars have questioned whether democracy might be in a moment of crisis all around the world, they have looked beyond elections—but not by much. For example, in their article "How to Lose a Constitutional Democracy," constitutional scholars Aziz Huq and Tom Ginsburg describe the three features of constitutional democracy as competitive elections, free speech and association, and the legal rules necessary to ensure democratic choices. In their bestselling book, *How Democracies Die*, political scientists Steven Levitsky and Daniel Ziblatt focus on the erosion of constitutional norms, including many associated with electoral democracy: a leader's weak commitment to democratic institutions, the denial of the legitimacy of political opponents, toleration of violence, and clamping down on civil liberties. Many other scholars and commentators have also emphasized that democratic norms and institutions are under assault, eroding slowly, or being destroyed altogether.[3]

But although the emphasis in recent years has been on norms and institutions, the restoring-norms approach cannot fully explain what makes democracy work—and its reform agenda is not designed to make democracy more inclusive. This is a problem because the most sustainable way to preserve norms and institutions is to make democracy more inclusive socially, economically, and politically. To see why, consider the conditions under which leaders adhere to political norms and support democratic institutions. Norms are simply informal practices that a group of people follow even when they would benefit immediately from breaking them. We can include in this category both informal courtesies that people grant each other (for example, civility on the Senate floor) and respect for institutions (for example, not attacking the freedom of the press or integrity of the judiciary).

The puzzle is figuring out why political leaders would ever restrain themselves by following these informal conventions. The first explanation is that political leaders actually have a long-term interest in adhering to norms. If political leaders are what social scientists call repeat players—that is, they are going to be participating in politics for a long time—then they might be better off in the long run by keeping the norm intact, even if breaking the norm is in their short-term interest. In the first two years of President Trump's administration, for example, Senate Republicans would have benefited from ending the filibuster for legislation so that any piece of legislation would only need a simple majority to pass. In a time of Republican control of the House of Representatives, Senate, and presidency, ending the filibuster would have enabled the Republicans to advance their legislative agenda successfully. But Senate Republicans anticipated that the Democrats would, one day, have control over Congress and the presidency. And in that situation, Republicans would be better off if Democrats did not have the power to pass legislation so easily. Because they are repeat players who want the other side to play by the same rules, the filibuster remains.

A second explanation for why norms hold is that those who adhere to them are part of a shared cultural community with many personal ties and common beliefs. For example, the diamond industry has not relied on courts and governments to enforce contracts or police the boundaries of sales for centuries. Diamond merchants rely on personal relationships and trust—norms—to make and enforce sales contracts. But this mode of exchange works because the industry is dominated by an ethnically homogeneous group of merchants who have intergenerational family businesses.[4]

Note that on both of these explanations, norms are fundamentally antidemocratic. In the case of reciprocity, norms are stronger if senators are entrenched in power for decades because they know they will eventually be on the losing end if the norm breaks. In the case of diamond dealers, the community is small and insular. In other words, clubby environments are better at preserving norms. Relying partly on this basic insight, some commentators have suggested that the problem today is too much democracy. Andrew Sullivan's broadside in *New York* magazine was thus titled

"Democracies End When They Are Too Democratic." Many in this camp hold that the rising populism of the era proves that elites are central to safeguarding liberty. But for the many people who are not willing to adopt some sort of aristocracy, a commitment to both norms and democracy is in serious tension.[5]

There is also a third situation in which political and constitutional norms hold—one that does not rely on insular elites. When the population as a whole believes strongly in a norm, leaders are unlikely to attack it. Leaders who violate norms will face the fury of public opinion and will be sanctioned at the ballot box. Under this theory, the real strength of norms and institutions does not come from leaders or elites but from the people themselves. The leaders simply reflect the sentiments of society at large.

With these explanations in mind, how should we understand the current assault on democratic norms and institutions? There are two explanations. First, democracy has broken the elite club, and the political movements that stormed the gates and elected new leadership are less committed to norms and institutions—and maybe even want to destroy them. In other words, the repeat player and common culture explanations for norms have failed because our political leaders are no longer a small group of homogeneous people who will serve in office together over decades. It is thus no surprise that the most prominent norm breaker, Donald Trump, never held any elected or appointed office of any kind and that outsiders are the ones most intent on eliminating long-standing laws, practices, and institutions. The second possible reason norms come under assault is that the elites remain in power but are responding to popular preferences to stay in power. Politicians who fear a primary challenger or worry about losing turnout from their political base might find themselves staying silent or even participating in an attack on norms if they think their constituents demand it.

Whether the people have broken into the elite club or whether the club members are responding to the people's demands, norms are violated and institutions are attacked because the people themselves are no longer invested enough in them to preserve them. The deep, difficult problem is thus not the erosion of the institutions or the breaking of norms per se, but the fact that the people no longer have sufficient respect for those norms and institutions. The crisis of democratic *government* is therefore really a crisis of democratic *society*. And this leads to a critical point: to have a functioning democratic government, we must fulfill the conditions for a democratic society.

For much of the neoliberal era, there was less emphasis on the necessary conditions for a democratic society. Conversations about democracy emphasized the expansion of the franchise and the right of individuals to participate in the political process. In America, it was the heroic tale of how the Jacksonians expanded the franchise to white men, abolishing property requirements for voting; how the Civil War and Reconstruction ended slavery and gave African Americans the right to vote; how suffragettes fought and won the battle for women voting; and how, ultimately, the civil rights movement made civil and political equality real throughout the country. With the franchise expanded, democracy was secure as long as basic institutions were in place. Democratic debates in the neoliberal era thus focused on whether individuals could actually exercise the right to vote, on how to increase voter turnout and reduce apathy, and on making democracy more participatory. The neoliberal era's vision of democracy divorced politics from economics and society and emphasized individual rights. The crisis-of-democracy theorists in the last few years have largely also focused on these features or on the associated institutions and norms that are necessary to sustain them.[6]

The problem is that the neoliberal era's approach to democracy only captures one aspect of democracy—the political aspect—and a narrow version at that. Political democracy is a critically important aspect of democracy, to be sure. But for a government to be democratic in any meaningful and sustainable sense, it must have more than elections and the associated legal institutions. The political realm cannot be separated from economic, social, and ethical commitments. Taking this broader view of democracy is far more demanding even though it has always been what democracy required to flourish.

First, democracy requires a measure of social solidarity and citizens who have an ethical commitment to the democratic community. The idea that neoliberalism could coexist with democracy was always going to be problematic. Neoliberalism's individualism and desire to privatize everything is in direct conflict with democracy's demand for social solidarity. A government founded on rule by the people requires the people to be part of a shared project. John Dewey once wrote that democracy "is the idea of community life itself," and a community, by definition, requires some kind of common culture. Politics will always feature minor divisions on a variety of issues, but when democratic societies become severely polarized—into rich and poor, North and South, free and slave, red and blue—it becomes a zero-sum game. In those situations, the democratic community is no longer engaged in the project of self-government but in warfare by other means.[7]

The fraying of our social fabric is thus a serious threat to democracy. Institutions that once facilitated social understanding—public schools, public parks and services, and the military—are increasingly segregated by class, race, or both. The media environment, which once featured only a few TV channels and therefore united everyone in a common news and entertainment culture, is now fractured with fewer gatekeepers and increasing personalization. Commentators on both the right and left recognize that neighborhoods are increasingly segregated—not just by race but by class and culture. Societies that are deeply divided are susceptible to being ripped apart by centrifugal forces, such as scapegoating "other" people for social problems. Democracy cannot withstand such violent clashes of opinion. This is also why, as intellectual historian James Kloppenberg has observed, democracy is "an ethical ideal." To participate in a democratic community means rejecting the selfish individualism that neoliberalism promotes. Democratic citizens must see true freedom as connected to the flourishing of the democratic community, and, paradoxically, that involves restraint and sacrifice.[8]

The second precondition is an economic democracy. For most of the history of Western political thought—from at least Aristotle in ancient Greece onward—philosophers and political leaders alike recognized that democracy cannot survive when there is extreme economic inequality; it requires a large, strong middle class. A society in which wealth is concentrated in the hands of the few will face one of two disastrous fates: either it will descend into oligarchy, as the rich use their wealth to rig the political system in their favor, or the divide between the rich and everyone else will lead to popular backlash, with a demagogue leading the revolt. Economically unequal societies are therefore inherently unstable and, one way or another, become undemocratic. In contrast, in a society with a substantial middle class, people will largely have shared economic interests. Political conflicts will be less likely to lead to polarization or to destabilize the republic. An economic democracy also ensures that no private actors—whether individuals or corporations—have so much power that they can dominate individuals or the government. This guarantees political and economic freedom for everyone. As Teddy Roosevelt once wrote, "There can be no real political democracy unless there is something approaching an economic democracy."[9]

Political democracy is, of course, what we normally think of as democracy. It might seem pithy and obvious to say that a representative democracy needs to be representative of all the people. But even amid worries about the erosion of democracy, our political system falls far short of this most basic principle. Reformers have long focused on how gerrymandering, voter suppression activities, and other election rules undermine the ability of everyone to have an equal voice in government. But a serious effort at political democracy will require more than voting reforms. Over the last decade or so, political scientists have shown that policy outcomes in government represent wealthy people and corporate interests and don't represent ordinary people well. Part of the reason is that wealthy people vote at higher rates, donate more, contact their representatives more, and serve as elected officials more. But again, the challenge goes much further than elections. Every branch of government is susceptible to influence. Congress is made up of people drawn from the wealthiest subsets of our population, and it is beset by lobbyists who "educate" members and their staffs and sometimes even draft legislation for members. In the executive branch, corporate interest groups wield considerable power over the regulatory process, both by commenting on the substance of regulations and by getting industry advocates appointed into government jobs. Even the courts are skewed: judicial appointees frequently come from backgrounds defending corporations; far fewer have spent their careers in the public interest or representing workers and consumers. Although there is a robust debate on how to balance majority rule with protecting the rights of minorities, a system that never has majority rule is hardly democratic and a system that channels the views of the wealthy is hardly representative. It is more like an oligarchy or an aristocracy.

Of course, "representation" can mean many things. The philosopher Hanna Pitkin wrote probably the most famous book on the concept, and she distinguished between two types of representation. Representation can mean standing for the people, meaning that the elected representatives resemble the people they represent. John Adams, for example, wrote in 1776 that the legislature "should be an exact portrait, in miniature, of the people at large, as it should think, feel, reason and act like them." Alternatively, representation can mean acting for the people. This meaning ranges from being an independent trustee that makes judgments in the people's best interest to acting like a transmission belt for their preferences. But here's the most important thing: neither theory of representation justifies rule by the wealthy, interest group domination of the policy agenda, or a small minority with idiosyncratic preferences wielding power over all of society.[10]

Each of the three conditions for democracy reinforces each other. Under conditions of economic inequality, stagnation, and scarcity, people become more susceptible to claims that other groups are to blame for the failures of public policy or for structural changes in the economy. As one scholar writes, "Political tribalism thrives under conditions of economic insecurity and lack of opportunity." In contrast, in a society with relative economic equality, attempts to use scapegoating find a less favorable social environment. The reverse is also true: in a society with a strong sense of solidarity, like the Scandinavian countries, people will also be more likely to support policies that expand economic equality.[11]

Economic inequality and political inequality also go together. The wealthiest people and interest groups use their wealth to reshape laws and regulations in ways that benefit themselves. This further deepens economic inequality. In contrast, in a society with relative economy equality, neither the relatively wealthy nor the relatively poor will be able to skew public policy because the middle class will pursue policies that help most people. Greater political equality also means greater economic equality, as the majority's preferences will be more likely to be put into law—and the majority is unlikely to support policies that disproportionately help the wealthy.[12]

Finally, a society with deep social divisions will also break down politically, as each tribe interprets all policy issues as part of a winner-take-all system, rendering compromise and cooperation impossible. In contrast, in a relatively homogeneous society, disagreements among people are relatively minor, rendering political compromises possible. "Societies thrive on trust," one political theorist notes, "but they need the widest possible radius of trust to do well." Social solidarity expands trust among people within the community—and that facilitates political cooperation rather than political conflict.[13]

Breakdown in any of the political, economic, and social conditions for democracy can lead to a breakdown in all three. Similarly, success in each arena strengthens the others. When people are economically equal, their political power is relatively equal, leading to more responsive policy choices. When people feel connected to their fellow citizens, they will be more likely to adopt policies to support them, leading to greater economic equality and therefore political equality. The choice is between a vicious cycle that destroys democracy and a virtuous one that sustains it.

Part of the problem today is that we have ignored the preconditions for a democratic society for too long. In the 1960s, the United States finally decided that the political community would treat all of our citizens as equals—white and black, men and women. But at the very moment in which our society was becoming politically inclusive, it failed to become more economically equal and socially united. The rising tide that lifted all boats in the post–World War II era started to recede in the 1970s. A brutally competitive global economy joined with neoliberal policies to bring a generation of wage stagnation and the economic collapse of communities across the country. Rather than getting closer to economic democracy, neoliberalism brought us to the edge of oligarchy. The civil rights movements of the 1960s promised to replace segregation with integration. But efforts to achieve social solidarity across race, gender, and geography also failed. Neoliberalism championed retreating into private cliques instead of confronting the hard work of building a national community. Attempts at racial integration led to white flight from the cities and eventually to informal segregation of many neighborhoods. Dog-whistle politics kept resentment simmering. And the culture wars increasingly brought division.

With the end of the neoliberal era, it is possible to succeed where past generations failed and fulfill the aspiration of democracy. Political leaders and activists have already begun to advance elements of this agenda. A new generation of elected officials, from Congressman Joe Kennedy to Mayor Pete Buttigieg, emphasizes the importance of public service and recognizes that service unites us. Some elected officials, including Congresswoman Alexandria Ocasio-Cortez and Senator Elizabeth Warren, have proposed higher tax rates on the very wealthy and investments in opportunity for all Americans. Federal Trade Commissioner Rohit Chopra and Congressman Ro Khanna have called for greater antitrust enforcement.

And a wide range of political leaders recognize the perilous conditions of our democracy and have supported sweeping reforms to voting, ethics, and conflicts of interest rules. If these emergent priorities are successful, the country will have more social solidarity, be more equal economically, and be more representative politically. It will become a great democracy.

As an approach for the future, the agenda for a great democracy stands in contrast to the last two eras of politics. Neoliberalism tries to put market processes before politics. Great democracy recognizes that people choose what kind of society to live in, and that includes choosing the rules for markets. Neoliberalism tries to separate economics from politics, imagining a separate sphere of economic action in which government should not operate. Great democracy recognizes that politics and economics are intertwined and that the accumulation of power in one can distort and destroy freedom in the other. Neoliberalism tries to place the individual above everything, atomizing people from each other in a competitive arena. Great democracy recognizes the importance of community with shared ethics, a common tradition, and joint ambitions.

Great democracy also isn't just a repackaged form of the liberalism of the post–World War II era. The old liberalism was based on public-private cooperation between big business, big government, and big labor. Great democracy instead seeks to establish a public realm—a set of shared institutions that everyone can partake in and from which everyone can benefit. The old liberalism was highly technocratic, seeking active management of specific processes and designs within industry. Great democracy aims instead to pursue structural regulations and policy programs that will be simpler and easier to monitor. The old liberalism also emphasized individual rights, and its era involved a great struggle for everyone to have those rights. Great democracy seeks to make good on the struggle for equality by working to build social solidarity across the country.

Great democracy also has a chance to build a new political coalition. Although the foundation and the vanguard of great democracy will likely be progressives, conservatives who are worried about the collapse of our constitutional system should also find common cause. With the specter of nationalist oligarchy on the horizon, conservatives should be willing to recognize that reform is better than revolution and that loosening their attachment to neo-liberal economics is likely the only way to preserve constitutional democracy for another generation. Populist conservatives should also find much to like in great democracy. Like progressives, they recognize the widespread corruption of the American political and economic system and seek a way out—a path for change. Great democracy emphasizes our American community and celebrates and exalts patriotism in defense of democracy.

Great democracy can be the future of politics after neoliber-alism, but for it to succeed, we need to understand it at the level of ideas and advance it forward through policy. This means delving deeper into great democracy as a worldview that can replace the neoliberal ideology—and connecting that worldview to a detailed policy program for the future. This is the task to which we now turn.

6

UNITED DEMOCRACY

There is a tension at the heart of liberal democracy. Liberalism is founded on the equality of individuals. It leads ultimately to the belief that all people, all around the world, have equal moral and political worth. Many liberals therefore become cosmopolitans. For a democracy to exist, there must be a demos, a people who are in the democracy. And that, in turn, suggests there are people outside of the democracy. Those who are part of the democratic community should be equal, but we have different duties to people who are outside our democratic community. Throughout history, many of the most fiercely contested political and moral questions have been about the boundary of the democratic community: Should everyone inside the country's borders—including women, minorities, young people—be considered full members of the political community? When should foreigners be allowed to join the political community? And how deep must the connections among members of the political community be? Of course, philosophers and dreamers might imagine a cosmopolitan democracy, a democracy of all humanity. But such a thing would require world government, and that is highly unlikely in the short or even medium term.[1]

For a democratic community to succeed, the people must be relatively united. There must be some degree of solidarity. If people are fractured by wealth or economic interests, if they are divided sharply by ideology, if they are separated by strong, even tribal, identities, it becomes more likely that one group will seek and use power to oppress the other groups. At the extreme, the result could be violence, civil wars, or revolutions. The less divided, the less risk of conflict along such cleavages. The stability of a society is thus partly based on social solidarity.

The second reason democracies require solidarity is freedom. The central premise of democracy is that the people themselves should determine their own fate. We the people decide our future *together*. If a group of people does not share a common purpose or common cause, if they are highly fractured in the direction they want to take the future, then it becomes hard for them to exercise their democratic freedom jointly. This is not to say that there will never be disagreements and differences. Hundreds of books and articles by philosophers, constitutional scholars, and political scientists have been written on how to manage societies that are divided in one way or another. Indeed, when any two people come together, there will be differences. But there is a breaking point. For a democracy to be sustainable, it must be relatively united.

This is why many of the most important political philosophers in history believed that republics had to be small in size. In a small republic, the people would be relatively homogeneous—in their culture, manners, views, and wealth. As a result, citizens and leaders could easily pursue the public good. In an expansive, large republic, there would be greater diversity among people and, with it, differences in opinion, culture, and wealth. The common good would become harder to discover, as people would confuse their own personal, selfish interests with the public interest. "In a small [republic]," the celebrated French philosopher Montesquieu said, "the public good is better felt, better known, lies nearer to each citizen."[2]

James Madison, writing in *The Federalist*, offered the classic response to the problem of size. He posited that in a large republic, there would be so many interests, so many different groups, that no single group would be able to dominate society. But it is worth remembering that Madison's political community—the demos he was thinking about—was itself relatively homogeneous. Women and minorities were excluded, and most of the new nation's citizens were of British descent with a shared language, culture, and religion. Within this political community, there was also relative economic equality. No feudalism, no hereditary aristocracy, and lands to the west meant any white man could be a property owner. As one of Madison's contemporaries observed, America had "a greater equality, than is to be found among the people of any other country."[3]

Over time, however, American democracy has expanded geographically, economically, and demographically. The country has become more and more diverse in every sense of the word. Madison's solution has thus come under greater strain, particularly as the country has become more polarized. "Social cleavages today," writes political scientist Lilliana Mason, "have become significantly linked to our two political parties, with each party taking consistent sides in racial, religious, ideological, and cultural divides." The fracturing of society is one of the classic threats to the persistence of democracy.[4]

To prevent this kind of extreme fracturing, individuals must have a democratic ethic. Democratic citizens have duties to each other that differ from—and are more demanding than—the duties we have to all of humanity. The liberal ethic of individualism and the neoliberal ethic of selfishness can come into tension with democracy's foundational premise: we are part of a shared project. The ethic of democratic citizenship requires that we think not just about ourselves but about others—about everyone in our community, about the community itself, and about its future. This ethic cannot be completely selfish or individualistic because it requires individuals to sacrifice to preserve and fulfill the promise of democracy.[5]

The hard task is building—and sustaining—a united democracy. Democratic virtues and ethics don't spring from thin air; they have to be nurtured actively. Identity divisions are easy to exploit and hard to transcend, so they have to be bridged deliberately. We cannot just assume that civic culture and community spirit will persist.

Part of the problem today is that many institutions that tried to unite our democracy have eroded or been deliberately dismantled. Public schools and the military draft. Bowling leagues and civics classes. The other problem is that history, political tactics, and technological developments conspire to keep us divided. Racial, economic, cultural, and geographic segregation. The proliferation of media and personalization of social media. Public policy and social trends have fostered the political and cultural tribalism that can threaten democracy.

Building a united democracy stands in an uncomfortable tension with liberalism and neoliberalism, both of which look askance at any effort to shape a shared community identity. Liberals and neoliberals often worry that such efforts lead invariably to totalitarianism. But it is worth remembering that liberalism's eras of greatest success have been in times when there was in fact a shared culture and a common enemy—times when we recognized the need for a united democracy and understood that there were people outside of it. Cold War liberals, for example, facilitated a national culture that exalted constitutional freedoms in opposition to communism. Civic unity thus nurtured liberalism but was then destroyed by neoliberalism. Today, if we are to become a great democracy, we will need to unite our democratic community.

Race, Class, and the Politics of Divide and Conquer

One of the most difficult problems in American history—and in America's present—appears at the nexus of race and class. Since at least Bacon's Rebellion in 1676, when a biracial coalition of black slaves and poor whites threatened to overthrow economic elites in early Virginia, American politicians have fanned the flames of racial antagonism to prevent the emergence of a coalition of working-class whites and working-class African Americans, Latinos, Asians, and other minorities. If working-class whites believe racial minorities are to blame for their problems, they'll vote with wealthy whites, who can then preserve an economic system that perpetuates their wealth and power at the expense of working people, white or black. Divide and conquer: as long as working-class whites and minorities are divided, the elites in power conquer.[6]

One of the most famous and tragic attempts to break through the divide-and-conquer strategy took place in the early 1890s. Tom Watson was elected to the Georgia state legislature in 1882 and then to Congress, where he championed the interests of farmers and was the driving force behind the postal service bringing free delivery to rural areas. In 1892, the agrarian campaigned on a different platform, one of uniting poor blacks and poor whites against the white planter aristocracy that dominated the South.

"You are kept apart that you may be separately fleeced of your earnings," Watson thundered. "You are made to hate each other because upon that hatred is rested the keystone of the arch of financial despotism which enslaves you both. You are deceived and blinded that you may not see how this race antagonism perpetuates a monetary system which beggars both." Watson appeared alongside black speakers. He gave speeches to mixed-race audiences. He wanted the Populist Party to "make lynch law odious to the people." Watson's political coalition would be transformative: a union of working-class blacks and whites would form a majority that would fundamentally change the rigged economic and political system.

The white planter aristocracy knew it, and they would not let Watson's growing power go unchallenged. "They have incited lawless men to a pitch of frenzy which threatens anarchy," Watson commented. "Threats against my life were frequent and there were scores of men who would have done the deed and thousands who would have sanctioned it." He wasn't wrong. Georgia governor William Northen allegedly said that "Watson ought to be killed and that it ought to have been done long ago." The planter aristocracy didn't stop there. Black voters were intimidated with violence and force. The election was marred with fraud and bribery, all to prevent Watson from winning—and from transforming politics.[7]

In the years after Watson's spectacular defeat, the planter aristocracy in the South would ratchet up the strategy of divide and conquer to ensure that there would never again be another Tom Watson. Poll taxes, literacy tests, and white primaries were the tools, in addition to the weapons of fear and violence. But divide and conquer also came with an ideology. After marching from Selma to Montgomery, Martin Luther King Jr. described the emergence of segregation and white supremacy in the populist era. "The segregation of the races was really a political stratagem . . . to keep the poor white masses working for near-starvation wages." And when poor whites didn't have money and couldn't feed their children, the "southern aristocracy" fed them Jim Crow, "a psychological bird that told him that no matter how bad off he was, at least he was a white man, better than the black man." Jim Crow's divide-and-conquer politics, King said, "eventually destroyed the Populist Movement of the nineteenth century." As for Tom Watson, that profile in courage ended in capitulation. More than a decade later, seeking another chance at political office, Watson reinvented himself as a vicious racist. And won.[8]

Watson's defeat happened during the Gilded Age, but as King understood, the use of this tactic never ended. Indeed, four decades after the Civil Rights and Voting Rights Acts, in 2005, Republican National Committee chairman Ken Mehlman admitted that his party had spent years exploiting racial divisions through dog-whistle politics and that it was "wrong" to have done so. Today, racism is increasingly out in the open, and if we keep divide-and-conquer tactics in mind, the rising visibility of racism over the last generation seems hardly surprising. After decades of broad-based economic growth, things changed in the 1970s. Wages stagnated for the median-income white male. The United States began running trade deficits for the first time since World War II. Then came the neoliberal era. Deregulation, privatization, liberalization, and austerity combined with technology to accelerate economic inequality. After decades of economic stagnation and insecurity, there had to be someone to blame. Right-wing neoliberals surely were not going to blame themselves for their opposition to inclusive social policies or for the neoliberal ideology of upward redistribution to the wealthy. Indeed, they deliberately linked neoliberal policies to racial dog whistles to win elections. As Republican strategist Lee Atwater famously said, "You start out in 1954 by saying 'N[*], n[*], n[*].' By 1968 you can't say 'n[*]'—that hurts you, backfires. So you say stuff like, uh, forced busing, states' rights, and all that stuff, and you're getting abstract. Now you're talking about cutting taxes, and all these things you're talking about are totally economic things and a byproduct of them is, blacks get hurt worse than whites."[9]

Nor were center-left neoliberals going to admit their complicity. They could have blamed the wealthy, corporations, and their political partners for sacrificing the middle and working classes of all races on the altar of profits. But they had joined forces with those very groups to secure electoral victory in the Age of Reagan.

It is also hardly surprising that some were susceptible to an explanation that placed the blame squarely on minorities themselves. The Democratic Leadership Council's chairman, Chuck Robb, said that the New Democrats would address the "uncomfortable truths" about black poverty. Their emphasis wouldn't be public policy or structural racism. "It's time to shift the primary focus from racism—the traditional enemy without—to self-defeating patterns of behavior—the new enemy within." Although some of the blame certainly lies with individuals and their choices, Robb's shift from policy and racism to individual responsibility turned a blind eye to Atwater's explicit, intentional strategy of using neoliberal policies to harm working-class whites and minorities while mobilizing whites through racial antagonism.[10]

Racism went from covert to overt with the rise of President Trump, but this should not be surprising. These patterns were stitched into the neoliberal era's reinforcing cycle of economic insecurity and scapegoating. What is far more surprising is how mainstream Democrats initially responded. During the 2016 presidential primaries between Hillary Clinton and Bernie Sanders, for example, many liberals unwittingly fell backward into something akin to a divide-and-conquer posture themselves.

In January 2016, prominent commentator Ta-Nehisi Coates, who himself supported Bernie Sanders, criticized Sanders for being unimaginative on racial justice policies—and in particular for opposing reparations. Coates argued that Sanders's economically populist ideas wouldn't end structural or systemic racism in the United States: "Raising the minimum wage doesn't really address the fact that black men without criminal records have about the same shot at low-wage work as white men with them; nor can making college free address the wage gap between black and white graduates." Coates was obviously right that these policies alone couldn't end structural racism, and advocates for them were not arguing they would.[11] A few weeks later, in a speech at Henderson, Nevada, candidate Hillary Clinton picked up on Coates's critique, asking the crowd, "If we broke up the banks—and I will if they deserve it, if they pose a systemic risk, I will—would that end racism?" Again, the answer is, of course, no. But what if we did break up the banks? What if we did raise the minimum wage? What if we did have free college? At a minimum, working people would have a better shot at making ends meet, and their kids could get an education without taking on a huge debt burden. And perhaps the economy wouldn't be prone to major financial panics, during which working and middle-class families—often African American and Latinx—lose their homes and savings, while bankers get taxpayer bailouts and get to continue gambling with other people's money.[12]

Instead, Clinton belittled important economic reforms in a play for minority voters. Perhaps minorities should be willing to accept such a trade if it meant *ending* racism. But no one could have seriously believed Clinton or any other president could end racism in the United States. This rhetorical tactic has serious consequences: it undermines the case for structural economic reforms, saps popular energy to mobilize for such reforms, and gives the impression that economic and racial reforms are an either-or proposition. The results are predictable: no end to racism *and* no end to a rigged economic system—a liberal variant on the divide-and-conquer strategy.

As the "party of the people," the Democrats might have been expected to lay the blame on the elites that had governed America into the ground. They might have called for uniting *all* working-class and middle-class people—regardless of their race, gender, identity, or geography. They might have said that minorities aren't to blame and that both whites and blacks are oppressed by a rigged political and economic system—by structures of economic, racial, and political power. But instead of a union of whites and minorities, instead of the radical Tom Watson, some Democrats doubled down on identity without emphasizing cross-racial economic justice. During the protests after President Trump's inauguration, one democratic political operative on MSNBC commented, "You are wrong to look at these crowds and think that means everyone wants fifteen dollars an hour. . . . It's all about identity on our side now."[13]

Reformers didn't always think this way. Dr. Martin Luther King Jr. understood that the choice between race and economics was as pernicious as it was false. King's "I Have a Dream" speech took place at the March for *Jobs* and Freedom. King organized the Poor People's Movement in the years before his death. And it was King who said that "the inseparable twin of racial injustice was economic injustice." King understood that economic greed could bring with it injustice. "Capitalism," he wrote, "is always in danger of inspiring men to be more concerned about making a living than making a life. We are prone to judge success by the index of our salaries or the size of our automobiles, rather than by the quality of our service and relationship to humanity."[14]

Liberation from divide-and-conquer strategies, King recognized, could only come from acknowledging that race and economics cannot be separated. Battles must be fought and won along both lines, and people must be united across race and class to win those battles. In recent years, a new generation has taken up King's mantle, refusing to see opposition between race and class. As Congresswoman Alexandra Ocasio-Cortez has said, "I can't name a single issue with roots in race that doesn't have economic implications, and I cannot think of a single economic issue that doesn't have racial implications. This idea that we have to separate them out and choose is a con." Divide and conquer is a con, a deception that has always been used to prevent both economic justice and racial justice.[15]

Indeed, when the term *identity politics* was first used in 1977, it wasn't intended to be a synonym for group tribalism. Its first proponents were working-class black lesbian women. Their insight was that they couldn't be put into just one category—whether working class, black, lesbian, or woman—because they were all of those things. Fighting injustice meant addressing all kinds of injustice, not just one. As a result, they forged alliances rather than retreating into their own tribal corner. As Demita Frazier commented, "We found ourselves in coalition with the labor movement because we believed in the importance of supporting other groups even if the individuals in that group weren't all feminist. We understood that coalition building was crucial for our own survival."[16]

Uniting across groups, recognizing the commonalities we have, seeing ourselves in each other's struggles and successes—this builds solidarity. And solidarity is the alternative to divide and conquer.

Soulcraft in a Complex Society

Solidarity requires that people see other members of the community as part of themselves, that we recognize the duties we have to each other. In recent years, a few conservative commentators have taken the lead in criticizing how the prevailing individualism of the neoliberal age has undermined the moral and ethical foundations of community. Yuval Levin's essay "Taking the Long Way" argues that too many people on both the right and left are committed to a thin vision of liberty, defined simply as the absence of constraints on individual action. Democracy and the market economy presuppose individuals who are not simply free "from coercion by others" but also "from the tyranny of unrestrained desire." Citizens, he says, must be "capable of using their freedom well." Patrick

Deneen's *Why Liberalism Failed* similarly criticizes liberalism for seeing liberty as nothing more than the lack of constraints rather than the virtue of self-mastery. The result has been the destruction of moral and community values that are essential to human flourishing. Both Levin and Deneen seek a richer notion of liberty, one that involves moral formation, or what Levin calls "the long way to liberty." We might think of Deneen and Levin as seeking a revival of the ethics necessary for democratic citizenship and community solidarity. And we might call the process of getting there *soulcraft*.[17]

Democratic freedom requires more than a mere license to act however one pleases. Because democracy means coming together as a people to govern, the people must consider the needs of others and of the community as a whole. Pure, unrestrained selfishness is simply incompatible with this imperative. The ancient Greeks and Romans thus saw liberty not just as the freedom to act, unconstrained from government or other people, but as freedom to act unconstrained by one's desires. True liberty involved not being a slave either to another person or to one's own passions. It required self-restraint and self-mastery. Many of the original Progressives and some who might be called progressives today, such as the political philosopher Michael Sandel, envision freedom similarly to Levin, Deneen, and the ancients. They recognize that soulcraft is critical to democracy. Across the board, progressives and conservatives in this vein recognize that one of the most important civic callings today is to reinvigorate the traditional soul-forming institutions of family, work, education, faith, and civil society.

The question is how to do it. And where Deneen, Levin, and conservatives often go wrong is in restricting soulcraft *only* to those traditional institutions. These traditional pathways did ease the tension between liberalism and democracy, but so did public institutions. Public schools and public libraries, the jury and military service—these public activities were also the means of soulcraft, of forming citizens with the ethics and morality needed for democracy to survive. In a complex, changing society, it will not be enough simply to reaffirm the private pathways of soulcraft.

This is particularly true because in a polarized era in which people are sorted into tribes, retreating to our neighborhoods or churches only segregates and polarizes us more. It deepens tribalism rather than alleviating it. Levin himself has said, "The biggest problem with our politics of nostalgia is its disconnection from the present and therefore its blindness to the future." Today, if we hope to move beyond nostalgia, we will need to reform the traditional pathways to soulcraft and, at the same time, to devise new ways to encourage moral formation.[18]

Consider family. Through these most intimate of relationships, we experience not only fulfillment and happiness but also the suffering and obligations that build responsibility. But the challenge is that the family of today does not look like the idealized 1950s vision of a happy couple with children. Families today are increasingly complex, with stepparents, stepsiblings, and half-siblings, multiple adults coming in and out of children's lives, and grandparents acting as parents. Even the idea of a single-parent household assumes a level of stability that is illusory: of mothers who are single at the birth of their child, 59 percent experience three or more residential or dating transitions before their child reaches five years old—and 33 percent have another child with a different romantic partner in those first five years.[19]

Family instability and complexity is linked to another shift: marriage and childbearing in marriage have increasingly become practices for economic elites. Over the last 140 years, marriage was only prevalent among *all* Americans during time periods when income inequality was shrinking or relatively low—in other words, *only* in the middle of the twentieth century. In the old Gilded Age of the late nineteenth and early twentieth century and in this new Gilded Age, the marriage gap has widened, with plummeting marriage rates among working-class Americans. Likewise, the practice of childbearing during marriage also seems increasingly to be the province of economic elites. And this is not solely a result of cultural devaluation of the institution of marriage. In an important study, Kathryn Edin and Maria Kefalas showed that many poor women aspire to and respect marriage so much that they don't believe in divorce. But they choose to have children outside of marriage because they see motherhood as existentially meaningful, independent of marriage.[20]

Do these trends and changes mean we should give up on families as a soul-forming institution? Absolutely not. But they also imply that we cannot just advocate for defending the family in some abstract, nostalgic way. If we really want contemporary families to play a role in shaping responsible individuals, we must address the underlying causes that put a strain on families' ability to play a moral role. Although there is considerable debate over whether culture or economic security is the main factor, it is hard to argue that economic security isn't an important factor. The process of building supportive families thus requires, at least in part, policies that build economic democracy.

Levin, however, says little about economic policy and implies that liberal redistribution policies give people license to live however they want. Deneen argues that progressive state-building policies undermine moral formation by sapping the energy of traditional institutions. But these arguments miss important parts of the relationship between economics and soulcraft. An America without economic opportunity for everyone isn't an America that facilitates soulcraft. When parents have no economic opportunities, it is harder for them to nurture their children and engage in the soul-forming activities Levin and Deneen desire. Likewise, a nation of Sisyphean workers, condemned to an eternity of hard labor without ever making any economic progress, is unlikely to believe that hard work, responsibility, and character lead to just results. What moral lesson does one learn from a lifetime of work without progress? Indeed, the neoliberal era's policies show little moral value in hard work. Our country's tax policies, to take just one example, reward heirs and heiresses who gain wealth without work—even as regular people who seek wealth through work pay full freight. The moral message of such a policy is precisely the selfishness that Deneen and Levin decry.

Criminal justice policy also contributes to the challenges that American families face. Over the course of the neoliberal era, between 1980 and 2015, the prison population in the United States quadrupled. This was not a function of rising crime rates, which hit their high-water mark in 1991. It was the result of harsher policies, including mandatory minimum sentences and an emphasis on punishment, not rehabilitation, as the central purpose of incarceration. Mass incarceration puts millions of Americans in prison. As a result, one in twelve children in the United States will see one of their parents put in prison. Incarceration breaks up families, leaves children traumatized, and can create distrust in government and institutions among entire communities. And punishment is not limited to time served. Those who get out of prison have a harder time finding housing and getting a job, leaving them with worse economic opportunities going forward. For African Americans, the consequences are particularly significant because they are more likely to be arrested and more likely to be convicted than whites for precisely the same crimes. If we truly value families, neighborhoods, and economic opportunity as ways to encourage soul formation, we cannot ignore how criminal justice policy has contributed to breakdown in these areas.[21]

Of course, it is not just family and work that can enable soul formation. Participating actively in civil society and local government can help build essential "habits of freedom," and both Levin and Deneen celebrate such institutions. But ours is a time when the problem of *Bowling Alone* has become the phenomenon of bowling online. The decline of civic and social institutions and their replacement with technological and social networks means that we cannot rely solely on participation in civil society groups to cultivate virtue. We must expand the fields of possibility and look for other institutions that can facilitate personal development.[22]

One of the most important sites for soulcraft is the workplace itself. Despite the rise of freelance work, millions of Americans still work for large corporations. Corporations can provide an avenue for soul formation, but only so long as they are organized to give employees initiative and responsibility. The original Progressives believed that the new industrial age required thinking differently about corporations for precisely this reason. For the Progressives, economic democracy not only prevented the vast accumulations of power that could undermine political freedom but also helped individuals build self-mastery in the increasingly complex industrial economy.[23]

In some countries, like Germany, corporate leaders believe that workers should have a say in the governance and operations of the company. Workers at Volkswagen, for example, are empowered on the shop floor and even included on the company's supervisory board. Not only is their narrow personal fate attached to the company, but they are also partly responsible for the success of the corporation in the long run. Think of how perspectives might change when workers have such great responsibility. Yet neoliberals are reflexively hostile to opportunities that would allow corporations to facilitate soulcraft. They fight attempts for workers to participate in the governance of their companies, even when, as in the case of Volkswagen in Chattanooga, the *corporation* wanted to empower workers. A true commitment to soulcraft requires being willing to think about how our existing institutions can adapt to facilitate the moral formation of democratic citizens.[24]

Of course, existing institutions may also not be sufficient. The family is a site for soulcraft because people are bound together in genuine relationships of care derived from blood or marriage. But we know that in our modern, complex society, families are not the only sites of relationships of care. Consider the United States military. Drill sergeants and officers may lecture on the virtues of courage, discipline, integrity, and honesty, but I suspect it is as much the experience of trusting another with your life, the pain and suffering of friends lost, and the joy of close camaraderie and intense effort with a team that builds the bonds of brotherhood and sisterhood within a unit. Service leads to soulcraft. Service for others and service with others builds relationships of care that lead to joy and obligation, responsibility and fulfillment. We must facilitate a new culture of service—whether civilian or military—so that everyone has the opportunity to build these relationships of care and experience the moral transformation that accompanies serving others.

Service for and with others also has one other effect: it develops the virtues of tolerance and compassion for those who are different. Levin says that liberals enforce an "ethic of pluralism" for "fear of compromising the freedom of others." But tolerance and understanding are just as important to the richer vision of freedom that Levin and Deneen advocate. Imagine an individual who encounters someone different and cannot but condemn the stranger's views, spew hatred for his lifestyle, and reject his opinions. Such a person hardly has self-restraint or self-control, and we would not think him emancipated from the tyranny of his own passions, biases, and emotions. In a complex society, it is not a weakness but a strength to engage productively with those who have different views, and it is a hallmark of a truly free mind to seek first to understand before making judgments.[25]

Ultimately, all individuals operate in a social context, with social institutions, political institutions, culture, and personal actions interacting in complex and organic ways. As a result, personal and social transformation are linked. Social transformations shape individuals and can help or hinder their opportunities for personal transformation. Likewise, a thousand personal transformations can recast a community's views, leading to social transformation. The path to liberty is not unidirectional. It is interactive. And we must not be afraid to look beyond the old ways of moral formation—or to advocate for public policies that foster the ethics needed for democracy.

Restitching Our Social Fabric

The great question, of course, is *how* to facilitate soulcraft and how to bridge social divides. There can be no single or simple path to uniting democracy because solidarity depends on so many factors—culture, economics, history, shared experience, and common aspirations. Still, there are policies that can help restitch our fraying social fabric. As we shall see in future chapters, economic reforms will help, as will greater political democracy and a well-designed foreign policy. In some areas, introducing a democratic policymaking process can help communities—reforming police practices is a good example. In others, like climate change, policy makers will need to infuse their thinking on a range of policies with a goal of bridging social divides. And on topics like national service, the media, and immigration, public policy can directly and deliberately help stitch people together. Let us take each of these areas in turn.

Democratic Policing. In recent years, the role of the police in our society has come under increasing scrutiny. White police officers have shot African Americans, with video footage showing that the use of lethal force was unnecessary. A federal judge declared New York City's policy of stop and frisk illegal. Cities have engaged in widespread surveillance of their citizens, including via drones. Police departments have become militarized, with SWAT teams that approach citizens as if they were enemies in a war zone. And the policy of civil asset forfeiture—seizing suspects' property permanently, even if they are not guilty of a crime—has gained widespread attention, with the Supreme Court even weighing in to restrict the practice. These problems all seem very different, but as legal scholars Barry Friedman and Maria Ponomarenko have argued, they all stem from the fact that policing in our society has very little democratic authorization or accountability.[26]

In our society, and unlike most other areas of government policymaking, police practices have almost no democratic authorization. It is true that many police departments operate under the supervision of a mayor or city council, that some jurisdictions elect sheriffs, and that state legislatures give general grants of authority to police forces. But legislative or regulatory authority for particular police actions are few and far between. For example, after the killings in Ferguson and in other cities around the country, a number of jurisdictions adopted laws requiring police to wear body cameras. These kinds of laws are the exception, not the rule. Normally, states and cities do not adopt policies for the police through the democratic lawmaking process. Indeed, even when police departments have manuals for their operations, these are generally adopted without public notice, participation, or explanation, and they are typically not publicly available. Instead, we have a system of general authorization for police powers, considerable discretion to the police, and after-the-fact judicial review of police actions. This requires people who feel their rights have been infringed upon to sue and then argue in court that the police undertook unconstitutional actions.[27]

This approach makes little sense. In policing, like other areas of public policy, not everything that is constitutional is desirable. The Constitution permits a lot of policies that might be undesirable. Because our system of government values both the rule of law and democratic authorization for government actions, we choose among many permissible policies through procedures that allow for democratic input. For example, federal government agencies that regulate individuals and companies go through an extensive process of providing public notice of their proposed regulations and inviting comments from members of the public. They are then required to explain why they adopted the regulations they adopted, and courts can strike down their policies if they do not have a well-reasoned justification. In other words, we require government to engage the democratic public before regulating—and to explain their reasons for regulating the way they did.[28]

If we want to bridge the divide between police and communities, one approach for doing so would be to introduce a similar system for police actions. Friedman and Ponomarenko call this "democratic policing." Police departments or cities should have more community participation in setting the rules that the police use in those communities. This would include providing notice, an opportunity for public comment, and publicly available justifications for their policies—whether it is general surveillance of the public, policies on the use of force, or civil asset forfeiture. Communities could design the specifics of the process differently, but the general theme would be to engage the community directly. This democratic process would help break down barriers in the community while increasing the legitimacy of police activities.

Uniting to Address Climate Change. Policing takes place at the local level, so it is possible to engage members of the community directly. Climate change, in contrast, is a global crisis that will affect everyone, everywhere, including future generations. From draughts and flooding, to famines, migration, wars, and the spread of disease, climate change will have profound and disastrous consequences for people throughout the world.

But these consequences will not be evenly distributed. Low-lying coastal geographies will be hit hard by storm surges and rising sea levels. Areas like the rural southeastern United States will be worse off than some other areas, particularly due to rising temperatures. And within any specific geographic area, low-income people, minorities, children, and the elderly tend to be the least resilient and the most vulnerable. They generally have less access to information about how to adapt and fewer resources to be able to adapt. For example, poor people and the elderly often have fewer options if they are displaced due to hurricane-induced flooding.[29]

Building a united democracy in the future will mean thinking about these uneven geographic and social impacts while designing policies to address and adapt to climate change. Part of the solution will be ensuring that vulnerable populations are more involved in the political and planning process. But the other part of the solution is considering equity as a goal in designing policy on climate change. A good example of this approach at work is in the embryonic proposals for a Green New Deal. The general premise of the Green New Deal is that the scope of the climate challenge is so great that it will require a New Deal–like effort—a national endeavor and a transformative set of policies across multiple economic and social arenas. Far from proscribing a single piece of legislation, the Green New Deal is an organizing principle under which many policies can fall—from upgrading infrastructure and adopting a smart electrical grid to moving toward clean, renewable energy and renewing threatened ecosystems.

From the perspective of building a united democracy, what is so striking and instructive about Green New Deal proposals is that its advocates have built questions of geographic, racial, and economic equity directly into the fabric of their thinking. They seek not just to pass legislation on clean energy or a smart grid but to ensure that when big changes come to communities, those communities are consulted and have input—and that there is a just economic transition that leaves no one behind. Advocates want to ensure that any policies, however technical, keep in mind the disproportionate effects of climate change on minorities, on the poor, and on indigenous communities. At the same time, they recognize that policy efforts to move toward a net-zero emissions society must also address these effects and the disproportionate impact on some geographies and industries. One proposal, for example, is to create a green industrial policy, including massive investments in manufacturing and deploying clean energy infrastructure. This effort would create millions of jobs in the United States while transitioning the economy away from fossil fuels. To ensure that everyone benefits from the influx of these new resources, advocates for a green industrial policy have focused on investing in all geographies and on equity across groups. The thinking behind the Green New Deal provides an example of how policy makers can infuse the values of a united democracy into a range of policies, many of which might not seem like they have anything to do with bridging our racial, geographic, economic, and cultural divides.[30]

Patriot Corps. Restitching our social fabric can also be done directly—with policies that attempt to bridge differences between people and develop a democratic ethos within individuals. As a pathway to soulcraft, public and community service has been understood across time, geographies, and religions to be one of the most effective. Service is not selfish. It requires devoting yourself to others—whether individuals, a community, or the nation. Historically, the military was the central way that populations engaged in service. Militaries train their members in the importance of the unit, not the individual; service members are expected to sacrifice for each other, not simply support their own selfish interests. Distinctions of race, religion, and national origin break down; what matters is the unit. Since the end of the military draft and the rise of the all-volunteer force, however, fewer people serve in the military. But that does not mean that service can no longer be a pathway for stitching together our social fabric. Indeed, in recent years, a number of countries have reinstated mandatory national service programs. Some, like Sweden, have done so in response to the rising threat of their neighbor Russia; others, like France, have adopted mandatory service as a way to address social fracturing.[31]

Patriot Corps would be a new national service program that links service and schooling. As part of a plan for economic democracy, as we shall see, the United States should offer up to four years of free public education after high school for anyone who wishes to attend. Patriot Corps would provide an additional benefit: members of Patriot Corps would get up to four years of education or training at a public *or private* college, university, or community college debt-free—tuition, fees, room and board, and books—through a combination of a Patriot Corps scholarship and need-based aid from the college. In return, they would serve the country for four years. Any person of any age would be eligible to participate, including retirees interested in a second (or third) career.

The model is the military, which covers students during the college years in return for military service. Patriot Corps would be similar, but members would serve in a variety of nonmilitary capacities: addressing the impacts of climate change as part of the Green New Deal; working for states or nonprofit organizations; installing new infrastructure from bridges to broadband; modernizing government services through the application of new technologies; serving as teachers, childcare providers, and home health care workers, and more. They would emerge from Patriot Corps with an education and real work experience.

The benefits to the country would be significant. Patriot Corps members would help address some of the country's biggest challenges, keeping the United States on the frontiers of the world. The country would not only guarantee that millions of Americans, young and old, get further education and training, but it would also help address the student debt crisis for new students. Currently, students have $1.5 trillion in outstanding debt. Not only does this massive debt burden weigh on students psychologically and financially, it harms the economy. A generation of debtors is a generation that can't put a down payment on a new house or start a small business. Finally, and most importantly, Patriot Corps would build an ethic of service and help create a more united democracy. Members would not only serve others but would also be part of a diverse community. As with the military, most members would be assigned to a different region of the country, where they would interact with different people and see the diversity of America in all its forms. Patriot Corps would also make private colleges accessible to those who otherwise could not afford them, helping to bring a more regionally, economically, and racially diverse student body to those institutions. The overall result would be to make Americans less isolated from each other.[32]

Patriot Corps would also merge all of the existing service programs—the Peace Corps, AmeriCorps, VISTA—under one single banner. This would help with recruiting and give the program a brand that everyone would recognize. The program would not be mandatory, but the benefit of a debt-free education at a private institution would be significant. Although the very wealthiest kids might opt out of Patriot Corps, over time, norms would change. As more and more people participated, eventually there would be an expectation of participation. The question "Where did you serve?" might even become an icebreaker that wouldn't just apply to members of the military.

Patriot Corps isn't a pie-in-the-sky idea. During the New Deal, Americans across the country were mobilized by the Civilian Conservation Corps, the Works Progress Administration, the National Youth Administration, and other alphabet-soup agencies. These agencies built public works, brought mobile libraries to rural areas, and made national parks usable. And after World War II, the GI Bill helped 2.2 million veterans become scientists, business people, engineers, and artists, sending a generation to college. For every dollar spent on the program, the country gained five dollars in productivity and taxes. But more importantly, these programs engaged Americans as members of their country, of our national community. They helped stitch us together as one people, aiming for a more perfect union.[33]

Fixing the Media. Over the past few decades—and particularly in the last decade—it has become clear that the changing nature of media has contributed to our social fracturing. In the mid-twentieth century, the sources of media were limited. There were only a few TV channels, and TV executives decided the content. Today, TV channels have proliferated, as have internet news sources. Gatekeepers like news producers no longer determine the content available to us; any individual can write up a story, post a photo, or make a video. Media now also tailor content to an individual's tastes and preferences. One result has been an explosion in the sources and content available to us. The other is that we are no longer part of a single, shared conversation. At the same time, the media has also become harder to trust. Social media and personalization mean that foreign governments, bots, and even individuals can make fake news go viral without any checks or balances. Powerful media conglomerates, like Sinclair, now push ideological content to their reporters, using their huge scale for what is effectively corporate propaganda. And in the midst of all that, local newspapers and investigative journalism—both critical to the functioning of democracy—have been under severe threat.

At the broadest, structural level, reinvigorating antitrust enforcement and regulating technology platforms form the foundation for addressing the crisis in our media environment. Antitrust enforcers need to block mergers that create massive media conglomerates that have power across geographies, types of media, and both content and distribution. This would prevent the Sinclair problem, by which one ideological company can buy up TV stations in hundreds of markets around the country and force news anchors to deliver centrally drafted messages. It would also prevent content producers (like Time Warner) from merging with distributors (like AT&T). Those kinds of mergers risk preventing customers of other distributors from gaining access to content. We will discuss these reforms more in the next chapter.

The second shift, as part of regulating technology platforms, should be to revisit Section 230 of the Communications Decency Act. That law has been called "the most important law in tech" and "the law that gave us the modern internet." Section 230 shields internet platforms from liability for the content that others put on the platform. What that means is that if someone posts defamatory, libelous, hateful, criminal, or violence-inducing content, the platform isn't responsible. This is a special rule that doesn't apply to other media companies. If the *New York Times* printed revenge porn or criminal incitements in its classified section, it would be held responsible. Although many people celebrate Section 230's libertarian consequences, the law wasn't designed for this purpose—in fact, quite the opposite. The goal was to protect providers who were trying to *block* obscene and offensive material from lawsuits in the event they weren't completely successful in removing that material.[34]

The perverse result, however, is that platforms have too little incentive to police who their users are or what they are posting—even when the users are bots or foreign governments and the posts are harassing, fake news, or indecent. In fact, some have business models that depend on precisely that kind of behavior. Instead of offering blanket immunity, Section 230 should be revised in line with its original purpose of providing immunity to platforms that are trying to be responsible. Platforms should get this immunity only if they verify their users and have a program to police their content. This would go a long way in preventing bots and trolls, in addition to fake news and problematic content. Platforms that seek to benefit from Section 230 immunity would also have to pay a tax because they allow for the sharing of news without any compensation. The proceeds of this tax would go toward funding the final aspect of media reform: the creation of a National Endowment for Journalism.

Right now, we face a crisis in journalism. Amid the talk of fake news and Russian bots, the news business has been under severe pressure for decades. Most frequently, the internet is fingered as the culprit, and to a great extent that is true. Eyeballs have moved to the internet, and aggregators and social media platforms repost news sources without paying the news organizations that produced them. But there have been other factors as well. Private equity firms have bought up, consolidated, and in some cases stripped and bankrupted local newspapers. And perhaps most surprisingly, government subsidies for news have plummeted. One of the biggest news subsidies began at the very start of the republic, in 1792. That year, Congress passed the Post Office Act, which subsidized sending newspapers through the mail. Washington, Madison, and the other founders of the country supported this policy as essential to ensuring that citizens of the fledgling democratic republic had access to the news. One hundred and eighty years later, starting with Postal Reorganization Act of 1970, Congress decided otherwise. It shrank the subsidy from covering 75 percent of periodical mailings in the late 1960s (about $2 billion in 2010 dollars) to only 11 percent of mailing costs (or $288 million) in 2010.[35]

The decline in subsidies is important because the journalism that is most critical to the functioning of a democracy isn't necessarily going to be produced through the market. The market can support writing about sports and entertainment and about clickbait stories about the most recent outlandish statement by a public figure. But the most important stories for sustaining democracy aren't on those topics. They are the local issues that might not have a huge national audience, the international coverage that is expensive and distant, and the dogged investigatory reporting that takes months—or even years—to come to fruition. The economic case for these stories is tough because once written, everyone knows the story, and the news organization can't capture the financial benefits of the hard work they've put into the reporting. This is a classic case for government action because the market fails to produce enough of this kind of journalism. But the case is broader than basic economics. Without serious reporting and journalism, it's much harder for a democratic public to hold accountable corrupt government officials or to discover and regulate fraudulent corporate behavior. It's much harder for citizens to discuss how to fix the problems in our local communities and in the country if we don't know what those problems are. And it's much harder to build public support to defend democracy from our enemies if we have no idea what's happening in the rest of the world.

The National Endowment for Journalism (NEJ) would give financial grants to news organizations and individuals who are reporting on issues of local or international importance or on investigatory matters. The NEJ would consist of thirteen members, with the Librarian of Congress serving in an ex officio capacity. All members would need a minimum ten years of experience as full-time working journalists, with representation in local, international, and investigatory news. These requirements would ensure that professionals from a diverse set of backgrounds would make decisions on how to allocate the NEJ's funds. The NEJ would give grants through a competitive application process, akin to how the National Endowments for the Arts and Humanities and the National Institutes of Health give grants currently. They would also give a preference to nonprofits, cooperatives, and for-profit entities with employee unions or with half the board comprising employees. The funds would be less likely, as a result, to subsidize already profitable corporate media.[36]

Funding for the NEJ would come from two sources. First would be a small tax on technology platforms. The tax would apply to any internet company that seeks to benefit from liability protection under Section 230; in effect, any online intermediary that hosts, publishes, or republishes third-party content would have to pay a progressive tax on their annual revenue based on their size. The tax would be a condition for receiving the legal privilege of Section 230 immunity, upon which online publishers that feature third-party content rely heavily.

The second source would be proceeds from auctions of the public's electromagnetic spectrum. The Federal Communications Commission periodically auctions off parts of the spectrum that media companies use to reach the public. Some of the proceeds of the auction go to covering costs and funding critical infrastructure, but a significant remainder—$7 billion in 2017—go to the Treasury. Fifty percent of this funding should instead be directed, by law, to the National Endowment for Journalism. This would ensure the production of high-quality content (which of course could be discussed on the very spectrum being auctioned). The remainder should help to fund a public option for broadband, thereby expanding high-speed access to the internet and communications for all Americans. The combined result would be to expand the number of people that media companies can reach (and the speed at which they can reach them) while simultaneously guaranteeing the production of serious journalism.[37]

Public funding for journalism isn't crazy, and it isn't even unconventional. The federal government subsidized newspapers from the very dawn of the republic, with Washington and Madison as champions of this policy. And journalism in the United States has always relied on a public-private model. In the mid-twentieth century, for example, media outlets were required to serve the public interest as a condition of receiving their licenses. Other developed constitutional democracies also subsidize their media, and most do so at far higher rates than the United States. As of 2011, Finland spent €130.7 per capita on all direct and indirect media subsidies, and the European low was Italy with €43.1. Comparing apples to apples, the United States spent the equivalent of only €5.2 per capita.[38]

Public funding is also unlikely to lead to improper government influence over the media. First, the design of the National Endowment for Journalism is insulated from politics. Funding is not dependent on congressional appropriations, as it currently is for the Corporation for Public Broadcasting, which—incidentally—is frequently under attack. Instead, both of the NEJ's funding streams are automatic. The composition of the NEJ also insulates it from partisanship; members require significant experience in journalism. Second, the government frequently funds activities—with little controversy—for which we might be worried about political influence. The government funds public defenders in the courts and research universities, yet few people (if any) think this has undermined academic freedom or the integrity of the lawyers representing the indigent. Indeed, the current model of corporate advertising–funded journalism has the potential to be bad as well. Corporate-funded journalists might have an incentive not to report hard-hitting stories that will lead to corporations pulling their ads. But it turns out this isn't much of a problem either. As Columbia University president Lee Bollinger has noted, "We trust our great newspapers to collect millions of dollars in advertising from BP while reporting without fear or favor on the company's environmental record only because of a professional culture that insulates revenue from news judgment."[39]

Democracy requires a free press and a serious press. The press is important not just to express opinions or even to report on daily events. It is important because it provides a check on the power of political leaders and of private actors who might seek to undermine democracy itself. This is precisely why would-be tyrants and oligarchs are so keen to delegitimize the press—or just buy it up. Without a strong, free press, it becomes easier to divide and conquer through propaganda and to manipulate the political system.

Welcoming America. Who should be allowed to become a member of our democratic community? How will they become members? And once welcomed into our community, how do we ensure we are all stitched together into one fabric? Every country around the world must address these questions, and throughout American history, immigration policy offered a range of answers.

In the nineteenth century, waves of immigrants came to the United States, fleeing monarchies and poverty in Europe for a better life. Ralph Waldo Emerson noted that America was a "smelting pot" of cultures, mixing "the energy of the Irish, Germans, Swedes, Poles, and Cossacks, and all the Europe tribes—and of the Africans, and of the Polynesians." Immigrants who declared their intention to become citizens were eligible to get grants of land through the Homestead Act of 1862, and perhaps more surprisingly, noncitizen immigrants were often allowed to vote until the early twentieth century.[40]

But people often fear change and the unfamiliar, and politicians throughout history have used immigrants as a scapegoat to blame for social or economic problems. So with the increase in the percentage of foreign-born people came nativism and ugly anti-immigrant sentiments. In the 1840s, 14 percent of Americans were foreign born, and nativists began to lash out against German and Irish immigrants. In the 1870s, when a massive financial panic led to economic depression, public opinion turned against the Chinese, leading eventually to the first federal restrictions on immigration by race and nationality. Over time, Congress put in place quotas based on national origin and largely shut the country to immigration in the 1920s. By the 1960s, the country had reopened to immigrants— and without discrimination based on national origin. By 2017, the percentage of foreign born was back up to 13.7 percent—the highest in a century. It is no surprise that politicians are once again blaming immigrants for problems.[41]

At the level of principles and abstractions, immigration is a difficult question that divides people on both the left and the right. Conservatives are divided between neoliberals who are cosmopolitans and want more open borders and nationalists who want to restrict entry. Liberals are divided between cosmopolitans who want more open borders and communitarians who embrace immigrants but also emphasize social solidarity. But for all the passionate debates over immigration today, many policy makers think the main contours of immigration reform have been clear for years. The first component is reform to the laws on who can come to the United States. Immigration has made our country stronger and more creative. Visa reforms need to preserve our country's long-standing commitment to the importance of families by allowing family members to reunify; they must be opportunistic to allow highly talented individuals who can contribute to our economy; and they must be humanitarian, allowing refugees and those seeking asylum to find protection. Second are reforms that address the population of people already in the United States, including a path to citizenship. The final component is border security. Countries must be able to regulate who enters and exits, especially for national security reasons. But border security and immigration enforcement are now practiced in ways that are an affront to American values, with little children separated from their parents, locked in cages, and marched like prisoners around detention facilities. Today, root-and-branch reforms to Immigration and Customs Enforcement and Customs and Border Protection will be needed to end the aggressive and outrageous operations that have shocked the conscience of the country.[42]

But immigration reform proposals have also largely overlooked an entire arena of policy. To have a united democracy, we must have a reasonable degree of social solidarity among our people. We have to see each other as part of a shared project, with shared values. Throughout our history, immigrants from many nations have become stitched into our national community, but too often immigrants have been isolated in pockets and it has taken a few generations before immigrants were considered full Americans. This not only slows entry into our broader American community but can also lead to resentment, alienation, and discrimination. At the same time, it takes time for people to get accustomed to people from other cultures, and some may fear that they are losing out to those who are different from them.

With the goal of building a united democracy, immigration policy needs to do more than just help immigrants come to America; it needs to welcome them to America. What we need is a transition process—call it the Welcoming America Program—to help those who have already arrived to become more connected to our national community. This does not mean erasing culture or assimilation; that has never been the American way. Even now, St. Patrick's Day is celebrated throughout the country—and by Irish Americans and non–Irish Americans alike. Chinese restaurants dot the country and are frequented by many non–Chinese Americans. I myself love eating Indian food and visit my Hindu temple regularly, but I'm also an Eagle Scout who grew up playing baseball and ice hockey, and I teach American constitutional law and love reading American history. Creating a welcoming America does not mean giving up culture; it means helping people join the American community.

The Welcoming America Program has a few goals. First is to welcome immigrants and help them transition into the country, in terms of culture, history, and customs, with a particular focus on civics. Second, the program signals to those who might fear immigration a commitment to ensuring that all immigrants will learn about American traditions and culture. Finally, the program would seek to create opportunities for positive encounters between communities and immigrants, so people could learn from each other—in both directions—and in the process build the familiarity and understanding that fosters not just harmony but friendship.

The program would consist of two parts. First, the government would offer civics classes and fully fund English as a second language for all immigrants who want to sign up. This would not include a requirement of English only or make English a national language. Immigrants to this country *want* to learn English. This program would provide the resources to ensure that they can—and as a result, it would accelerate their ability to become part of the American community. Second, Americans could "adopt" immigrants without family members in the country for a year to help them transition into their new communities. Institutions that hire or sponsor immigrants, like universities and businesses, would be required to pair each immigrant family with a person or family that would meet with them and help them with the many mundane things that can be challenging for immigrants—from opening a bank account to navigating customs and idioms. For those who come to the country without an institutional sponsor, the program would be voluntary, and the government would work with churches and other community groups to find families that would adopt these new Americans.

A program like this one is not unworkable. Canada has a similar program for Syrian refugees. Canadian families adopt refugees for a year and help them with a variety of transitional challenges—everything from getting set up at school to finding a doctor to preparing for a job interview. In the process, these families learn about each other's cultures and build personal and emotional bonds. They become a united community.[43]

* * *

Public policy in all of these specific areas—policing, climate, service, media, immigration—can help build solidarity and create a united democracy. But ultimately, uniting democracy will require approaching all areas of policy—from economic policy to political reforms to foreign policy—with a commitment to breaking down racial, cultural, and geographic barriers and to fostering soulcraft. If done right, these policies will reinforce each other and contribute to achieving a great democracy.

7

ECONOMIC DEMOCRACY

When Theodore Roosevelt said that it wasn't possible to have a political democracy without an economic democracy, he understood that democracy meant more than elections and voting. Roosevelt thought labor unions were indispensable and that they benefited workers and society as a whole. He condemned the conglomerates, monopolies, and trusts that aggregated power without responsibility. And he railed against corruption and special privileges.

The spirit of economic democracy gave life to his policies, and it has three components. The first is that society itself must be relatively equal economically. Political leaders and philosophers have long recognized that economic equality is connected to political democracy. The creator of the first American dictionary, Noah Webster, said that "an equality of property . . . is the very soul of a republic." Statesman Daniel Webster and Supreme Court Justice Joseph Story both believed the equality of conditions in early America was the foundation for popular government. Alexis de Tocqueville wrote in the very first paragraph of *Democracy in America* that the "equality of conditions" in the country was the most remarkable fact about the young republic and that this equality undergirded American democracy.[1]

Note that these thinkers didn't say equal opportunity or mobility, two things that neoliberal-era politicians champion. They instead emphasized the relative equality of conditions. They understood that, as we have seen, political power cannot be dissociated from economic power. This goes back to the "doom loop of oligarchy," but the basics are worth repeating. When some people have more economic power, they can use their wealth to gain political power and influence. "When the rich govern alone, the interest of the poor is always in peril," Tocqueville wrote. The result is not democracy, but oligarchy—rule by the wealthy few. At the same time, in an unequal society, the poor might rebel against the rich, leading to class warfare and revolution. Economic inequality brings with it political instability. Only in a country with relative economic equality is a stable democracy possible. Of course, for most of history, not everyone was considered part of the political community: women and minorities were systematically excluded. Today, we include people of all races and genders in the political community, and as a result, economic equality must extend to everyone.[2]

The second principle of economic democracy is that no entity should be so big or powerful that it evades democratic control. When any corporation has so much power that it can capture politics and defy regulation, it threatens democracy itself. Economic democracy therefore requires breaking up monopolies and conglomerates and instead fostering an economy of smaller businesses. Alternatively, if breaking up big businesses makes little sense, as is often the case with public utilities infrastructure and networked industries like telephones and railroads, economic democracy means regulating corporations or direct public provision of those goods and services. For there to be an economic democracy, economic power must be accountable to the people.[3]

The final principle of economic democracy is that the people themselves must have economic independence, freedom, and responsibility. In the age of artisans and yeoman farmers, the democratic spirit infused the idealized framework for the economy. The paradigmatic person was an owner of a small business—and thus was both empowered to succeed and responsible for failures. The school of commerce taught not just risk taking but restraint, and in the process, trained individuals in the kind of deliberation and measured reasoning that would help them participate in political democracy. With the rise of industrial wage labor and the corporation, this aspect of economic democracy increasingly fell by the wayside. Workers were left with routinized work that demanded little of them by way of discretion, responsibility, or creativity. Champions of economic democracy thus advocated for labor unions, worker cooperatives, and worker participation in corporate governance as ways to recapture some of the individual virtues that come with a truly economically democratic society.[4]

The three elements of economic democracy are, of course, related to each other. In a society with gigantic corporations, wealth concentrates in the hands of owners and managers, undermining the egalitarian foundations of democracy. The great corporations capture government, bringing special privileges to themselves and their leaders. And as workers are disempowered, they neither develop the civic capacities needed to arrest these changes nor do they have any say in their economic or political lives. The result is not democracy at all, but a condition of economic and political serfdom.

Achieving economic democracy will require reform along all three elements. Over the last generation, economic inequality has been widening and the middle class collapsing. Corporate consolidation has led to a new age of monopoly power, in which a small number of gigantic companies dominate entire sectors, cripple small businesses, and lobby governments. In the midst of these changes, workers are increasingly disempowered. No-poach and noncompete clauses restrict their freedom to work. Anti-union efforts restrict their freedom to participate in corporate governance and improve their conditions. Wages are stagnant, and opportunity feels like it is shrinking. The result is widespread dissatisfaction and even outright rebellion on both right and left. Minor tweaks cannot fix these problems. To confront the magnitude of these challenges, an economic democracy agenda has to be bold and transformative.

Fighting Monopolies and Concentrated Economic Power

We live in the second age of monopoly power. The first age, which spanned from the Gilded Age of the late nineteenth century through the Progressive Era in the early twentieth century, was marked by the growth of corporations into trusts. During the peak of 1894–1904, hundreds of corporations disappeared in the Great Merger Movement. The trusts wielded both economic and political power, and courageous politicians in both parties rallied to fight these monopolies because they threatened freedom and democracy. Republican John Sherman of Pennsylvania authored the Sherman Antitrust Act of 1890 and was joined by the Republican "Trust-buster" Teddy Roosevelt in seeking to rein in powerful corporations. Democrat Woodrow Wilson signed the Clayton Antitrust Act and the Federal Trade Commission Act, supported by advocate and later Supreme Court justice Louis Brandeis. Right and left, many Americans of that era understood that massive economic concentration was a threat not just to a free and competitive marketplace but a threat to constitutional democracy. The Sherman Antitrust Act made monopolization and monopolists' practices illegal in extremely broad terms. When the Supreme Court subsequently narrowed the law, declaring that it covered only unreasonable market practices, Congress passed new, broader antitrust laws and created the Federal Trade Commission (FTC) to serve as an antitrust agency.[5]

A century later, we are now in a second era of monopoly power. Four airlines now control 80 percent of the market. Three drug stores control 99 percent. Four beef companies control 85 percent. The Fortune 100 now makes up nearly 50 percent of GDP, with the top twenty firms capturing more than 20 percent. Commentators across the ideological spectrum have noticed and criticized America's monopoly problem: from progressives like Joe Stiglitz and neoliberals like Bloomberg's Noah Smith to conservative Breitbart columnist Virgil and establishment centrists at the Brookings Institution and the *Economist*. Even Congress has gotten involved, with members of the House creating an Antitrust Caucus and the Senate Judiciary Committee holding hearings on the goals of antitrust in 2017. There is such widespread interest in corporate consolidation because people recognize that the concentration of economic power is a threat to both the American economy and to freedom and democracy.[6]

The concentration of economic power harms consumers, increases inequality, and stifles economic growth and vibrancy. Monopolists have the ability to hold consumers hostage, raise prices, and deliver worse-quality goods and services. In a wide-ranging study, economist John Kwoka has shown that despite regulators' predictions, corporate mergers over the last few decades have led to an increase in consumer prices. Rising concentration also contributes to widening inequality. As megacorporations use their market power to squeeze suppliers and consumers to gain higher profits, those benefits accrue to wealthy executives and shareholders. Economists have also found that concentrated markets lead to lower wages for workers. In addition, the rise of monopolies threatens innovation and entrepreneurship. Powerful companies don't want competition and are likely to use their market power (and political power) to stop, delay, or otherwise prevent innovators from gaining traction. In recent years, economic researchers have confirmed this: the rate of new business formation is plummeting, and consolidation is an important factor.[7]

Economic power is also a danger because it turns into political power. The larger the company, the better able it is to contribute to political candidates, lobby legislators and regulators, dominate trade associations, hold cities hostage for economic giveaways, and shape the law to favor their interests at the expense of everyone else. Unlike small businesses or ordinary individuals, megacorporations have the resources to hire lobbyists to rig the law in their favor— gaining tax breaks, creating regulatory loopholes, and watering down campaign finance restrictions. When laws and regulations are created to rein them in, they can hire armies of lawyers to fight the government in court—sometimes for years—in order to delay or reverse sensible checks on their power. And even if they lose in court, they can still hire thousands of lawyers to help them exploit every loophole and ambiguity, something smaller businesses and individuals simply can't do.[8]

Why did policies the that brought an end to the first era of monopoly power fail to prevent the rise of this second era? The answer

131

comes down to three factors: ideology, the structure of the anti-trust agencies, and the emergence of new industries, namely digital technology.

The first failure was one of ideology. The United States had a robust anti-monopoly philosophy and movement from the found-ing of the country through the mid-twentieth century. But starting in the 1970s, a group of professors—largely lawyers and economists centered at the University of Chicago—adopted a new neoliberal approach to antitrust. The Chicago School argued that bigness was not a problem at all and that antitrust had nothing to do with polit-ical freedom, economic power, or even competition. The only thing that mattered in antitrust law was the welfare of consumers, and this was measurable by looking at prices. As a result, they focused antitrust law on reducing consumer prices and increasing economic efficiency, even if that meant allowing megamergers to create behe-moths that had more power than most governments. Over the course of the neoliberal era, the Chicago School's approach came to dominate antitrust law and policy.

The second failure is in the structure of government agencies tasked with policing competition. In most areas, Congress passes laws commanding federal agencies to regulate—the EPA regulates clean air and water, the National Highway Transportation Safety Administration regulates safety in cars and trucks, the Consumer Products Safety Commission regulates children's toys. In each case, the agency is empowered to use its considerable expertise to make regulations that set standards or regulate specific practices. Courts are able to review these regulations, giving deference to the sub-stance of the regulation as long as it is within the agency's discre-tion and the agency has used its expertise to come to a reasoned decision.

Antitrust doesn't work this way. Although the Federal Trade Commission has the power to make regulations, just like other agencies, it has failed to take up this role. Instead, the FTC and the Department of Justice take companies to court. What this means is that the Supreme Court—a group of unelected, unaccountable judges who have no expertise in business generally or in any specific sector of the economy—get to set antitrust standards and policies. Judicial lawmaking in this arena also ties back to the ideology problem. Normally, the courts provide a check on regulatory agencies, which utilize their expertise and follow a transparent process for making regulations. In antitrust, because the courts have no expertise, they have to rely on the parties in the case to teach them about markets and competition during litigation. A skewed set of intellectual inputs, and limited public participation, leads to judicial lawmaking that is disconnected from reality.[9]

The FTC itself is also badly designed to ensure the vigorous enforcement of antitrust law. The FTC is a multimember commission composed of five members with no more than three from any one political party. This design means that it is almost impossible to have a majority of active, aggressive regulators on the commission for any length of time, given compromise in the appointments process. And when the commission takes a strong action, minority commissioners often write dissents that legitimize opposition to regulations and act as a guide or roadmap for ideological judges who want to strike down those regulations. Taken together, a multimember competition agency is a roadmap for inaction and delay, weak regulations, and ultimately reversal of those weak regulations. In contrast, single-director agencies accountable to the president have significant benefits. They unify power, thereby empowering an active and energetic director to undertake serious actions. And they unify responsibility and accountability, creating a focal point for organizing the opposition against a failing director or one ideologically opposed to strong regulation.[10]

Beyond the FTC's own shortcomings, further problems arise because the FTC and Department of Justice share power. The division of labor across these agencies is haphazard and problematic. For example, the DOJ addresses agriculture, but the FTC covers food retailing. Both agencies have power to review proposed mergers. But the division of sectors hasn't been set by law and is frequently the subject of turf wars between the agencies. This division also means duplicative costs, inconsistencies in the application of the law, and confusion in the merger clearance process. In theory, division could mean competition and a higher standard of enforcement. In practice, it has meant the opposite: weaker enforcement and ineffective administration.[11]

The third failure has been a failure to adapt. Antitrust enforcers have not adapted to the rise of the most important industry of the twenty-first century: technology platforms. New technologies can often seem unprecedented, and it takes great effort to learn about how particular companies and industries work. Add to this neoliberal ideology and the structure of the antitrust agencies, and the result is that regulators have allowed numerous technology mergers to go forward and a variety of anticompetitive behaviors to go unchallenged, despite the fact that they run afoul of antitrust principles.[12]

Reversing the second age of monopoly power requires bold action along a variety of dimensions: challenging the ideology that has dominated antitrust for decades, reforming the substance of antitrust laws, and understanding and regulating new technologies. First, the FTC should be relaunched as a new Anti-Monopoly Agency (AMA), with a single director rather than a multimember commission. The second big change concerns what this new Anti-Monopoly Agency should do. To align with the normal model of regulation, the new AMA should be required to use its rulemaking power to define and specify violations of the antitrust laws—just like agencies in every other sector do. In exercising this power, the agency should abandon the neoliberal consumer welfare approach, with its narrow approach to prices, and return antitrust to protecting and promoting a competitive economy. The third change is to take on the technology platforms.[13]

Regulating Technology

One of the central questions of our time is how democracy will survive the rise of gigantic technology companies. In recent years, people around the world have recognized the need to regulate the technology sector. Scandals about data breaches and transfers, Russian infiltration and fake news, uncompetitive market practices, and constant surveillance have sparked widespread concern. It has gotten so bad that even tech company CEOs have been forced to admit that their companies need to be regulated. Apple's Tim Cook said, "Some well-crafted regulation is necessary." Facebook's Mark Zuckerberg acknowledged that the question isn't whether to regulate but "How do you do it?" The answer turns out not to be as hard as one might think. It will take three steps: regulating the platforms as utilities, breaking up tech companies through antitrust laws, and ending the business model of surveillance.[14]

Start with platforms. Technology platforms require a special sort of regulation because they have power over their users that most other companies lack. In many sectors, companies compete with one another on price and quality to sell products or services. Technology platforms, in contrast, often play the role of intermediary, connecting consumers with other sellers and advertisers, but many of them simultaneously compete directly with successful small businesses who rely on their platform.

Take, for example, Amazon Marketplace. John Q. Public can make custom bracelets at home and sell them on Amazon Marketplace. But Amazon both runs the marketplace and has its own business that competes on the marketplace, Amazon Basics. That means that if John Q. Public's bracelets do well, Amazon will notice because it collects data about its marketplace, and Amazon Basics can produce identical bracelets in China at a lower cost. Amazon can then feature Amazon Basic's bracelets on page one of its search results while relegating John Q. Public's bracelets to page three, four, or worse. The result is that John Q. Public will go out of business—not because his product was worse but because Amazon used its platform's data, its power over the marketplace, and its Basics business to put him out of business. Some companies have alleged that Amazon has done exactly this to them.[15]

The same kind of thing can happen with Google Search. Consider the conflict between Google and Yelp, which aggregates customer reviews of restaurants and other businesses. Because Google has a separate line of business reviewing and recommending businesses, Google can prioritize its content over Yelp's when a user searches for a business review—and even when they search for "Yelp" and a business review. This, too, isn't theoretical. In the summer of 2017, the EU antitrust authorities fined Google $2.7 billion because it did not place its shopping comparison tool on a level playing field with those of competitors. One start-up has also alleged that Google deprioritized its competing search tool. If the start-up gained traction, it might eventually threaten Google's dominance in online search, so they alleged Google prevented them from even being findable on the internet.[16]

The problem in these cases emerges from what scholars call vertical integration and market power. In these cases, vertical integration means that the company owns both the platform (the marketplace or search engine) and simultaneously competes on the platform. This gives a platform a motive to discriminate against its users and favor its own business over others. The market power problem is that platforms are so dominant that companies and individuals have to use them, and as a result, are at their mercy. Many people think tech platforms got so powerful because of network effects—that is, the more people using the platform, the better the service gets. But platforms can also become dominant if they discriminate against, exclude, and threaten possible competitors. For example, if a search engine doesn't allow a potential competitor to be searchable, the competitors might never have a chance to succeed.

The problems of vertical integration and market power are not new, and there are long-standing models for addressing them through regulation. Since the dawn of the industrial era, policy makers confronted a variety of industries engaged in similar practices to those of contemporary tech platforms. They recognized that these practices were destructive, and to address them, they developed a set of legal principles that have regularly been applied to sectors like transportation, communications, and electricity: nondiscriminatory access, separation or quarantine of the business, and (depending on the context) regulation of rates.

A few illustrations will help. Let's start with an industrial era example from the late nineteenth century. Imagine that railroad service is competitive, with many train companies (each of which owns its own track) operating on the East and West Coasts. But the railroad terminal in St. Louis is owned by one train company, and any other train company that wants to send its trains from the eastern United States to the West must pass through it. If the company that owns the terminal refuses to let any other company use it, there would be no competition on the routes through St. Louis. Because of the extremely high cost of building a new terminal and rerouting tracks to it, competition might be impossible. The terminal and train company could price gouge both consumers and other train companies while providing poor service.

Historically, under the essential facilities doctrine, it would be illegal for the company to discriminate against other companies for access to the terminal. The idea was that it was impractical to build another terminal, and the terminal was basically a public utility or piece of infrastructure, essential for commerce to work. This doesn't mean that the company can't recoup its costs by charging a fee (it can, though that rate has to be reasonable), nor does it mean that the company can't limit access to the terminal to prevent congestion. But it can't charge different prices to different users or bar access altogether. The law recognized that monopolists have the extraordinary power to choke off commerce (and, in this case, transportation) and that no entity should be so powerful as to be able to exploit and pressure consumers, citizens, or the government.[17]

Another example comes from the law of public accommodations, also known as the law of innkeepers and common carriers. Innkeepers and common carriers were required to accept all comers, meaning that they could not discriminate against customers. The justification for the rule was similar to the one undergirding the essential facilities doctrine. Think back to the early republic, when travel between cities took weeks and there were few roads and few places to stay along those roads. If an innkeeper could discriminate against travelers, then it would be impossible to travel. The nondiscriminatory access rule recognized that innkeepers served an important public function on highways and held extraordinary power over the free flow of commerce in the country.[18]

A third example is public utilities regulation, which can apply when a particular service is a natural monopoly or networked industry. In the telephone industry, for example, it was extremely costly to provide phone lines to every household, and the network was more valuable the more people were on it (because they could communicate with each other). As a result, it made sense to have a single provider of telephone service. But if telephone service was a monopoly, what was to stop the monopolist from raising rates? What was to stop the monopolist from using its power over phone lines to weasel its way into other adjacent sectors? Electricity and water were similar. It was costly to build pipes and power lines—and we didn't really want multiple sets of competing pipes and power lines everywhere—but that meant that a monopolist over these essential services could exploit users.

The answer in these sectors was public utilities regulation. The basic idea was that monopolies might be necessary, but instead of government providing the service directly, the government would regulate the private monopolist. First, it would separate or quarantine the business line that had monopoly power from the rest of the company, restricting a company to owning only the monopoly element and thereby preventing them from exploiting other adjacent sectors. Second, there would be regulation of rates and terms to prevent the monopolist from jacking up prices on captive consumers. Third, there was usually a protected franchise and a mandate to provide service to everyone. The utility was given exclusive domain over its sector so that competitors could not undercut the utility's business by skimming off the most valuable customers.[19]

The common themes in these approaches provide principles for how to regulate tech platforms. Platforms like Amazon Marketplace and Google Search should be required to offer nondiscriminatory access to their services, and vertically integrated business lines should be divested—broken off—from the platform. This separation, or quarantine, prevents exploiting power, including the power that comes from surveillance and data collection, and giving preferential treatment to their own business lines. The nondiscriminatory access provision is a complementary obligation to treat all users with fair and neutral terms. In some industries, rate regulation might also be a necessary companion to nondiscrimination and quarantine. If a platform charges users and becomes so dominant as to serve as an effective monopoly, then the platform might raise rates on captive users. Competitors won't be able to challenge the platform because they might not be able to build an alternative platform.[20]

The new Anti-Monopoly Agency should be directed to break up tech platforms along these lines. But even in the absence of Congress creating a new agency, the Federal Trade Commission can currently act in accordance with these principles on a case-by-case basis or by issuing regulations. Because the FTC has the power to regulate unfair methods of competition and unfair or deceptive practices, it could, for example, determine that discriminatory platforms are engaged in an unfair method of competition or unfair practice.[21]

The new Anti-Monopoly Agency, or a more steel-spined FTC, should also apply antitrust laws far more aggressively and seriously to the tech sector to prevent mergers and unwind already-completed mergers. When tech platforms merge, they don't just create a bigger company. Mergers allow a company to collect and combine data from different platforms. For example, when Facebook bought WhatsApp and Instagram, it significantly expanded the amount of data under its control and prevented the emergence of two full-scale rivals to the social network. The acquisitions made Facebook even more dominant than it had been. Google's purchase of Nest means that it has access to data on when people are at home and in what rooms, and its purchase of DoubleClick, which ran the platform for online advertising, enabled Google to dominate online advertising by integrating brokers, dealers, and the exchange on which they bought and sold ad space.

In some cases, data and the merger problem also work in tandem. If a platform like Google or Amazon uses search or sales data to identify companies that are starting to gain traction, it might purchase them before they even threaten to become competitors. This problem has gotten so bad that venture capitalists now speak of a "kill zone" that exists around these big-tech platforms; they refuse to invest in start-ups in this zone because there is no chance of success. The result, once again, is the further accumulation of power and the erosion of a competitive, dynamic economy.[22]

In addition to regulating and breaking up tech platforms, we must end the business model of surveillance. Many big tech companies conduct widespread surveillance of individuals in order to develop personalized profiles of people to offer targeted advertising and direct individuals toward specific products. This mass collection of personal data threatens individual privacy from corporate and government intrusion, increases the risks of hacks and identity theft, and enables companies and governments to engage in population control, behavior modification, and psychological experimentation. Companies (and the government) can now identify how often someone goes to church, whether they look at pornography, whether they have a physical or mental illness, and whether they are gay or straight. They can direct people toward specific emotions, products, or political candidates. The risks to security range from hackers seeking financial information to foreign governments rigging elections. And unless individuals want to move to a remote wilderness, there is no choice but to offer up their data—and even there, Google Earth captures images from above.

As we have already seen, when perfected, these technologies lead to digital authoritarianism, in which the fusion of tech and government enables population and behavior control. Given the risks from the mass collection of data, it is astonishing that there aren't comprehensive regulations on how companies should store, protect, and use personal data. Instead, we have a neoliberal notice-and-consent regime that is toothless because people have to accept the terms and conditions and have no ability to negotiate the terms or make choices about the use of their data.

There are different ways to address the problems of surveillance capitalism. *The American Prospect*'s David Dayen has offered one of the simplest solutions: ban targeted advertising. Dayen identifies a variety of negative consequences of targeted advertising, from racial discrimination to scams targeting vulnerable people. The business model of personalized, targeted advertising also leads to monopolization in the tech sector because bigger companies can harvest more data and target individuals more precisely. This, in turn, further concentrates economic and political power. Targeted ads also offer few benefits—if ads were not personalized to individuals, consumers would still be able to identify products that would appeal to them. Dayen's proposal is to "disallow all individually targeted ads." "Nothing tied to a user's identity," he writes, "should be used to serve them a particular message."[23]

Another option is to adopt a technology bill of rights. Under this bill of rights, consumers would have five rights: the right to use a tech product without giving up any of their personal data, the right to use a tech product without any targeted advertising, the right to use a tech product without transferring data to any third parties, the right to be free from behavioral experimentation, and the right for children to be free from all data collection, surveillance, and targeting. The tech bill of rights would fundamentally reshape power over data.

In both cases, companies would have to change their business models. But there is no reason to think they couldn't adapt. Google would still have an incredible search product, and Facebook would still have billions of users (and that's true even if it spins off WhatsApp and Instagram). But because both approaches change the rules on surveillance and data collection, companies would no longer be able to pursue a strategy that is deliberately designed to exploit user information for financial gain.

Reforming Finance

As applied to the financial sector, fears of the second monopoly era were ahead of their time. The financial crash of 2008 showed how central the financial sector had become to the economy, how risky and unregulated its practices were, and how big the biggest banks had gotten. Indeed, these developments were related. With neoliberal policies deregulating the sector over the last generation, finance became a bigger and bigger part of the economy—a process that scholars call "financialization." In 1950, the American financial sector was responsible for 2.8 percent of GDP. In 2012, it was responsible for 6.6 percent. Financialization takes talent and resources away from the productive, real economy, shuffling them instead to speculation and short-term gains. It makes the economy more susceptible to economic crashes and volatility. And it also increases inequality. Some economists estimate that rising wages in the financial sector are responsible for 15–25 percent of the increase in wage inequality since 1980.[24]

Although the 2010 Dodd-Frank Act reformed the financial sector, it did not go nearly far enough. Coming in the waning years of the deregulatory neoliberal era, political leaders were only able to muster support for technocratic reforms, not serious structural changes to the financial system. The result is that the biggest Wall Street banks today are bigger than they were before the crash. To fundamentally change the structure and organization of the financial system, reduce risk, and enable economic democracy requires two major reforms: creating a modernized Glass-Steagall Act to break up the banks and establishing a public option for bank accounts.

Until it was formally repealed in 1999, Glass-Steagall required a separation between depository banking, investment banking, and insurance companies. In recent years, the idea of resurrecting the law has had surprising support across the political spectrum. Progressive Democrats have advocated for its reinstatement consistently since the financial crash of 2008. The 2016 Republican Party platform embraced bringing back Glass-Steagall. Former heads of Citigroup have said it was a mistake to repeal the law. And, for a short time at least, even the Trump administration seemed open to the idea of revival. Although there has been a great deal of debate over Glass-Steagall and its repeal, much of the discussion misses the core point: the idea behind the law was that different financial functions should be in different financial institutions and that these functions shouldn't be commingled. Today, we need to break up financial institutions along functional lines.[25]

The core of the case for a modernized Glass-Steagall starts with asking a broad and farsighted question: How should the financial sector be structured? Breaking up financial institutions along functional lines rests on two premises. The first is the general opposition to concentrated economic and political power that is normally associated with anti-monopoly thinking. Indeed, we can think of a modern Glass-Steagall as something like a ban on mergers that create conglomerates. The purpose is to fragment power. When firms are smaller and separated by function, it is more likely there will be competition along specific business lines. Take a financial start-up that wants to enter the depository sector. It will be harder for that start-up to compete with conglomerates that can cross-subsidize business lines. Concentration isn't just bad for competition; it's also bad for democracy. Too much economic power spills over into politics, giving massive firms an advantage in lobbying Congress or influencing regulators. In other words, concentration makes it more likely that government gets captured by corporate behemoths and that regulations are written to stack the deck in their favor.

The second premise is that we should break up big financial institutions by separating their functions rather than by capping their size. Of course, it is not inconsistent to support both reforms, and some proponents of modernizing Glass-Steagall do. But there are many reasons to desire a financial sector that is fractured by function specifically. Separation means government guarantees won't cross-subsidize risky business lines—and that banks cannot leverage their market power in one sector to dominate another sector.

Separation can also help reduce the risk of a business infected with bad bets taking down the entire financial system. And it will make firms smaller, even though it would still be possible for a firm to become large within a single business line. Overall, these factors make the financial system less susceptible to systemic risk.

Separation along functional lines also has a variety of legal and political benefits. It will improve the ability of regulators to monitor and regulate financial entities, indirectly making simpler regulations more viable. It also breaks up political power based on types of financial activities, meaning that lobbyists for different parts of the financial system are more likely to find themselves on opposing sides of policy questions. That should, in turn, enable policy makers to design smarter and fairer regulations.

Financial institutions themselves might also benefit from such separation. Separation along functional lines makes compliance easier for banks that have become too big to manage. With fewer divisions and complex structures, management will have an easier time preventing bad apples in the company from illegal or improper behavior. Indeed, employee culture within these institutions would likely change over time. Depository bankers, for example, could redevelop a culture of being boring, while investment bankers would remain risk takers.

Of course, there are drawbacks to reviving a Glass-Steagall-like regime. For example, monopoly-sized firms and massive conglomerates are more likely to offer one-stop shopping and can more seamlessly integrate financial practices for customers. But any effort at making public policy has trade-offs. The reality, however, is that a modernized Glass-Steagall will make the financial system less concentrated, more competitive, easier to regulate, and give it less political power.

The second transformative reform would be to institute what finance scholars Morgan Ricks, John Crawford, and Lev Menand have called "central banking for all." Like all businesses and individuals, banks need their own bank accounts. But unlike businesses and individuals, banks get to have their accounts at the Federal

Reserve. These accounts have huge benefits: higher interest rates, no minimum balances, no fees, immediate clearing between payments, and no need for deposit insurance because they are pure, sovereign, nondefaultable money. Central banking for all would make bank accounts at the Fed available to all Americans and American businesses. These FedAccounts would give people the same deal that banks currently get. Although FedAccounts would mostly be electronic, brick-and-mortar ATMs and tellers could be located at post offices around the country, which would ensure that every community had a location if individuals needed in-person assistance.[26]

Perhaps the most obvious benefit of FedAccounts is that it would make serious headway in bringing everyone into the financial system, regardless of wealth, race, or geography. In the old days, when people earned cash and could pay for goods and services in cash, government-backed paper money worked seamlessly. But with the popularization of checks in the mid-twentieth century, and then credit cards, debit cards, electronic payments, and other innovations, cash has increasingly fallen by the wayside. But 8.4 million American households—comprising some fourteen million adults and more than six million children—don't have a bank account, which is essential for easily accessing these financial innovations. Another twenty-four million households have accounts but don't fully use them. Banks charge fees and have minimum balance requirements, and a significant percentage of these people are too poor to afford these accounts. As a result, to spend their hard-earned money, these unbanked and underbanked households have to rely on check cashers, money orders, prepaid cards, and other so-called fringe banking services—all of which charge one-off fees and sometimes interest. In effect, millions of Americans pay a tax just to use the money they are entitled to simply because they are poor and because most people and businesses have moved away from cash. FedAccount would give these people a way into the financial sector. It would serve as a basic piece of the modern economic infrastructure.[27]

There would also be other significant benefits. For small (and big) businesses that choose to open a FedAccount, payments made by or to other account holders would clear instantly. Small business would no longer have to wait days for checks to clear, credit cards to pay out, or wire transfers to be logged and accounted. Individuals wanting to transfer money also wouldn't have to worry about delays—payments would be instantaneous. For consumers and retailers, FedAccount would also eliminate interchange fees, like those that debit card networks charge retailers every time a consumer uses their card. So if a consumer and retailer both have FedAccounts, then the retailer won't pay fees and can pass along some of that savings to the consumer.

More broadly, FedAccount would have major systemic benefits for the economy and the financial system. First, it would make monetary policy work better. The Fed sets monetary policy by increasing or decreasing the interest rate it gives banks on their accounts. The idea behind this approach is that banks will pass along that interest rate change to their customers, thereby increasing or decreasing the supply of money in circulation. The problem is that banks keep part of the interest changes for themselves instead of passing all of it along to consumers. The Fed's monetary policy is thus less effective, and it is subsidizing banks. FedAccounts would end the subsidy and improve monetary policy. The second systemic benefit is that FedAccounts would make the financial system more stable. The immediate cause of major financial crashes throughout history has been financial panics—people fearing their assets were at risk and pulling them out of the financial system. Federal Deposit Insurance ended bank runs in depository banks in the 1930s. But modern banking panics still happen, now just in other sectors with names like repo, money market mutual funds, and Eurodollars. Businesses often rely on these other kinds of funds because they want to park their money in something with a decent return. FedAccounts would serve that function and lead to a shift away from these runnable assets, thereby making the financial system more secure.

Corporate Democracy

Antitrust laws break up big, powerful companies into smaller ones that are less threatening to political and economic democracy. Public utilities regulation allows for massive size and scale, but it places restrictions on the threats that come from corporate gigantism. A third strategy is to democratize the corporation itself—that is, to reshape its internal power structures by giving voice to workers. Since the New Deal, labor unions have been the primary way that workers gained voice inside corporations. But today, with labor unions under fierce attack and corporations gaining in power, reforms to both corporate governance and labor law can help achieve corporate democracy.

For much of the early American republic, corporations didn't exist in the form that we now think of them. Corporate charters were considered a special privilege, and state legislatures issued them on a case-by-case basis when the creation of a corporation was essential to the public good—and with restrictions that the corporation not expand the scope of its activities. Many people worried, however, that legislatures were captured by wealthy and well-connected individuals and that charters were not available on fair and equal terms to everyone. Reformers in the middle of the nineteenth century therefore pushed for general incorporation laws, which allowed anyone to start a corporation as long as that person organized it according to specified criteria. Although these reformers were often hostile to corporations, their solution actually unleashed more and more corporations into the American economy. Because general incorporation laws were passed at the state level rather than the federal level, states eventually began to compete for corporate charters (and the incorporation fees that came with them). The result was a race to the bottom in which states offered less and less restrictive charters. Today, that race leads to Delaware, where two-thirds of the Fortune 500 are incorporated, in addition to some 1.2 million other companies.[28]

The rise of the corporation in the late nineteenth century created a second problem that cut to the heart of economic democracy.

In the old world of artisans, shopkeepers, and yeoman farmers, economic democracy was largely a reality because the owners of a business also ran that business. In the new world of corporations, ownership and control were divided: the managers who ran the corporation were not the same people as the shareholders who owned it. Whatever this system was, it wasn't an economic democracy. Some commentators, like Walter Lippmann, argued for the independence of managers who ran the business, so they could do what was in the long-term best interest of the business rather than simply in the best interest of shareholders. They would become "industrial statesmen," the private sector counterparts to political statesmen, and they would be devoted to their craft while keeping the social good in mind. In contrast, shareholders were transient and absentee. They were nothing like actual owners and were ill-suited to corporate control.[29]

Something like this approach existed for many years, but in the late 1970s, a new theory emerged. Scholars argued that managers were merely the agents, or servants, of the owners—the shareholders. Under this theory, managers should maximize value to shareholders, and this was accomplished by boosting profits. This approach birthed the shareholder primacy movement. In its purest form, shareholder primacy holds that the interests of workers, the community, the environment, or the public or social good do not matter. The only concern for managers is value to the shareholder, and that value is easily measurable: stock price.[30]

By the turn of the twenty-first century, shareholder primacy had become the dominant approach to corporate governance, even as it had perverse consequences for businesses and society. Companies began to shift their earnings from reinvesting in their workers, equipment, and future into paying their shareholders. Between 2003 and 2012, more than 90 percent of the earnings of S&P 500 companies went to shareholders in the form of stock buybacks or dividend payments. On the theory that share prices are what matter, corporations started compensating CEOs through stock options so the CEOs would have an incentive to boost share value.

The result was massive inequality within corporations. In 1965, the ratio of CEO to worker pay was 20 to 1. In 1989, it was 59 to 1. By 2016, it had skyrocketed to 271 to 1. More broadly, because most Americans don't own any stock at all, the focus on boosting share prices has increased inequality by funneling money from workers to shareholders.[31]

The story of the rise of corporate power must be told alongside the story of labor power. In the late nineteenth century, populist reformers observed that corporations had undermined another aspect of economic democracy: small farmers and artisans were becoming wage laborers. In many cases, these workers had little control over their lives, livelihoods, or economic destinies because corporate bosses called the shots. The populists therefore argued that corporations had to be transformed. Some advocated for requiring all corporations to become cooperatives, with joint ownership and control by employees. Others, like future Supreme Court justice Louis Brandeis, argued for industrial democracy, a form of worker participation short of becoming a full cooperative. "The employees must have the opportunity of participating in the decision as to what shall be their condition and how the business shall be run," Brandeis said in 1915. Brandeis meant that workers would have a real say and stake in corporate governance—and that they should bear the consequences of their mistakes. Neither cooperatives nor industrial democracy came to pass. Instead, labor unions mobilized, organized, and won a system of worker-management bargaining.[32]

Under the National Labor Relations Act of 1935, workers would organize into unions within companies and be able to negotiate and bargain with their employers for better terms and conditions of their employment. By the post–World War II era, about one-third of the American workforce was unionized. But neoliberalism's attack on labor unions undermined the precarious détente between workers and companies that existed for the generation after World War II. Companies took an active role in breaking unions. They classified workers as independent contractors to avoid having employees in the first place. And they lobbied hard for anti-union laws throughout the states—laws that would make it harder for unions to grow and organize and, in the process, would crush the ability of unions to advocate for the interests of working people in the political process. They largely succeeded. By 2012, union membership had plummeted to only 11 percent of the workforce.[33]

Achieving economic democracy will require serious reforms in corporate governance and in the role of workers in companies. One of the key lessons of the history of corporate law is that corporations don't exist in nature. They only exist because we the people, acting through our democratic government, have passed laws that allow for their creation. As a result, we can change those laws to tame corporate power. We should start by passing a federal law to require that large corporations be chartered at the federal level rather than the state level, with conditions on receiving a federal charter. We should create a new Bureau of Corporations within the Department of Commerce, which would be tasked with licensing the biggest corporations that operate in America based on revenue and number of employees.

Federally chartered corporations would be required to meet a number of criteria. First, they would have to adhere to principles for benefit corporations. Benefit corporations are traditional corporations, but their charter requires that they engage in publicly beneficial activities and sustainable value in addition to generating a profit. This requirement would prevent corporate managers and boards from pursuing shareholder profits alone, instead of also considering the interests of the business, its workers, the environment, or the public good more broadly. Second, federally chartered corporations would be banned from compensating any of their senior managers with anything other than a salary (for example, they couldn't get paid through stock options). This would delink the managers from the short-term incentives of boosting stock prices for themselves and investors. Finally, federally chartered corporations would either have to be organized as cooperatives, with full employee ownership and governance, or they would have to be

unionized and half of all board members would have to be representatives of employees. This latter approach to corporate governance is called codetermination.

The idea of a federal incorporation law is not a new one. In 1908,
Theodore Roosevelt called for a federal agency with the power to
license, control, and supervise corporations. Today, the case for a
federal incorporation law is strong. Federal chartering of the largest companies in the country would both prevent the race to the
bottom in corporate governance standards and reduce the power of
companies that pose the greatest threat to political and economic
democracy. The conditions placed on federally chartered companies would end the problematic shareholder primacy approach
to corporate strategy, which exacerbates inequality, undermines
long-term value, and harms workers. And the internal governance
reforms would empower workers to have a say over the company.
This would not only mean that the company would be better to its
workers but would also inject a significant new perspective into
corporate decision-making. Indeed, the case is so strong today that
political leaders again have picked up and modernized Roosevelt's
idea along similar lines to those proposed here. Senator Elizabeth
Warren, for example, has proposed an Accountable Capitalism Act
that would require federal charters for large companies and worker
participation on their boards.[34]

Although new federal charter requirements would make the
largest companies more democratic, reforms to labor law would
also help empower workers at midsized companies and ultimately
enhance the political power of working people. First, we could
adopt a rule of automatic unionization of workplaces, unless workers opt out. Under current law, workers have to vote in order to
create a union. These elections are beset with problems, including
corporate managers and even politicians interfering in the electoral
process to prevent unionization. Another approach is to flip the
default so that all workers who are covered by the labor laws will
be members of a union unless there is an election and a majority opt out of the union. This change would help rebuild labor

union membership all across the country. Second, many countries around the world have works councils, a collaboration between workers and managers at the worksite to discuss improvements, best practices, and other issues. Unlike codetermination, works councils don't bargain for wages or engage in high-level policy-making. Instead, they bring together, for example, autoworkers and managers in a single plant to talk about how to improve the line, increase productivity, enhance safety, and innovate. Works councils are democracy on the assembly line, democracy in the cube farm. They empower workers, turning them from cogs in the machine to participants in the enterprise. Works councils are illegal under current law, in part because they might undermine unionization. But this is much less of a concern if works councils are combined with default unionization.[35]

Finally, we need to shift to a sector-based approach to collective bargaining. Labor bargaining at the company level doesn't always make sense. Companies in many sectors face serious competition, and increased labor costs could make the difference between success and failure in the marketplace. But if every company in the sector adopted the same prolabor policies, for example, on wages or safety standards, there would be no competitive problem. Making policy along these lines is called sectoral bargaining, and it exists currently in countries around the world. But the sector-based approach is far from common today in the United States. A new statute establishing a process for sectoral bargaining could have a significant impact for workers while solving a serious competitive problem for corporate managers.[36]

Of course, the reality of work today is that not everyone works for a corporation. Some people strike out on their own and are self-employed or start small businesses. Others are independent contractors or gig economy workers. For these people, corporate democracy and reviving labor unions might be helpful for the broader economy and for advancing economic democracy as a general matter. But these reforms are less likely to get them health care coverage and retirement savings. For their economic security and opportunity, we will also need robust public options for the basic preconditions for a flourishing life.

Public Options

As we have learned, during the liberal era after World War II, the dominant model for providing many of these essential social and economic goods was called the Treaty of Detroit. Under the Treaty of Detroit, automakers and labor unions agreed to a system of employer-based benefits: for example, workers would get health insurance from their employers. Since the treaty, much of the American social safety net operates this way. Health care, unemployment, pensions, retirement accounts—all are provided through employers. In the neoliberal era, this started to change. Neoliberals preferred a system in which people would fend for themselves in accessing these necessities—education, health care, and childcare would be available, they argued, through the marketplace.

Today, however, neither of these approaches makes much sense. The economy is precarious, and workers and families are financially insecure. Workers no longer work for a single employer for a career (if they ever did). The reality is that many people are now independent contractors and freelancers, workers who don't have a single salaried position—and as a result, can't get health care, childcare, or other benefits through an employer. At the same time, leaving their fate to the marketplace means they are highly vulnerable to fraud and predation, assuming they can afford to shop in the marketplace at all.

Having access to these basic elements of everyday life is a precondition for being a full citizen in both an economic democracy and a political democracy. It is very difficult to participate in the economy, or in democracy, when you're sick. It's difficult when you don't have childcare. It's difficult when you don't have transportation infrastructure to get to work or the ballot box. It's difficult if you don't know how to read or never got a basic education. As a result, we can't just rely on employers providing basic social goods to their employees. We need another approach. And throughout

American history, we the people have provided just that, through a public option.[37]

What is a public option? A public option is a universally accessible, government-provided good or service that coexists with private sector options. A public school is a public option. Any kid can attend—without fees or preconditions—but if you don't want to go, you can attend a private school instead. A public swimming pool is a public option; a private swimming pool is in your backyard. A public park is open to all; your backyard is a private option. Public libraries mean you don't have to build your own private library for books you might read just once or not at all. Public transportation, like buses, subways, and trains, means you can get around town, but you can also opt for the private option of a car. Public options are critical to democracy because they enable everyone in our democracy to improve themselves civically, morally, culturally, and economically.

Historically, public options haven't always been perfect, and they haven't always been inclusive. But when designed right, they have significant benefits. They provide universal access to important goods and services. Anyone can use them, regardless of race or gender. And because the fees are reasonable to ensure widespread access, wealth isn't a factor either. Public options thus not only expand equality, they also enhance freedom. A public option can also introduce competition into markets that are highly concentrated, forcing private monopolists to offer better services or lower their prices. In addition, public options help build community and stitch Americans together as one people. Public libraries, for example, offer a place for people to come together to enjoy educational programs, storytime for children, and other activities.

Today, however, the economy and society are changing rapidly. It now takes more than a public library and a public school to thrive in the modern world. To have an economic democracy, everyone needs to have the basic opportunity to succeed in the economy. As a result, we now need a new set of public options so that all of our citizens can be full members of our economic and political democracy. Consider a few examples of public options that are critical to the future.

In the modern economy, having high-speed internet access is as critical as it was to have electricity a hundred years ago. But 6.5 percent of Americans don't have any access to even moderate-speed internet, defined as 25 Mbps download speeds. For the roughly 25 percent of rural communities that have no access, the absence of broadband keeps them disconnected from the national and global economy. In places where there is access to high-speed internet, the problem is different: often, internet service is a monopoly. If we move up to high-speed internet—100 Mbps downloads—almost half of neighborhoods have only one provider, and 36 percent have none at all.[38]

A public option—a government-provided internet service that would compete with the private sector—would help solve these problems. Some cities have already taken steps to build municipal broadband networks as a public option. Chattanooga, Tennessee, for example, offers internet through a fiber network. Residents get 1 Gbps service from the city's Electric Power Board for less than seventy dollars per month. By 2019, more than one hundred thousand residents and businesses were taking advantage of the city's broadband service. The city experienced a tech boom, with new jobs and businesses popping up, and it even used the new network to improve electricity service. Importantly, Chattanooga didn't ban Comcast or AT&T or anyone else. It just offered a simple, straightforward service—without frills, gimmicks, or hidden fees. Cities around the country should follow Chattanooga's model and provide broadband service as a public option. The consequence would be a stronger economic democracy—broader access, better service, and more competition.[39]

The most hotly debated public option today is for health insurance. The idea is that the government would let anyone have access to Medicare (or a similar government-provided health insurance plan). If people don't want to use it, they can buy private health insurance instead. Commentators often point out that the public option is different from another proposal: single-payer health care. The argument is that single-payer is the exclusive government provision of health insurance with no private option. But in reality, although single-payer health care is not a *competitive* public option, it is a *baseline* public option. In countries with national health insurance systems, and even for Americans on Medicare, there is often a private market for additional health insurance above and beyond what the government option provides. The private market finds opportunities where they exist, but there is a baseline of public provision that ensures universal access to health care.

What could a public option in health care look like today? The passage of Obamacare in 2010 set up exchanges—or marketplaces—in every state. People can go to the marketplace and purchase health insurance there, and the plans have requirements as to what they must offer to ensure a basic quality of coverage. The simplest short-term possibility for a public option would be for the government to offer its own health care plan, like Medicare, on the exchanges. People could then choose to get Medicare or whatever private plans are available. A broader reform would eliminate the state exchanges, create a single national exchange with many competing plans, and offer Medicare on the national exchange. A final approach would be single-payer reforms. Everyone would be enrolled in Medicare from birth and have lifetime guaranteed health insurance. Private insurers would then compete to provide additional or complementary coverage for those who wanted it.

Childcare is another arena in which a public option could be helpful. For most families, taking care of children while juggling work is a real challenge. Kids don't go to school until kindergarten, the school day is short and rarely coincides with the workday, and schools don't run year-round. As a result, parents are forced to think up (and, if they can afford it, pay hefty sums for) ways to have people watch their kids: latchkey programs, babysitters, neighbors, childcare providers, after-school programs, summer camps. If they can't find a way to take care of the kids, a family might have to forgo a necessary second income or just leave the kids to their own devices.

A public option for childcare could help alleviate this challenge for millions of families. It would have three parts to it: infant care for children under the age of three, full-day preschool that would be integrated with public schools, and before-and-after-school care that would also be integrated with public schools. This optional service would allow parents who want to use it to be able to work, even when their children are little, and provide supervision, care, and enrichment to children during work hours before and after the school day. This system isn't a pie-in-the-sky idea. It's been road tested—most of it already exists in France. In France, *crèches* care for infants under age three. The *écoles maternelles* offer pre-K. And then the public schools take over from there. In the United States, cities and states are already moving toward creating universal pre-K programs. A public option for childcare simply acknowledges that the challenges are broader than just the pre-K years.

Of course, such a program would have to be designed well, it would require qualified personnel, and it would be costly. But it would also be hugely beneficial. A public option for childcare would enable parents to get back to work, prevent kids from getting into trouble when parents aren't home, and help remove a major stressor and financial burden on families that can't afford to hire a nanny or pay for the fanciest childcare centers.

Education is critical for democracy and for the economy. In a democracy, the people determine their futures, and that requires them to debate over public affairs. Education—and particularly education in civics and history—is essential for citizens to develop the ethics and sense of community that sustain democracy. Education is also increasingly tied to success in the economy. Some kind of post–high school training is increasingly important for everyone, just as a high school education was increasingly important a century ago. And as technology changes our society, continuing education throughout a lifetime is also critical for workers to succeed.

A public option for higher education would help on both of these fronts. Public training programs, colleges, and universities should be free to all attendees—tuition and fees, room and board, books, and other expenses. A public option for college would guarantee that anyone who needs an education can get it without taking on mountains of debt. Those who want to attend private schools wouldn't get the benefit of free college (private schools are not a public option) unless they joined Patriot Corps and participated in national service.

One of the most successful public options is Social Security. Social Security is effectively a baseline public option for a pension—it provides Americans who work with a pension for their retirement years. Workers can supplement with another pension and additional retirement savings, and they don't have to draw their Social Security benefits if they don't want to. Social Security has helped keep millions of Americans from a life of abject poverty in their old age, and, as a result of this reliable safety net, it is extremely popular.

But Social Security was never meant to be the sole way that Americans financed their retirement. It was meant to be part of a three-legged stool, alongside employer-based pensions and personal savings. Over the course of the neoliberal era, however, the other two legs of the stool have collapsed. First, as economic inequality has increased, more and more Americans simply do not have sufficient retirement savings. According to Boston College's Center for Retirement Research, half of Americans don't have enough money for retirement. The problem is so bad that almost one in four Americans, according to a 2019 survey, say they will never retire. Second, employers largely eliminated pensions for their employees during the neoliberal era and instead shifted to defined contribution investments like 401(k) plans. Under a traditional pension, the employee would get a fixed sum of money every month during retirement. In contrast, under a defined contribution plan, the employee pays into a 401(k) and then can invest that money in the stock market. The result is that these new plans shift risk onto the employee. If you retire after a big economic crash, for example, you'll find yourself without much in your employer-based retirement plan. On top of that, many investment firms charge hefty fees and even steer people to fee-charging investments because they get kickbacks from the funds. Employees thus bear the risks of market downturns and can be manipulated and cheated out of their money in the process.[40]

The path forward is to reinvigorate the public option for retirement in two ways. The first is to increase Social Security benefits, thereby improving the baseline of secure finances people have for their retirement. The second is to create a public option for 401(k)s. Ideally, this public option would offer coverage to all workers, regardless of where they are employed, whether they change jobs, or if they are independent contractors. It would offer a simple set of sound investment options with low fees. Finally, it would pay out benefits as annuities so that retirees would get a reliable stream of income over their later years. Right now, in fact, the government offers a plan pretty close to this one. It's called the Thrift Savings Plan (TSP), and it is open to federal government employees. Making the TSP open to all, and expanding Social Security, would go a long way in providing economic security during retirement.

Taxes and Democracy

"Taxes are what we pay for civilized society," Oliver Wendell Holmes Jr. once wrote. From World War II until the early 1960s, the top marginal tax rate was between 80 and 94 percent before ultimately settling in at 70 percent until the Reagan administration. But in the neoliberal era, the spirit of Holmes's maxim was barely tolerated—and certainly not celebrated. Taxes were seen as a burden, and the central thrust of tax policy was to cut taxes, not to achieve a "civilized society," as Holmes put it. Right-wing neoliberals did not worry that tax cuts would mean lower revenues; they opposed government action, seeking instead to "starve the beast" and privatize its functions. And they did not see taxes as essential to redistribution because "greed is good," as the movie *Wall Street* reminded us. The center-left neoliberals of the Third Way were worried that raising taxes would be bad politics, and they saw cutting middle-class taxes as both good politics and good policy.[41]

Since the Reagan administration, Republican presidents made tax cuts one of their central priorities, with Democrats eventually going along, albeit emphasizing tax cuts for the middle class. The top marginal tax rate for individuals dropped below 40 percent. The capital gains tax rate—a tax on investments by which many wealthy people make money—plummeted from 39.9 percent in 1977 to 15 percent. Taxes also dropped on estates, the ability to pass along wealth to one's children. In 1976, more than 7 percent of estates paid a tax. By 2011, it was 0.14 percent. Corporate taxes also dropped from 52 percent in 1960 to 35 percent, and then in the Trump administration to 21 percent.[42]

With this downward trajectory over the neoliberal era, it is worth asking the question squarely: Why does taxation matter in a democracy? There are three answers. The first is to generate revenue. Every government—democracy or not—needs to generate revenue to fund itself. The national defense, diplomacy, police, and firefighters all require funding. In a democracy, the people choose to build the future however they desire. When "we the people" create a Constitution to "promote the general Welfare," as the preamble to the US Constitution says, we need to fund the activities that lead to the general welfare.[43]

But why fund these activities through taxes instead of other forms of revenue? The answer gets to the second reason: taxes keep citizens engaged in democracy, and at the same time, they keep government dependent on the will of the people. The American Revolutionaries did not seek freedom from all taxation but "taxation with representation"; they wanted a government that was accountable to the people for its actions and responsive to the people's demands. Taxes are one way to keep that linkage strong. The people set the government's agenda, and they fund it.

The third reason taxes are important is to ensure a relatively equal society. Commercial activity will inevitably create winners and losers. Eventually, the "vast inequality of wealth is socially destructive," a leading tax scholar notes, "because it degrades relationships among people (cultural, social, and political), and eventually undermines the sense of community on which a democratic polity must rest." On one side, taxation allows for redistribution that makes society more equal, both through spending on public programs and through financial transfers. In the process, this equalizing effect tends to make the community more similar economically. On the other, taxes prevent the creation of a class of wealthy individuals who can use their economic power to undermine democracy. Although some people might protest that wealth itself does not automatically translate into power, the wealthy themselves recognize that it does. As James Stillman, a Gilded Age banker and investor admitted, "'Twasn't the money we were after, 'twas the power. We were all playing for power. It was a great game."[44]

With these purposes in mind, achieving a great democracy will require tax policy to change. Personal tax rates should be designed to protect economic democracy from the emergence of an oligarchy. This means, first, having a more progressive income tax structure. The top tax bracket currently starts at $500,000 for an individual and $600,000 for married couples. There should be new brackets at higher levels—$1 million, $5 million—with higher top marginal rates. Congresswoman Alexandria Ocasio-Cortez, for example, has called for returning to a 70 percent top marginal tax rate. Many economists have agreed with her proposal—and some have said she did not go far enough. All income should also be treated the same to better capture how many wealthy people currently earn their income. Right now, for example, investors who make their money primarily through the stock market pay a capital gains rate, which is lower than the ordinary income tax rate. These rates should be aligned. Second, we need to institute oligarch taxes, a tax on enormous levels of wealth that threaten political and economic democracy by their very existence. There are many ways to do this. Senator Elizabeth Warren, for example, has proposed an Ultra-Millionaire Tax on those who are worth more than $50 million. From a democratic perspective, the source of the income is not as important as the fact that accumulated wealth, however it is gotten, threatens our constitutional system.[45]

Third, we need to prevent the creation of a hereditary aristocracy in the United States by either reinvigorating the estate tax or establishing inheritance taxes. Currently, upon death, a couple can transfer $22 million to their heirs without paying any estate taxes. This is a gigantic sum of money, enough that the heirs will never need to work again—and would have money to spare. This policy does not value work; it supports the creation of heirs and heiresses who didn't earn any of their wealth. The usual justification for such transfers is that the wealthy parents should be able to give freely to their children. Although this individualistic argument has some merit, it conflicts squarely with the ethos of democracy. The purpose of estate and inheritance taxes is to prevent the creation of a hereditary aristocracy—a class of people who, generation after generation, have wealth and exercise power. The Founding Generation understood this, even though their economic situation was different. Writing to John Adams in 1813, Thomas Jefferson said that one of his proudest accomplishments was abolishing the entail and primogeniture. These were legal rules that allowed landowners to pass property on to their heirs in a concentrated fashion. Property was the central form of wealth at the time, and ending these laws made sure that property would be divided among children, rather than placing it in the hands of the oldest son. Jefferson said his abolition of these laws in Virginia "laid the axe to the root of the Pseudo-aristocracy." When North Carolina passed a similar law, the bill noted the purpose of the law: "It will tend to promote that equality of property which is of the spirit and principle of a genuine republic." The contemporary version of this policy is estate and inheritance taxes.[46]

The other side of taxation in a democracy is distribution. Economic democracy requires that everyone has opportunities. It has no place for hereditary aristocracy or hereditary poverty. James Madison thus noted in 1792 the importance of having laws that would "reduce extreme wealth to mediocrity, and raise extreme indigence toward a state of comfort." Today, many commentators have argued for cash transfers to the poor, either through an expanded earned income tax credit (which transfers additional money to the working poor) or through a universal basic income. These direct tax-and-transfer policies, in conjunction with others, can help realign economic democracy, but it is also worth noting that other policies, like public options, are effectively redistributive as well. When the government offers universal access to public schools and public libraries—or Social Security and health care—it benefits the poor and working class.[47]

Corporate taxes also need to be reformed. In recent years, many policy makers have been skeptical of corporate taxes for two reasons. They argue that corporations are made up of shareholders and that shareholders are already taxed. So corporate taxation is really double taxation. Perhaps more prominently, they argue that the American corporate tax rate is too high, which makes the United States less competitive than other countries for investment. Based partly on these justifications, under the Trump administration, Republicans passed a bill reducing the corporate tax rate from 35 percent to 21 percent.

These arguments misunderstand the role of corporations in a democracy. Corporations only exist because we the people allow them to exist. It is perfectly legitimate to condition the privilege of operating as a corporation on paying a fee like a tax. The other justification for the corporate tax is to regulate and reduce corporate power. Although corporations have shareholders, corporations are not simply the sum of their shareholders. Managers have significant power internally over corporate decisions and, through corporate spending, have considerable public power as well. And corporations last long after shareholders die. One purpose of the corporate tax is to allow the public to have control over what these important, legally created entities do. Imposing a corporate tax, as one tax professor notes, "reduces the economic resources available to corporate managers [and thus] also reduces the power of corporate management." Information from tax filings and the tax's regulatory power also give the government another way to oversee corporate activity and prevent the bad behavior of corporations. As President

William Howard Taft said on the passage of the corporate tax in 1909, with "knowledge of the real business transactions and the gains and profits of every corporation in the country, we have made a long step toward that supervisory control of corporations which may prevent a further abuse of power."[48]

The global competitiveness problem is also solvable. The United States taxes corporations that are in residence in the country and taxes income from foreign corporations or subsidiaries when that income is repatriated into the United States. As globalization has made capital more mobile, corporations increasingly move residency or operations overseas to tax havens. Economist Gabriel Zucman has shown that about $200 billion, or 8 percent of global wealth, is held in such tax havens, forcing the middle and lower classes to pay more in taxes to cover the shortfall in revenue. Luckily, there is an easy way to solve this problem. The global tax problem is similar to the problem of corporations operating in different states within the United States. Companies could move their residency to low-tax states to avoid paying higher rates. The way that we have solved this problem domestically is that we do not try to attribute specific income to specific states and charge taxes based on it. Instead, we calculate national income and apportion it to the different states in which a company operates. This same approach could work globally. Calculate worldwide income, and then apportion it to all the different countries in which the company operates. There are a lot of technical details for how such a system would be adapted to the international level, but the key point is that global companies exist and our tax system needs to start from this premise. A race to the bottom with tax havens isn't good for democracy.[49]

Trade Policy for All

The 2016 election marked the end of an era of go-go trade liberalization, with candidates Clinton, Trump, and Sanders all opposing the Obama administration's signature trade policy, the Trans-Pacific Partnership. Since taking office, President Trump has raised tariffs on rivals and allies alike, waged a trade war with China, and renegotiated NAFTA. In the midst of all of these changes, little has been articulated on what the United States' trade strategy should be. A reformed trade policy should include three parts: redistributing the gains from trade to help the so-called losers from trade deals, addressing the economic threat from nationalist oligarch governments by developing and executing a comprehensive economic growth and security strategy, and fixing the rigged domestic trade policy process.[50]

For the last generation, the trade consensus had three parts. First, policy makers believed that trade deals would be a rising tide that would ultimately lift all boats. The losers from trade, they argued, would be able to adapt, transition, and bounce back after a short while. Second, policy makers believed that trade liberalization would push undemocratic foreign governments to open up both their economies and their politics. Countries like China would, over time, become more market friendly and more democracy friendly. Finally, policy makers believed that what was good for American companies was good for America, and they gave companies privileged access to trade negotiations.

All three of these assumptions have now been proven wrong. Although trade agreements have been a powerful force for economic growth in many parts of the country, both academic research and the lived experience of many communities demonstrate that trade liberalization has also created serious distributional consequences that persist over time. In a series of papers looking at the consequences of economic integration with China, economists David Autor, David Dorn, and Gordon Hanson have demonstrated that some areas of the country have been disproportionately impacted. More importantly, these areas have not bounced back even a decade after the "China Shock." The long-standing view has been that the winners from trade liberalization could compensate the losers, ameliorating these festering consequences of trade liberalization, but that such compensation should not come from trade policy itself. Yet time and again, we have watched as a trade deal passes and, with it, the political leverage for serious redistribution.[51]

Americans should require that any trade agreement include policies that will ensure that the winners help lift up the losers. First,
Congress should direct the US International Trade Commission
(ITC), which conducts assessments on the impact that a trade deal
will have in different sectors of the economy, to conduct geographic
impact assessments. We should know which parts of the country
are going to be disproportionately harmed by a trade agreement.
Second, Congress should include tax-and-transfer policies in trade
agreement implementing legislation. Ideally, this would include a
tax on those who the ITC projects will benefit from the trade deal.
These dollars should then be placed into a trust fund that would be
used for economic growth in areas that are harmed by trade. Third,
trade agreements should include a development component requiring countries to spend on programs like infrastructure and education that can help regions adversely affected by trade liberalization.
The United States, as part of these development efforts, should also
engage in an industrial policy that invests in communities across the
country. This industrial policy would jump-start areas with investments in research and development and infrastructure and require
that manufacturing take place in the United States when products
are built on breakthroughs from public investments in R & D.

The second thing Washington got wrong was the foreign consequences of trade deals. Despite the optimism about trade liberalization, trade agreements did not lead to more democracy or more
open economies. Instead, countries like China have benefited enor-
mously from joining the global economy, have not reformed their
undemocratic governments, and use state capitalism and crony capitalism to stack the deck in favor of their own companies, steal
technology and trade secrets, and, according to some reports, infiltrate American companies through secret back doors in tech products. Economic integration, in other words, has created a variety of
national security and economic security threats—threats that the
United States currently has no long-term strategy to address. Unfor-
tunately, our government is also not designed in a way to either
develop or execute a strategy to combat these threats. International

economic policymaking is split across a variety of departments and agencies—the United States Trade Representative, Commerce, Treasury, State, plus a variety of smaller agencies. This means that there is no single institution thinking in a holistic fashion about the relationship between economic integration, domestic inequality and distribution, and economic security.[52]

To promote the development of long-term economic policy, Congress should create a new Department of Economic Growth and Security that would merge all of the government's disparate offices that work on trade liberalization, trade promotion (that is, helping US businesses find markets abroad), domestic economic development and industrial policy, and economic security. This new department would have the power and responsibility to develop a comprehensive strategy—and to execute it.

Finally, the trade policy process has been stacked in favor of well-organized and powerful economic interests—particularly corporations and industry associations—that have predictably pursued their own profits over the interests of working Americans. The general public, for example, could not see drafts of the Trans-Pacific Partnership during negotiations because they were classified. Even members of Congress could only look at drafts of the trade deal in a secured facility, and they were not allowed to take notes or have a staff member present. At the same time, members of the USTR's trade advisory committees—85 percent of which are company or industry representatives—were allowed to see the agreements.[53]

We should reform this rigged system by requiring a more transparent, participatory policy process. First drafts of trade agreements should be treated similarly to proposed regulations in other areas of policymaking. Prior to beginning negotiations, the government should make the draft (or part of the draft) available to the public for comment. The government would then have to explain publicly how and why it responded to the comments before it could table the draft with negotiating partners. This would allow everyone— ordinary citizens, small businesses, and nonprofits—to provide comments on how the proposals would impact them. The advisory committees should also be reformed to include a much wider group of interests, including labor and public-interest advocates on every industry-specific advisory committee. The result of these changes would be a trade strategy that takes seriously the demands of democracy. It would be a trade policy for all Americans.

The Geography of Inequality

In recent years, commentators of different political stripes have converged on an important point: our society is fracturing geographically. Robert Putnam, on the left, describes how his hometown of Port Clinton, Ohio, once an integrated middle-class town, is now deeply divided—by race, culture, and economic success. Conservative Charles Murray makes a similar point in his book *Coming Apart* through the discussion of the fictional but representative Fishtown and Belmont. Americans are now sorting ourselves into groups, increasingly living in communities with people who are similar—from the TV shows we watch to our political views.[54]

It wasn't always this way. In the liberal era of the mid-twentieth century, incomes across geography were converging. In 1940, for example, Missourians earned 62 percent of what Californians made, but that number gradually increased to 80 percent by 1980. In the 1960s, the top twenty-five wealthiest metro areas included a wide variety of American cities, including "Rockford, Illinois; Milwaukee, Wisconsin; Ann Arbor, Michigan; Des Moines, Iowa; and Cleveland, Ohio."[55]

The era of economic convergence among regions began to come to an end in the 1980s, coinciding with the rise of neoliberalism. Bigger cities got richer and richer as other regions were soon left behind—with massive economic and social consequences. Economists have shown that mobility is highly variable across the country; in some areas, the very poor have only a miniscule shot at making it. Huge swaths of the country are afflicted with an opioid epidemic that ravages families and communities. And in many areas, Americans are literally dying—mortality rates have been increasing for middle-aged white Americans. Harvard sociologist William Julius

Wilson once argued that it was the decline of jobs and economic security that led to the social crisis in poor minority-dominated cities. Reflecting on Wilson's theory, Paul Krugman has commented that in recent decades, "when rural whites faced a similar loss of economic opportunity, they experienced a similar social unraveling."[56] One approach for addressing the geography of inequality is to encourage people to move. Scholars have argued that leading cities attract talented people, spark innovation, and therefore grow. This creates a natural divergence between some places and others. As a result, the goal should be to get Americans moving from low-wage, low-opportunity places to higher-wage places. They argue for changing zoning and land use laws that prevent cities like San Francisco from building. More housing would reduce housing prices and thus make it more affordable for people to move to and live in the Bay Area. They also suggest creating mobility vouchers, which would help facilitate people moving. These proposals have an economic logic to them. But they are less satisfying from a democratic perspective. What happens to the people and communities that are left behind, hollowed out by stripping all their talent and sending them to the big cities? Why should a democratic political system write off entire swaths of the country as dead or dying? And if abandoning parts of the country means further inequality, what about resentment that builds up and the possibility of backlash?[57]

A second approach, most prominently offered by former treasury secretary Larry Summers, Edward Glaeser, and Benjamin Austin, is to adopt what they call "place-based policies," policies targeting areas with the worst unemployment. They identify four types of policies—public investment, tax benefits and grants for businesses, tax benefits and grants for individuals, and deregulatory efforts—and they focus primarily on tax benefits.[58] This center-left approach comes from their skepticism of public investment as the route to addressing geographic inequality. "It is impossible to know," they comment, "whether a relocation of capital and labor from Los Angeles to Kentucky will lead to benefits in Kentucky that are large enough to offset the losses in Los Angeles." Perhaps

that is true, but why should we only care about the economic benefits offsetting the losses? Why is this policy choice being made on
grounds of what is most economically efficient? And why isn't it
taking into account political consequences, like the skewing of the
Senate toward overrepresenting a minority of the country or moral
consequences such as health and mortality? A democracy should
care about all of its people. We should want the people of both
Kentucky and Los Angeles to have good jobs, flourishing livelihoods, and vibrant communities.[59]

To be fair, both zoning changes and tax benefits might have places
in reshaping the geography of inequality. But both approaches are
too quick to take the geography of inequality as a given, as a natural state of affairs. Geographic inequality is a function of public
policy. The policy choices we make determine whether there is geographic inequality or geographic equality—and that means those
choices can help alleviate inequality.

Consider a few areas. For decades, trade policy hollowed out
some communities while bolstering others. The theory, as we have
seen, was that the winners would compensate the losers and that
communities would bounce back or people would move. But communities hit by the China Shock didn't bounce back. Meaningful
compensation has never been a serious part of the policy conversation. And for a generation, industrial policy has been more focused
on corporate profits than on vibrant communities. Policy makers
could have considered these regional impacts and addressed them
or could have just said no to the trade agreements. Those were policy choices.

The failure of antitrust enforcement and the coming of the second monopoly age is another policy shift that contributed. Antitrust laws prevent corporate consolidation, creating an economy
of small and medium-sized businesses. And an economy with a
large number of flourishing small and medium-sized businesses
is one in which wealth and power are distributed throughout the
country. To consider a new example, look at the banking sector.
From the 1920s to the 1980s, nationally chartered banks were not

allowed to have branches in more than one state, and some states even prevented banks from having multiple branches within the state. This effectively meant that the United States had a nation of relatively small banks. In that context, a local bank president was likely to be wealthy enough to sponsor the little league team but unlikely to be one of the richest people in the country. In the 1980s, however, some states began deregulating their banks, and in the 1990s, President Clinton signed the Riegle-Neal Act, a federal law that deregulated bank branch restrictions and allowed for interstate banking, and the Graham-Leech-Bliley Act, which repealed the Glass-Steagall regulations and allowed for depository banks to merge with insurance companies and investment banks. Over time, the banking industry saw merger after merger, consolidation into regional banks and eventually national and international banks. Now we have a small number of gigantic banks that span the country, concentrate wealth and power, and are too big to fail. There are still some community banks and credit unions, but these smaller players compete with global behemoths whose executives are far better compensated than the president of a single bank branch ever could have imagined. Other laws, like the Robinson-Patman Act of 1936, served similar functions. Robinson-Patman was designed to protect small retailers from chain stores, which could use their size and scale to undermine local retailers. The people of the era wanted to preserve their economic democracy and designed the law to achieve that purpose. By the neoliberal era, Robinson-Patman largely went unenforced.[60]

Public investment is a third policy choice. Americans in the past invested in massive public works projects to ensure that the whole country would have economic and social opportunities. One of the oldest examples is the US Postal Service. At the very start of the republic, mail was the cutting-edge communications network, and the post office stitched together even the far-flung parts of the new nation. The land-grant college system is another example. Massive public investment in these educational institutions created decades of economic growth, opportunity, and intellectual and social vibrancy in all parts of the country. During the New Deal, the Rural Electrification Administration brought power to remote areas, creating opportunity for millions. New Deal programs also built schools, trails, and other infrastructure throughout the country—from funding the expansion of the hospital in Winnemucca, Nevada, to building a post office in Belleville, Kansas, and a school in Danville, Virginia. Public projects were not designed with economic efficiency alone in mind; they were designed to support communities all across the country.[61]

A final factor shaping geographic inequality is perhaps the most surprising—regulation. A number of sectors of the economy—trains, buses, airlines—are network industries. In a network industry, a bigger network is more valuable. For example, if you can fly anywhere in the country—including small cities—that is more valuable than if you can fly only to a handful of cities. At the same time, however, some places are much more expensive to add to the network. Flights to small cities might have a lot less volume, meaning that access will be limited or prices will be extremely high. Regulation solved these problems, guaranteeing widespread geographic access to these important networks.

Under the system of airline regulation that existed until 1978, the Civil Aeronautics Board (CAB) assigned airlines routes and regulated the prices of routes. This ensured that airlines would serve small and medium-sized cities and that prices were equitable—the longer the flight, the higher the price. The CAB would give airlines some highly profitable routes and some less profitable routes that were nonetheless important to serving farther-flung communities. The profitable routes subsidized the less profitable routes, and competition among airlines was all about the quality of service.[62]

After deregulation and a few bursts of new competition, the industry saw wave after wave of mergers. The airline industry transformed from a "regulated oligopoly . . . to an unregulated oligopoly." This had a few consequences. First, airlines shifted from serving many cities on a point-to-point basis to a hub-and-spokes model. Hubs like Atlanta and Dallas would have hundreds of flights, and travelers to smaller places would have to connect through the hubs. This meant fewer direct flights for passengers. Second, some airlines succeeded in creating fortress hubs, in which one carrier could have 70–90 percent of the market into that airport. This effective monopoly means they can charge travelers higher prices. Finally, the airlines reduced services and increased prices on small and medium-sized cities. These were never profitable routes, and there was far less reason to cross-subsidize them in an era without regulation.[63]

These seemingly minor shifts, tied to what is usually considered a great public policy success, have had a devastating impact on many communities across the country. Chiquita—the banana company—had been headquartered in Cincinnati, Ohio, for decades. But in 2011, the company announced it was moving to Charlotte, North Carolina. Why? The airport. Once a high-traffic international airport, Cincinnati's airport lost two-thirds of its flights between 2004 and 2012 and saw increased fares due to airline consolidation and the shift to a hub-and-spokes model. "If you're a global business like Chiquita, which operates in seventy countries and needs to be able to attract global talent," two journalists noted, commenting on Chiquita's departure, "the situation is untenable." With the company's move to Charlotte went four hundred jobs, not to mention all the economic activity that its employees engaged in—trips to the movies and restaurants, shopping at local stores—and the company's philanthropic efforts in the community. Nor is this story unique. After a massive decline in air traffic in Memphis, combined with higher fares, the Folk Alliance music convention departed for Kansas City; the Church of God in Christ moved its annual meeting too. The law firm K&L Gates moved its annual firm-wide gathering from Pittsburgh to New York and Washington. Getting to Pittsburgh had just become too difficult.[64]

Economic inequality, social problems, and community vibrancy are all tied together. Whether we have opportunity across geographies is a policy choice. Restitching our social fabric and alleviating the economic and social suffering across much of the country will require considering how *all* types of policies—trade, tax, public investment, industry, and even regulation—impact communities across our expansive democracy.

8

POLITICAL DEMOCRACY

The most familiar understanding of democracy focuses on its political aspects. Political democracy simply means that the political system is responsive to the people. Or, to put it in more obvious terms, a representative government should be representative. But our political system today isn't representative. From voting and elections to legislation, regulation, and even litigation in the courts, every branch of government is failing in its responsiveness to the people. Indeed, for all of the country's deep tribal divisions, we share at least one thing in common: according to polls, the number one fear for most Americans—more than 70 percent—is government corruption.[1]

Americans recognize that our democracy is no longer working for the people—and the failures of political democracy stand in the way of achieving an economic democracy and a united democracy. The vast majority of Americans, for example, support gun control legislation, yet nothing happens. The vast majority of Americans support increasing Social Security, yet nothing happens. The vast majority of Americans think climate change is real and are concerned about it, yet nothing happens. The vast majority of Americans support higher taxes on the wealthy and putting limits on campaign spending, yet these things never happen either.[2]

In the last decade, political scientists have issued a barrage of studies showing how unresponsive the political process is to ordinary Americans. Larry Bartels, in an important study of the Senate, found that the views of the poorest one-third of constituents had no impact at all on senators' behavior. Martin Gilens ends his extensive study comparing the political influence of the poor, middle class, upper middle class, and the richest 10 percent of Americans with this depressing conclusion: "Under most circumstances, the preferences of the vast majority of Americans appear to have essentially no impact on which policies the government does or doesn't adopt." We have instead what scholars call a "democracy by coincidence," in which the views of ordinary people prevail only when they coincide with the views of the wealthiest elites.[3]

Part of the problem is electoral. The basic act of voting turns out to be pretty difficult for many people. Election days are Tuesdays, making it harder for working people to get to the polls. Voter ID laws, deliberate efforts to purge the voter rolls and suppress the vote, and registration requirements add to the challenge. And if you do make it to vote, in many places, there's a decent chance that your district has been gerrymandered to help one party or the other preserve its power, making it less likely that the election was competitive.

On top of all that, the wealthiest people—who systemically have different preferences than the majority of Americans—tend to vote more, volunteer on campaigns more, contact their members of Congress more, and run for office themselves more. Their higher rates of participation combine with our campaign finance system to skew politics even further. Many people decry money in politics, and for good reason. Some members of Congress are transparent that access to them is based on money. For example, Mick Mulvaney, the simultaneous director of the Office of Management and Budget and acting White House chief of staff under President Trump, said explicitly that when he was a Republican congressman from South Carolina, the only lobbyists he would meet with were the ones who gave him money. Most members, however, are not so brazen. Rather, they are unconsciously shaped by their funding sources. Elected officials can spend up to four hours a day on the phone raising money, and that means listening to rich donors opine about the issues of the day. Of course, what elected officials *aren't* doing is actually learning about legislative proposals and coming to their own judgments.[4]

Pressed for time, members of Congress turn to lobbyists. Lobbying isn't fair and balanced. In a study of tens of thousands of lobbying organizations in Washington over a thirty-year period, political scientists have shown that lobbying groups disproportionately represent businesses and wealthy people. Less than 1 percent of organizations represent the poor. Although blue-collar workers are 24 percent of the population, they are only 1 percent of economic organizations in Washington. White-collar workers make up less than 10 percent of the public, but they are represented by almost 74 percent of economic organizations in DC. To take just one area, the financial, insurance, and real estate sectors employed 2,397 lobbyists in 2017. That's more than four lobbyists for every member of Congress. The dollar amounts are also staggering. In 2018, Google spent $21 million on lobbying; Amazon spent $14.2 million, and Facebook spent almost $13 million. Lobbyists don't just advocate for policies; they also educate members of Congress and their overworked staffs. They even draft legislation to help members. This work pays off: one study finds that for every dollar a firm spends on lobbying, it gets between six and twenty dollars in tax breaks.[5]

With such a lucrative lobbying industry, members of Congress and their staffs have a powerful financial motive to leave public service and join the influence-peddling industry. For example, after the Republican Congress and Trump administration pushed through the 2017 tax bill, many staffers who worked on the long, complicated legislation cashed out. The Senate Finance Committee's head tax staff member joined the tax group at accounting firm PwC, an aide to Senate majority leader Mitch McConnell joined lobbying and law firm Akin Gump, and other tax staffers joined lobbying firms, corporate lobbying shops, and trade associations. *Politico* said the authors of the bill were "leaving the Hill in droves." Of course, with all these departures, members of Congress are left with junior staff with less expertise, which in turn means that they'll have to rely even more on lobbyists to help them.[6]

But the problem goes further than Congress. The executive branch is also skewed toward serving the interests of the wealthy and powerful. Instead of being the home of expert administrators or even a "team of rivals" from different political perspectives, federal agencies have become a weigh station for industry insiders and lobbyists, who roll back and forth from government to the private sector. Consider the fact that two of the last four Democratic secretaries of the treasury worked for Citigroup either before or after their government service, and the other two worked elsewhere in finance. Or that despite President Trump's desire to drain the swamp, his administration has hired at least 187 lobbyists— including slotting lobbyists in jobs where they are responsible for shaping the regulations that impact their former industries. This revolving door between government and industry is a problem in both directions. People coming in from industry might be overly sympathetic to industry arguments and might shy away from enforcing the law against their former friends and colleagues. People planning a future career in industry might go easy on a company in hopes that they'll be offered a job.[7]

In addition to staffing the government, corporations and their lobbyists also have outsized influence over the writing of regulations. Business groups provide the vast majority of comments to proposed regulations, and on important issues sometimes engage in dozens of preproposal meetings in which they can shape the views of the agency officials who are designing the regulations. If a regulation makes it through the process, it must then be reviewed by the Office of Information and Regulatory Affairs (OIRA), a little-known outfit within the Office of Management and Budget. There, too, officials meet disproportionately with industry representatives— and political scientists have shown that lobbying OIRA leads to further proindustry changes in the regulations.[8]

So we have a political process that is stacked to favor the wealthy and corporate interests, a legislative process dominated by lobbyists, and a regulatory process often staffed by lobbyists and susceptible to their influence. If, by some miracle, the laws and regulations are sharp enough that corporate interests feel their sting, the courts provide one last opportunity to evade the long arm of the law. Here, too, the deck is stacked. One 2008 study of the federal courts showed that 85 percent of judges had worked in private practice, largely for corporate firms, while only 3 percent had worked for nonprofits—and only one judge out of 162 had experience in consumer protection. Supreme Court watchers have shown that the groups best at getting their cases before the highest court are a who's who list of powerful corporate lobbyists: the Chamber of Commerce, National Association of Manufacturers, the pharmaceutical lobby, and the American Bankers Association. And when they get to the court, these groups find some of the most probusiness justices in American history. According to scholars Lee Epstein, William Landes, and former judge Richard Posner (a Reagan appointee), prior to Justice Antonin Scalia's death in 2016, the five conservative judges on the Supreme Court were in the top ten of the most probusiness justices in history—and numbers one and two were Chief Justice Roberts and Justice Alito.[9]

With all these problems, it is no surprise that Americans' greatest fear is that our government is corrupt. What we need now is not cynicism and resignation, but a plan to fight corruption—a bold, fearless anti-corruption agenda. This agenda has four parts: electoral reforms, legislative reforms, executive branch reforms, and judicial reforms.

Electoral Reforms

Thin versions of democracy focus on the ability of people to vote, but democracy goes beyond simply casting a ballot. It is a way of life that imposes civic requirements—political, economic, ethical, and social obligations—on every person. One of those obligations is that everyone participates in the political process. Right now, we have an opt-in system of political participation, which means that people don't have to participate, often aren't encouraged or formally expected to participate, and are sometimes even prevented from participating.

To move toward universal participation, in the short term, we should make voter registration automatic and adopt same-day registration, early voting, and a nationwide vote-by-mail system. This would mean that any time a person engages with the federal government or a state government, they would be automatically registered to vote if eligible. If, by chance, there's a failure, they could also register at their polling place and cast a ballot. And to make voting itself easier, every jurisdiction should be required to offer early voting and vote-by-mail. Under vote-by-mail, every registered voter gets a ballot in the mail and can fill out the ballot at home and then either put it back in the mail or return it to a drop-off site, such as a public library or fire station. This approach has already been implemented in Oregon, Colorado, and Washington, as well as virtually all of Utah, half of North Dakota, and other parts of the country too. Studies show that a vote-by-mail system increases turnout, and it has the virtue of making voter suppression and fraud more difficult because individuals can't intimidate or turn away voters when they vote in their own homes. Voters don't get frustrated with long lines or have to deal with work schedules or childcare issues. And a vote-by-mail system creates a paper trail that makes it much harder to hack an election.[10]

Over the longer term, we could also try to move away from an opt-in model for voting to an opt-out model. In Australia, for example, voting is universal, and the failure to show up at the polls comes with a small fine. Universal voting recognizes that we all have the duty to participate in shaping our shared future. It also solves many of the problems of political responsiveness. With everyone voting, elected officials can't just rely on the wealthy to build political coalitions. They have to attend to the needs of working people, the poor, and the otherwise ignored. Indeed, some studies suggest that universal voting might decrease economic inequality; because candidates are responsive to all the people, they can't support policies that only support the wealthy elites. This is also why would-be nationalist oligarchs have always feared the franchise. They know that the best way to stay in power is to stop the people from exercising their voice—and they know that if the people exercise their voice, they won't support oligarchic policies that only benefit the elites.[11]

Those with libertarian sympathies might object: What about those who don't want to vote or want to protest through their vote? The answer is simple: universal voting can come with an option to vote for "none of the above" or simply submit an empty ballot, thereby registering disapproval of all candidates. Indeed, this protest option will also increase political responsiveness and make the system more attentive to everyone in society. A rising share of votes for "none of the above" would give incumbent parties a powerful incentive to reform to compete for those voters. If the parties don't change, they face the looming threat of new parties that might emerge to capture those who feel unrepresented.

In addition to expanding access to voting, we need to eliminate gerrymandering and move to a neutral system of legislative districting. Gerrymandering legislative districts is just a form of rigging politics to preserve the power of one faction over another. It is also an important strategy for nationalist oligarchs who might not be able to win in a neutral, fair election. By drawing district lines that benefit one party, a minority can retain political power even if popular majorities oppose them. Citizens must demand that independent commissions draw legislative districts.

Achieving political democracy will also require reducing the power of big money in elections. The Supreme Court has interpreted the First Amendment to block virtually all efforts to stop the rigging of our political system through large campaign donations. Thus, the starting point for reform is an amendment to the Constitution that will allow Congress to place restrictions on money in politics, undoing both the famous *Citizens United* case and the less famous case of *Buckley v. Valeo*.

What rules should Congress then place on money in politics? There are different approaches it could take. First, Congress could simply place far greater restrictions on the size of campaign contributions and spending. This would prevent the wealthiest people from dominating candidates' time and the political airwaves. Second, Congress could restrict the geography of contributions. Right now, people in New York or Texas can contribute gigantic sums to determine who should represent the people of Iowa. If democracy is to be representative, however, constituents should pick their representatives free of interference from outsiders. Restrictions could limit contributions or outside spending to a candidate's constituents only. Third, Congress could establish a system of campaign finance vouchers. On this approach, every voter would get a voucher worth a small amount of money to give to any candidate (or candidates) the voter chooses. To fund their campaigns, candidates would have to compete for citizens' voucher dollars. Thus, instead of spending time dialing for dollars from the wealthy, they would spend time hearing the concerns of ordinary people. Finally, Congress could mandate public financing of elections, setting aside a limited amount of money for elections at every level and requiring candidates to work within that budget. Of course, these reforms could also be combined.[12]

Election reform also requires thinking about who is in the electorate—and making sure that *all* Americans are represented in our democracy. Right now, our system excludes many citizens from meaningful representation. Around six million citizens are excluded from voting due to conviction for a felony, including more than 7 percent of the adults in Alabama, Florida, Kentucky, Mississippi, Tennessee, and Virginia (though Florida recently undertook a serious effort to reform this status). Felon disenfranchisement has far-reaching effects in skewing representation particularly on racial and class lines when there are no opportunities to earn back the right to vote.[13]

In addition, millions of American citizens are excluded systematically from representation because of their geography. The citizens of Puerto Rico; Washington, DC; and the United States' island territories (Guam and the Northern Mariana Islands, the Virgin Islands, and American Samoa) are US citizens and pay federal taxes. Yet they do not have representation in Congress. Representation for these people matters. When Hurricane Maria hit Puerto Rico in 2017, the response from the federal government—Congress and the Trump administration—was tepid at best and disastrous at worst. Without real representation in Congress and the power to exercise a meaningful vote, the pressure on the administration to help these American citizens was limited. The answer here is clear: states can be admitted to the union by simple majority vote in Congress, and Congress should admit Puerto Rico, the Island Territories, and the District of Columbia as three new states if those areas seek to join the union.

Congressional Reforms

Of our branches of government, Congress is supposed to be the most representative of the people. But instead, Congress seems perennially to be in the pocket of big interest groups, whose aims diverge significantly from ordinary voters. There are three basic ways to reform Congress to address this divergence.

The first is to make members of Congress more independent of interest groups and lobbyists. Although campaign finance reforms are a good start, we must go further and institute a lifetime ban on members of Congress becoming lobbyists and a multiyear ban on staff becoming lobbyists. Members of Congress should also not have financial conflicts of interest when they are making policy. They should all be required to move their investments in stocks into the Thrift Savings Plan (TSP), a set of mutual funds, independently managed, for federal employees' retirement. Members should also have to relinquish any ownership stake in a company beyond mutual funds and release their tax returns.

The second strategy is to increase the power of congressional staff vis-à-vis lobbyists. Many congressional staffers are in their twenties and are overworked, underpaid, and have too little expertise in any particular area. The result is that staffers turn over frequently—and often depart to lobbying firms, where they can parlay their relationships and influence into lucrative careers. This phenomenon was always present, but it wasn't always as bad as it has become. In the early 1990s, when Newt Gingrich became Speaker of the House, he "moved quickly to slash the budgets and staff of the House Committees," Republican Bruce Bartlett writes. This "permanently crippl[ed] the committee system and depriv[ed] members of Congress of competent and informed advice on issues that they are responsible for overseeing." One way to address this problem is not only to rebuild the committee staff system but also make congressional staff more professional, akin to the civil service. Staff salaries should be increased so members can recruit and retain top talent without fear that they will depart to become lobbyists after only a few years. There should also be a regular pay scale so staff can be promoted and build seniority in salary and benefits.[14]

A third approach is to decrease the power of the lobbyists. Senator Elizabeth Warren, for example, has called for banning lobbyists from giving gifts to members of Congress, ending contingency fees whereby lobbyists get paid only if they get a certain policy outcome, and banning political donations from lobbyists to members of Congress. She has also proposed placing a tax on excessive lobbying—defined as more than $500,000 in expenses annually—and using the proceeds to fund the creation of a public advocate who would represent the general public in legislative debates.[15]

Executive Branch Reforms

The executive branch is also susceptible to influence, but the corruption of the executive branch is in some ways more pernicious because it is less publicly visible—and therefore more difficult to ferret out. Some of the same solutions for members of Congress should apply to top executive branch officials—a lifetime ban on lobbying for cabinet secretaries and other top officials and a multiyear ban on lobbying for junior officers, including banning them from lobbying the agency they worked in until the end of the administration. In addition, rules should seek to slow, or stop altogether, the revolving door by which officials roll in and out between regulators and the very industries they regulate. Officials should be prohibited from working for any company that the official had jurisdiction over for at least four years.

Reforms to the regulatory process can help ensure that regulations serve the public interest rather than rig the economy on behalf of powerful corporations. One of the great virtues of our rulemaking process is that it offers public notice and a period of comment in which anyone can give an opinion about a regulation. This allows agencies to get a wide variety of information in order to make a reasoned decision. But sometimes seemingly scientific studies are funded by interest groups who have designed the study to support their position. If an agency is going to rely on such outside studies, there should be independent peer review to prevent these conflicts of interest. In addition, many groups seek to lobby government after the notice-and-comment period by approaching the Office of Information and Regulatory Affairs (OIRA), which reviews regulations from its perch in the White House. This office should be barred from taking these meetings. Everyone should have to participate on a level playing field, with no special access or second bites at the apple for those who have wealth and connections.

Finally, some commentators and officials have called for creating and empowering a single agency to address issues of government corruption, ethics, and transparency. Rohit Chopra, now a commissioner on the Federal Trade Commission, and Julie Morgan, a former Senate staffer, have proposed establishing a Public Integrity Protection Agency that would unify the work of the office of government ethics and the inspectors general of the various federal agencies. This single agency would be able to promulgate rules for government officials on ethics issues, investigate violations, and bring enforcement actions across the executive branch.[16]

Judicial Reforms

In this era of polarized politics, the Supreme Court has become a pawn in the battle between Republicans and Democrats. The Republicans blocked well-regarded Judge Merrick Garland from the court because they knew their 5–4 ideological majority was at risk. After Justice Kennedy announced his retirement, the toxic confirmation process of now-Justice Brett Kavanaugh not only solidified a reliable conservative majority on the court but also left many liberals feeling that two seats on the Supreme Court had been filled illegitimately.

The court's legitimacy and the legitimacy of the rule of law and our constitutional system more broadly depend on people knowing that the court makes decisions based on law, not on crass partisan politics. If half the country doesn't see the court as an impartial arbiter of justice, the consequences are dire. Imagine the Supreme Court striking down signature accomplishments of a progressive president along party lines. The political branches of government might then ignore court decisions, creating a constitutional crisis. Indeed, many are already calling for the next Democratic president to pack the Supreme Court— by adding new justices— or for Congress to strip the court of its jurisdiction to hear certain cases. If we want to save what is good about the Supreme Court, we will need serious—even radical—reforms.

One promising solution would be to appoint *all* federal court of appeals judges as associate justices of the Supreme Court. The Supreme Court would then hear cases in panels of nine justices selected at random from the full list of justices (that is, all the judges on the federal court of appeals). Once selected, each panel of justices would hear cases for only two weeks before another set of judges would replace them. Alongside this reform, the court would also need a supermajority to strike down a federal statute.

This approach would have significant benefits. It would get rid of high-stakes Supreme Court appointments, taking the court out of the electoral and political realm. It would also significantly decrease the ideological partisanship of court decisions. No judge would be able to advance an ideological agenda over decades of service or develop a cult of personality among partisans. And it would be very difficult to be a judicial activist on any given case because the next court—arriving no more than two weeks later—might have a different composition and take a different tack. Judges would be restrained both by the need to preserve stability in the country and by the supermajority requirement preventing them from overturning federal statutes.

Cases would also be chosen behind a veil of ignorance. While serving their two weeks, the justices would consider petitions for Supreme Court review. But with such short terms of service, the justices would know that another slate of justices, perhaps with different partisan dispositions, would hear the cases they select—leading to greater caution. Activist lawyers would also not be able to game the system, bringing legal arguments and cases tailored to the particular preferences of a justice or a few justices. In the run of cases, the court's decisions would likely be far more deferential to the democratic process and far more tightly linked to precedent.

Some commentators have proposed that Supreme Court justices serve an eighteen-year term instead of a lifetime term. Each president would therefore get two appointments, and appointments would be predictable, removing the pressure to appoint younger and younger justices. Although this is a well-intentioned reform effort, it is unlikely to solve the problem and instead will likely make it worse. First, it guarantees that the Supreme Court will be a campaign issue in every single presidential election because each president would get to shape the court with two nominees. During the appointment process, movement activists on both sides would still jockey to make sure only the purest ideologues would be appointed. And once on the bench, the justices themselves might actually become more political: a term-limited justice might see the court as the perfect jumping-off point for a presidential run, decide cases in hopes of retiring into a lucrative lobbying gig, or play to the public to secure a future as a talking head on Fox or MSNBC.

To be sure, even under the lottery approach, there would still be politics related to the appointment of federal court of appeals judges. But there are many more such judges, and they would still serve lifetime appointments. Over time, both parties would get a variety of appointments—and there would inevitably be more ideological, methodological, and experiential diversity from this larger bench of judges. Combined with short terms of service on the Supreme Court, this diversity would make it harder for any willful judge to impose a particular agenda on the country.

Our goal should be to make the court less political. A less political court is good for the political system, for the Supreme Court's legitimacy, and for the rule of law. Despite the importance of judicial review within our constitutional system, the Supreme Court was never meant to be, as Justice Elena Kagan has written, "black-robed rulers overriding citizens' choices." Judges were meant to interpret the law, fairly and without an ideological agenda. Selecting them by lottery would restore that basic constitutional commitment.[17]

*   *   *

A democracy that is unrepresentative of the people is hardly a democracy. American democracy today is in crisis—but the crisis in our political democracy is not limited to the breakdown of constitutional norms. The crisis is much more fundamental: the combination of voting rules, money in campaigns, lobbying, the revolving door in and out of government, gerrymandering, and other features of our political system mean that democracy is simply not representative of the people. Nationalist oligarchy only promises to make politics less representative, not more—further rigging the rules to sustain a minority in power. For anyone interested in preserving democracy in America, the path forward must be to transform democracy in America. Every branch of government and the electoral process itself require significant, structural changes. If we welcome citizens into the political process and enhance representation, the result will be a new era of political democracy.

9

DEFENDING DEMOCRACY

"Great nations need organizing principles," former secretary of state Hillary Clinton once said of foreign policy. For thirty years after World War II, containment provided the organizing principle for American foreign policy. Then neoconservativism and liberal internationalism took over, organizing American foreign policy around American primacy and the promotion of democracy, human rights, and neoliberal economics. With the wars in Iraq and Afghanistan and the global financial crash, American foreign policy was adrift.

In those last days of neoliberalism, Clinton noted that Obama's phrase "'Don't Do Stupid Stuff' was not an organizing principle." Of course, it's unclear that Clinton's preferred slogans—"Peace, Progress, and Prosperity" and "Smart Power"—would qualify as organizing principles either. Indeed, "Smart Power," meaning the use of all foreign policy tools, not just the military, was consistent with the technocratic ethos of the time. Complex problems in the world require smart foreign policy technocrats to address them in smart ways. Fair enough. But what problems? And what directions should the solutions take?[1]

Today, the single greatest national security threat to most democracies is not military invasion from abroad but erosion from within. Democracies might cease to exist, but in most cases, there won't be a revolution, a new Constitution, or even the declaration of a new regime. The trappings of democracy will remain while the reality disappears, replaced instead by oligarchy.

This threat, the threat to democracy itself, should be the highest national security priority, and preserving and protecting democracy at home from becoming a nationalist oligarchy—and from nationalist oligarchies abroad—should become the new organizing principle for American foreign and national security policy. This principle has widespread consequences. First, it means breaking down the silos between foreign policy and domestic policy because domestic resilience and strength—economic, political, and social—are foundational for national security. More specifically, it requires protecting democratic institutions from political attacks and cyberattacks. Second, national oligarchies can weaponize economic interdependence to gain leverage and power. Democracies must therefore develop economic resilience and capabilities, selectively disentangle from these countries, and forge countervailing alliances. Finally, preserving and protecting democracy at home means taking a more restrained approach to international interventions abroad.

Let's start with defending democracy at home. National security begins with achieving political, economic, and united democracy. For too long, national security and foreign policy have been disconnected from explicitly domestic goals like building an equitable economy and fostering social solidarity. But policies in these areas, whether antitrust or public options, campaign finance or judicial reform, are all national security policies. Democracy at home cannot be secure without attending to what makes democracy possible. Achieving the political democracy, economic democracy, and united democracy agendas described earlier in the book is therefore as important as any other homeland security or foreign policy endeavor and, indeed, is the foundation for them.

More specifically, the structures and institutions of American democracy have already been the subject of ongoing attacks. The Russian government targeted dozens of state election systems in the 2016 elections, and they even succeeded in infiltrating some voter registration databases. During that same time, hackers breaking into voter files in Illinois attempted to change voter information, potentially compromising up to ninety thousand voters.[2]

Part of the problem is that the election system is extremely vulnerable. Voting machines are electronic, and many of them allow for remote access. Although this access is intended for troubleshooting, it can also serve as a back door for hackers. This is particularly problematic because twelve states use machines that do not produce a paper ballot, and thirty-two states allow electronic ballots for absentee voters or voters who are abroad. Many machines are so old that vendors no longer make security updates for them. When results are transmitted over cellular phone lines or modems, they can be intercepted through the use of stingray machines that mimic cell towers. And because election administration is decentralized through states and local governments, hackers and foreign governments can focus on the weakest links. Given that election officials in ten states don't receive any cybersecurity training, American democracy has a very soft and vulnerable underbelly.[3]

Defending political democracy will require national reforms to election administration. As cryptographer Bruce Schneier has observed, "The U.S. against Russia is a fair fight. Fifty separate states against Russia—that's not a fair fight." The Constitution allows the federal government to take action, giving Congress the power to pass laws on the timing and manner of elections. Congress must do so. At a minimum, Congress should mandate cybersecurity training for election officials and cybersecurity standards for voting machines; all machines should have to produce paper ballots; and officials should conduct randomized postelection audits. These are not simply a matter of good government but central to American national security.[4]

Protecting economic democracy and fostering a united democracy also requires defending critical infrastructure—energy facilities, banking and economic infrastructure, water and utilities systems, and air traffic and transportation infrastructure. In early 2018, for example, the Trump administration's Department of Homeland Security and the FBI jointly accused the Russian government of targeting the US energy grid and, in particular, hacking into nuclear facilities. The threat to critical infrastructure is not simply one of inconvenience from a minor power outage. One of the greatest transformations in the history of warfare was the shift from warfare between armies to total war. Total war involves the full mobilization of a society's military, economic, and social power to wage war, and its central feature is that more than just military targets became part of military campaigns. For example, General Sherman's March to Sea during the American Civil War and aerial bombing campaigns during World War II were designed as much to break the will, spirit, and solidarity of the enemy as they were for narrowly drawn military purposes. Now, as every aspect of life becomes linked to technology, as robotics and the internet of things expand in scope and influence, total war has a new set of tactics. Shutting down electric grids or spreading propaganda and disinformation can spark social crises and unrest, breaking the unity required for democracy—and it can all be done from afar. As Senator Kamala Harris has said, "We have to be prepared for wars without blood."[5]

Addressing these threats will require more than just regulating tech companies, improving security, and educating people about the misuse of social media. Right now, most cyberoperations are run through each of the different branches of the military—army, navy, marines, air force—or are run through piecemeal efforts by the private sector and local and state governments. Each trains its own cyberwarriors, drawn from its ranks. This approach suffers from serious problems. First, cyber is its own domain of conflict, with its own threats, strategies, language, training, and operations. Second, because the United States has a law preventing the military from operating within the country, cybersecurity operations should not solely operate through the military. Third, piecemeal efforts mean that we have a patchwork of cyberdefense systems that is uneven and leaves significant vulnerabilities.

In a world defined by technology, the defense of democracy requires a dedicated Cyber Guard, akin to the National Guard, with the sole purpose of protecting the country from technological attacks. Creating a single, independent Cyber Guard would address the problems with fragmentation across the different military branches and assist the private sector. It would also help with recruiting talent. The kid who watches an advertisement for the army or the marines and wants to join up to serve in the field is probably not the same as the one who wants to sit at a computer and write lines of code. At the same time, the person who is only interested in cyber issues might not want to join one of the other services for fear of ending up an infantryman or a submariner. A Cyber Guard would be able to recruit from a population exclusively interested in cyber issues.[6]

Cybersecurity and election security might not seem like classic foreign policy or national security topics. Neither do trade and international economic policies. But economic policy is central to foreign policy because economic interdependence can be weaponized for the powerful to gain leverage over weaker countries. When it comes to engagement with nationalist oligarchies, this poses a serious threat—and requires fundamentally reforming how foreign policy and economic thinkers have approached international economics over the neoliberal era.[7]

For decades, American foreign policy makers believed that including and engaging foreign countries—even autocracies—in international institutions would inevitably lead to them liberalizing their politics and economies. The Washington Consensus, shock therapy, and democratization efforts of the 1990s and 2000s were thus partly predicated on the view that reforms would lead to stable liberal democracy. In perhaps no area was this approach truer than policy toward China. As Kurt Campbell and Ely Ratner have said looking back at more than forty years of US-Asia policy, "The assumption that deepening commercial, diplomatic, and cultural ties would transform China's internal development and external behavior has been a bedrock of U.S. strategy."[8]

This strategy, however, suffered from a number of problems. First, it turned out to be wrong. All good things—economic openness, political democracy, and human rights—do not go together, and international institutions do not necessarily change the character of a national government. "Diplomatic and commercial engagement have not brought political and economic openness," Campbell and Ratner write in their important reckoning with Asia policy. "And the liberal international order has failed to lure or bind China as powerfully as expected."[9]

The second problem is that international institutions are not necessarily good for democracy. If international institutions are designed badly or pursue policies that undermine economic equality, social solidarity, and political responsiveness, they can contribute to the collapse of democracy. Indeed, there is a good case that some international economic institutions—especially the IMF—have had precisely this effect. By pushing countries to deregulate, liberalize, privatize, and impose austerity, the IMF led them into a future of economic crises, rising inequality, and backlash to democracy. China's entry into the WTO had somewhat similar effects in the United States. As we have seen, economists have shown that the Asian country's admission to the trading body led to a China Shock that disproportionately affected some American communities. Even a decade later, these communities had not bounced back or adapted.

Finally, entanglement theory was not attentive to the threat that comes from becoming more economically interdependent with countries that do not share core democratic values. Nationalist oligarchies are not designing their policies to fit the theories of Adam Smith or the Chicago School economists. Their central, defining feature is the fusion of economic and political power. What that means is that economic integration gives the state the ability to wield political power and exercise leverage through the economic channels opened from integration. China, for example, has not shied away from using economic power for geopolitical purposes. For example, to punish Norway for the 2010 Nobel Peace Prize going to Chinese dissident Liu Xiaobo, China banned imports of Norwegian salmon. China also prevented the importation of Filipino bananas in 2012 to gain leverage during a maritime dispute. Integration raises other security concerns as well. According to a

Bloomberg News report, which companies have denied, Chinese manufacturers secretly placed microchips on motherboards destined for the American market, in the process creating a backdoor entrance into networks that use those chips. A more common complaint is that American companies operating in China are forced to turn over trade secrets and technology and partner with Chinese companies in order to gain access to the market. This benefits not only the Chinese companies but also the Chinese government, as many of these partner companies are state-owned or state-supported enterprises.[10]

Call this reverse entanglement: while liberal democracies were trying to entangle the Chinese through economic integration, they themselves became ensnared. Economic power has always been one of the foundations of global power, and the ability to have economic leverage over a country has always been important for pursuing geopolitical goals. Because politics and economics are intertwined in China, as China's economic power grows and it becomes more globally integrated into the economy, other countries will increasingly find themselves at the mercy of the Chinese government. These dynamics apply to nationalist oligarchies generally.

Responding to the reality of reverse entanglement requires three strategies. The first is an economic development and industrial policy to support and strengthen innovation and industry. This means massive investments in research and development and an active manufacturing and innovation policy that ensures the development of industry within the country's borders. Development increases resilience in the face of economic threats. But it cannot be implemented through economic policies that support and entrench monopolies and megacorporations. Democracy requires dispersing economic power internally; so, too, must its strategy for development.

The second strategy is selective disentanglement. Selective disentanglement means uncoupling the American economy from corporations, investments, and the economies of nationalist oligarchies in sectors that are of critical importance to national security. In the short run, selective disengagement would require the Committee on Foreign Investment in the United States (CFIUS), which can block foreign companies from making acquisitions in the United States, to act far more aggressively when dealing with nationalist oligarchies. It will also require the United States to adopt stringent, perhaps even draconian, policies to protect against both legal and illegal technology transfers and theft of intellectual property. Corporations that give up important technology, particularly when funded through US government grants, enhance the ability not just of companies within nationalist oligarchies but the states themselves.

In addition, the United States should push our allies to engage in similar policies. Former ambassador to Russia Michael McFaul has argued, for example, that Germany should cancel its plans to build a natural gas pipeline with Russia. The new pipeline would increase German dependence on Russia for critical energy needs, which is both a military and economic threat. Democracies also need to be far more attentive to Russian attempts to hide wealth in the West and to Chinese and Russian purchases of companies, technology, and even property. These efforts can not only have problematic economic effects (like increased real estate prices) but also economic security consequences (like spying, hacking, and theft).[11]

The final strategy is diversification of economic partners. As of 2017, China was not only the United States' largest trading partner in the world for goods but also the largest supplier of imported goods. It is also the largest holder of US government debt. As we have seen, dependency on nationalist oligarchies can be a vulnerability because economic power can be used for political purposes. This is why it is important to support international economic cooperation with democratic allies. But diversification must be done in a way that simultaneously expands connections abroad while preventing inequality and the concentration of economic power at home.[12]

Diversifying economic partners will mean rethinking and reforming critical alliances. Alliances help us defend our democracy from internal and external threats. Consider NATO. Since its

founding, NATO was based on two premises. The first was preserving security and stability in Europe. In the classic formulation
by Lord Ismay, after two World Wars that started in Europe, the
goal was to "keep the Soviet Union out, the Americans in, and the
Germans down." The second was that its member countries shared
liberal democratic ideas and practices. In the post–Cold War era,
the first premise had lost much of its force, leading to endless discussions of whether NATO was still relevant. The second premise,
perhaps unsurprisingly given the neoliberal character of the age,
was reduced to promoting a thin notion of electoral democracy
combined with neoliberal market economics for the countries of
the former Soviet bloc.[13]

Over time, three serious problems with the decades-old alliance
have become clear. The first, as Celeste Wallander has argued, is
that "there is no price for violating NATO's liberal democratic
standards, and some weak links are indeed backsliding." Countries
like Hungary and Turkey are no longer robust liberal democracies,
and their links to Russia in particular make it harder for NATO to
defend the democratic foundations of its members.[14]

The second problem is that NATO's vision of liberal democracy
was relatively thin to begin with. With a goal of democracy promotion and the expansion of capitalism, countries could be admitted
for making democratic reforms with respect to elections and political changes and without regard for their degree of economic equality. Rather, NATO (and the EU as well) saw the alliances as ways
to induce reforms over time—to engage in democracy promotion
rather than democracy protection. Many of the ensuing neoliberal
reforms, however, actually eroded the middle class. They undermined the very foundations of the democracies they were trying to
promote. After the 2008 financial crash, populations in countries
that had more insecure economies unsurprisingly engaged in various forms of political rebellion—against the EU and against their
own governments.

The third problem is that the threat to transatlantic liberal
democracies has evolved—but foreign policy and the alliance have

not fully refocused on the nature of the new challenge. The Soviet Union's threat to Europe during the Cold War was largely understood to be a military threat—a threat of invasion. Today, the Russian threat to democracy "operates through shadowy financial flows, corrupt relationships, bribes, kickbacks, and blackmail." Cronyism and corruption are not a bug but the central feature of the model. For this system to continue, nationalist oligarchs need a steady diet of economic resources so they can pay off their clients. Because every domestic economy has limits, nationalist oligarchies look abroad to make deals with foreign countries, gain influence over foreign companies, and steal foreign technology. At the extreme, think of it as a foreign policy Ponzi scheme. To keep power, you need to continue to get more and more wealth to buy off your supporters. A foreign policy of aggressive economic influence, deal making, and theft enables the corruption that sustains the regime. Ideologically, Russia now spreads "the same combination of intolerant nationalism, xenophobia, and illiberalism that is on the rise in Hungary, Poland, Turkey, and elsewhere in Europe." Combined with the technology—hacking, cyberwarfare, and social media disinformation campaigns—the current challenge may be even greater than the military threat was during the Cold War. Instead of taking over Europe by force, nationalist oligarchies might be able to break democracy through corruption and fraud.[15]

Today, the central purpose of our alliances must be to defend democracy. We must recognize the existential threat to democracy that comes from hacking, election vulnerabilities, social media disinformation, and other forms of electronic attacks and cyberwarfare. These are areas in which democratic countries can help one another by sharing intelligence and learning from attempted attacks across the West. For example, NATO countries that want to meet their 2 percent of GDP spending commitment, as President Trump has undiplomatically asked them to do, should be able to invest in cybersecurity as long as the benefits can be shared with other members of the alliance.

Economic democracy in transatlantic countries is also at great risk, as inequality reaches historic levels and power is increasingly concentrated in the hands of wealthy families and corporations. International institutions from the Organisation for Economic Co-operation and Development (OECD) to the European Union to NATO can work together to disseminate data and information and coordinate policy that will help fight oligarchic policies. Another proposal is for alliances themselves to build incentives into their structure to prevent democratic backsliding. Wallander thus argues for changing NATO's voting rules so that a majority of members can strip countries of voting rights and funding to punish countries that pursue undemocratic practices.[16]

Perhaps the boldest proposal would be to create a new alliance of democracies, which some commentators, including 2008 Republican presidential candidate John McCain, have alternatively called a league, or concert, of democracies. As a path forward for defending democracy, this idea has merit, particularly if President Trump undermines NATO to the point of no return. But for it to work, its goals would have to diverge significantly from those of its original promoters.

Advocates for an alliance of democracies came up with the idea after the intervention in Iraq in 2003. They were largely responding to the failure of the United Nations Security Council to intervene in a variety of conflicts and humanitarian crises with sufficient haste and attention. Although proponents argued that a concert of democracies would cooperate on a wide variety of issues of common concern, they also believed that this new international institution would be able to engage in foreign interventions more easily than the United Nations. And far from being exercises of power by Western elite democracies, the alliance's military and humanitarian interventions would be legitimate because the alliance would include upward of sixty countries, including the Philippines, India, and Brazil. As James Lindsay wrote in 2009, the concert of democracies "would be composed of a diverse group of countries from around the globe—small and large, rich and poor, North and

South, strong and weak." Some others, like Anne-Marie Slaughter and John Ikenberry, saw an alliance of democracies as updating the architecture of the international system for a new era and hoped the alliance would form a bloc that could push for the reform of traditional international institutions, like the UN, World Bank, and IMF. Opponents of the idea were primarily worried that an alliance of democracies would cause backlash. China, Russia, and other nondemocracies would see the alliance as a threat, leading to a downward spiral of mistrust that could potentially end in conflict.[17]

Today, the case for an alliance of democracies is stronger than it was in the post-Iraq context—but for different reasons. By now, it is clear to everyone that we were never at the end of history, at a unipolar moment where the United States and other democracies had time, money, and military power to spend engaging in adventures abroad. Even those who once believed that now recognize that the global context has shifted. Today, the primary goal of an alliance of democracies would not be to engage in interventions or promote democracy. It would be defensive—to maintain democracy *inside* each of the member countries.

An alliance today would also focus on deepening economic cooperation in order to build collective, countervailing economic power vis-à-vis nationalist oligarchies. The original proponents of an alliance argued for "eliminating tariffs and other trade barriers among member countries." But as Trump's election, Brexit, and data on the China Shock suggest, the liberalization of trade barriers without regard to the consequences is destructive for economic democracy and is a threat to social cohesion. Instead, the alliance's economic agenda should be to enforce antitrust and antimonopoly rules across borders, to prevent tax havens and simplify the financial system, to regulate tech platforms, promote corporate democracy, reinvigorate worker power, and fight corruption. In other words, an alliance of democracies would seek to facilitate international cooperation on the agenda that each country must pursue to achieve economic democracy at home. This cooperative effort is critical because individually each democracy is vulnerable to lucrative offers from nationalist oligarchies abroad. The enemies of economic democracy can play countries against each other, creating a race to the bottom that ultimately undermines democracy itself. Cooperation is critical to helping solve this problem.[18]

Importantly, building alliances among democracies is not the same as promoting democracy in places that do not have it. And although the United States and an alliance of democracies like NATO should advocate for the conditions that allow democracies to flourish, they should not focus on the kinds of aggressive military interventions that defined the neoliberal era's foreign policy on both the right and the left.

The logic of this more restrained foreign policy stems from the nature of democracy itself. As we have seen, democracy demands much more than holding elections or adopting formal political and civil rights. Because democracy has an economic and social component, it is not easily exported or created unless the preconditions for democracy are already in place. And if the preconditions for democracy are in place, there is a good chance democracy is already in place. Changing deeply held values, social structures, and the distribution of wealth is inevitably a long-term process. Attempts to rush it or impose solutions from abroad can backfire.

This is precisely where aggressive proponents of democracy promotion have gone wrong for decades. It wasn't just a matter of sufficient planning for postwar reconstruction. The idea that foreigners who knew nothing about a country's history, culture, customs, and language, didn't care enough to learn, and didn't want to stay for decades could somehow transform Iraq, Afghanistan, or any other country into a democratic paradise was misguided from the start. Add that the tactics for democracy promotion were elections and neoliberal economic policies, and it is unsurprising that these interventions often left behind chaos, corruption, and crisis.

What true democracy involves is that communities take charge of their own destinies. Philosophers from John Stuart Mill to Michael Walzer have understood that a commitment to self-determination actually requires restraint, not adventurism. In "The Moral Standing of States," Walzer argued that believing in self-determination paradoxically required nonintervention. For a people to be free, they must be free to engage in rebellion and overthrow their government—or free not to rebel and to retain their government even if it might seem, from abroad, to be undemocratic or illiberal. Intervention undermines the ability of a people to shape its own destiny. True democracy means the people themselves must determine their own fate. We cannot do it for them.[19]

The idea that restraint is a function of our commitment to democracy does not mean humanitarian interventions are never possible. Walzer himself argued that intervention would be permissible if there is an internal rebellion in a state, if intervention is necessary to counter the use of force by a foreign country, or in the case of slavery or mass murder. The common theme is that in each situation, self-determination is being violated. None of this, of course, means that intervention is mandatory. It might be too expensive, judged to be counterproductive, or simply politically unpopular at home.

Restraint in promoting democracy and intervening abroad isn't isolationism, and it doesn't morally endorse corrupt and oppressive regimes. It is a hardheaded recognition that stable democracies require not only political democracy but also a good measure of economic equality and social solidarity—all of which cannot be imposed from abroad. Democracy is fragile and rare, and people must achieve it on their own. In this sense, "American restraint abroad is not an abandonment of democratic values but rather an expression of them."[20]

*   *   *

Democracy might have ended with imperialism, or fascism, or communism. But with each challenge, democracies adapted and outlasted those rival forms of government. Today, the greatest threat to the persistence of democracy is nationalist oligarchy, both at home and abroad. The stakes of this challenge are about the struggle for global power and influence, but also the very character of our country. Crony capitalism and authoritarianism already threaten to undermine democracy from within. Nationalist oligarchies abroad seek the power to redefine world affairs and the leverage to dictate domestic ones.

The defense of democracy has the potential to be the foundation of a new grand strategy for the United States—the guiding principle for foreign and national security policy in addition to domestic policy. In some cases, this will mean significant shifts that foreign policy elites will find objectionable—for example, taking a far more restrained approach than go-go economic liberalization. In other cases, this approach will be consonant with trends in foreign policy that have already begun, like extreme skepticism toward optional military interventions. This is as it should be. The foreign policy of the past will not work for the future. We can't step in the same river twice, and there will be no return to normalcy no matter how comforting that dream might be.

CONCLUSION
THE POLITICS OF ACHIEVING A GREAT DEMOCRACY

The battle for a great democracy will not be easy. Legislation does not pass on its own. The bolder and more transformative an agenda is, the harder it is to accomplish. And creating a new political equilibrium is even more daunting. "Nothing is more difficult to handle, more doubtful of success, nor more dangerous to manage, than to put oneself at the head of introducing new orders," a political philosopher once warned. So what will it take to achieve a great democracy?[1]

First: Be Willing to Play Hardball

We live in an era of political and constitutional hardball, but for the most part, only one team is playing. Scholars who write about constitutional hardball mean that leaders approach political tactics and negotiations with the understanding that the stakes are so high and the consequences of losing so great that leaders must sometimes take drastic, controversial actions.[2] But we can understand political hardball in a broader sense: political leaders need to negotiate hard and push the boundaries both substantively and tactically.

Right now, only one side recognizes that this is no time for politics as usual. They know it is a winner-take-all moment and that whoever wins will set the terms for a generation. Senate Majority Leader Mitch McConnell thus announced that Republicans would not approve *any* Supreme Court nominee after the death of Justice Antonin Scalia until after the 2016 election so Republicans would preserve their 5–4 hold on the Supreme Court in the event of a Republican victory in the presidential election. When Republicans in Wisconsin and Michigan lost statewide elections in 2018, they did not go quietly into the minority, as would happen in ordinary political times. Instead, they played power politics, seeking to strip new Democratic governors and statewide officials of the traditional powers of those offices. These are not normal events; they are extraordinary—a political minority frustrating the will of the people in an election, all to retain power.[3]

Many centrists, liberals, and even some moderate conservatives worry about tactics like these, but they also worry about fighting hardball with hardball. They are concerned, for example, about proposals to reform the Supreme Court, change filibuster rules, or regulate money in politics. They oppose nationalist oligarchy and want to preserve democracy, but they fear that more hardball will simply unleash a never-ending tit-for-tat process—an era of permanent escalation in which politics spins out of control. Although we cannot rule that possibility out, this view assumes that neither side can win outright. But this assumption might be wrong. Shortly after Lincoln declared that a "house divided against itself cannot stand," he added, "It will become all one thing or all the other." When nationalist oligarchs are playing hardball to rig the rules so they can never lose power, when they strip institutions of power after they lose so the other side cannot govern, they are playing for keeps. It will not be possible to go back in time or return to normalcy.

In moments of extraordinary politics, in moments of transition between eras, the struggle is not to save the old regime, and political hardball is not a permanent status. The struggle is to achieve a new equilibrium. Political scientists call these moments of realignment. Jefferson, Jackson, Lincoln, Roosevelt, Reagan—all of them realigned politics. They consolidated power and created a new equilibrium different from the one that existed previously. Their heirs and followers advanced the banner, and each of these eras eventually collapsed—at which point the cycle started again.[4]

In the midst of the struggle, the founders of these new eras were all decried as tyrants themselves, precisely because they tried to create a new equilibrium—and because they often played hardball themselves. "King Andrew" Jackson was depicted standing on the Constitution after his veto of the Bank of the United States. Lincoln was called a despot because he unilaterally suspended habeas corpus, freed the slaves with the Emancipation Proclamation, and blockaded Southern ports. Roosevelt was called a dictator for taking bold action during the New Deal and seeking to restructure the government to adapt to the challenges of a modern economy. In the past, the extraordinary political moments that reshaped politics required bold actions, which then set the foundations for the new era.

The struggle between nationalist oligarchy and great democracy today is a struggle to establish a new equilibrium. Nationalist oligarchs play political and constitutional hardball to entrench minority power. Policies redistribute wealth to the rich, new laws disfranchise voters, and rhetoric and rules divide people and fracture society. Each policy reinforces the others and makes it more and more difficult for the other side to win. Incrementalism and timidity cannot defend against this offensive. They will only guarantee the death of democracy.

But hardball in service of building a great democracy has the chance to create a new, alternative equilibrium. Hardball that achieves political democracy can break the dam that holds back progress. The new political democracy can then put forward highly popular policies that not only build economic democracy but simultaneously reshape how political power is exercised, reinforcing the new political democracy. The result will be greater trust and support in government, continued popular support for economic democracy, and the chance to unite our political community under a new banner. The future is not necessarily an era of permanent escalation. More likely, one side will win. "It will become all one thing or the other."

Second: Find Leaders with Courage

Political change is impossible without leadership. Leaders are needed to navigate reforms through the legislative process and implement them forcefully at the federal, state, and local levels. Leaders are needed to inspire, educate, and champion policies. Leaders are needed to devise strategies and coordinate action to execute those strategies.

But extraordinary moments require certain kind of leaders—leaders with courage and ferocity, steel spines and bold vision. In extraordinary moments, leaders without courage and vision cannot deliver on the transformative change that establishes a new equilibrium. Playing a timid, incrementalist game virtually guarantees defeat because the other side plays hardball. Leaders must play to win—and to win not just their election but to win a new era and a new equilibrium.

This means, first, running to win a mandate for change. Not all mandates come from offering a specific agenda. Roosevelt's mandate in 1932 was for change—but the type of change needed was not obvious. Roosevelt championed "bold, persistent experimentation"—doing *anything* in the midst of uncertainty and persistent hopelessness. Today's context is different. There is no national crisis on the level of the Great Depression, and trust in government is not at the level needed to ask the people for leeway to experiment. Leaders need a diagnosis of the problems and a vision for how to solve them. Running on bold policies has the virtue of building popular support for those policies, educating elites and the general public about those policies, and, upon victory at the polls, giving the leader a mandate to implement those policies. Of course, the conventional wisdom for candidates is not to offer details because they give opponents something to attack. But a candidate who runs and wins on a specific plan will have more leverage—both in the legislative process and with the general public—to push for their agenda.

Second, leaders must continue to sell their vision and policies while in power. Mario Cuomo, the former governor of New York, famously said that politicians campaign in poetry and govern in prose. The idea was that campaigning could offer broad, appealing visions of the future, but governing is boring and detailed. If ever true, it is only so in ordinary times. In extraordinary moments, leaders must campaign and govern in both poetry and prose. Campaigns need to include details—the prose—to win a mandate for their policies. And governing to establish a new equilibrium requires poetry to build popular support for the new policies. Throughout history, attempts at transformative change have broken down because leaders failed to carry the people with them. Losing a midterm election might prevent a second round of reforms. Losing the presidency might reverse change altogether. It is striking that the founding presidents of new eras in American politics were all followed by a successor of the same party. Van Buren followed Jackson. Truman followed FDR. Bush followed Reagan. In Britain, Major followed Thatcher. Repeated victory indicates popular support for the new equilibrium—and it forces the other side to adapt to the new equilibrium. But repeated victory means winning the public while governing. It requires poetry and prose.

Third: Organize and Mobilize the Grassroots

Playing hardball is not easily done without popular energy. Achieving a great democracy will require the people to make demands of their leaders—to march in the streets, to organize and mobilize, to spread the gospel of democracy. This is because the system will not produce change on its own. Over and over again, political scientists have shown that politics works to support the preferences of wealthy individuals and powerful corporations. If the system is rigged to favor these groups, we should not expect them to go along with changes that undermine their power.

So how does progress happen? Historically, some of the most transformative moments have coincided with wars or crises—situations in which the ordinary rules of politics go out the window. But progress has also been possible when there is overwhelming, unrelenting popular pressure. Around the turn of the twentieth century, populists and progressives pushed forward a variety of extraordinary changes—minimum wages, maximum working hours, campaign finance reforms, constitutional amendments, income taxes, antitrust laws. These changes came, in part, because there was popular demand all across the country. Working people went on strike, people organized, and they voted. During the 1960s, the civil rights movement put pressure on leaders to end Jim Crow segregation in the South. Popular pressure is critical for transformational democratic change.

Today, we already see signs of this change happening. Millions of women march in cities large and small year after year. When the Affordable Care Act was on the chopping block in 2017, people packed town hall meetings to tell their members of Congress how important health care was to them and their families. Many more people are running for office for the first time—including for local offices—and in the process they bring new voters into the political process. None of this offers any guarantees, but sustained popular mobilization will be needed for success.

Popular pressure can also push leaders away from timidity and toward transformative solutions. We already see this happening today. The democratic socialists—most prominently Bernie Sanders and Alexandria Ocasio-Cortez—have had an indelible impact on the Democratic Party already. They have mobilized people to support bold ideas from a Green New Deal to Medicare for All, they have brought new voters into the political system, and in the process, they have moved the center of gravity within American politics away from incrementalism and toward bigger thinking. Even if one disagrees with the specifics, people who oppose nationalist oligarchy should not see these new entrants to politics—or the grassroots pressure they bring to bear—as an irritant but as an opportunity. They are opening up possibilities for change that would not otherwise exist.

Fourth: Sequence Policy to Build Power

People often think that what is politically possible is static. They believe that what is politically viable is the same today as it will be tomorrow and as it was yesterday. But this is manifestly wrong. Actions today can reshape the political context and open up possibilities that were not previously available. For example, the idea of significant regulation of the financial sector was virtually unthinkable before the financial crash. After the crash, it was inevitable.

Achieving a great democracy will require sequencing policies with an understanding that politics is not static. Policy victories today can unlock policy options tomorrow. For example, as neoliberals waged war on unions, they eroded the central countervailing power against corporations. As unions became less powerful over time and less able to fight back, deregulation became increasingly possible. Neoliberals also cut taxes, knowing that doing so would put pressure on government budgets. Sharp reductions in taxes gave further power to their argument that balanced budgets required cutting spending.

The key to using policy for power building is to push first for policies that build power and popular support, not policies that sap power and popular support. Although some policies might be extremely important and even urgent, if pursuing them first undermines popular support, those policies will threaten to derail the rest of the agenda needed to achieve a great democracy. Such policies should only be pursued in a genuine crisis—and even then counterbalanced with power-building actions.

The first step in winning the battle for democracy is therefore an anti-corruption and political democracy agenda. Victory on this agenda opens the possibilities of reform and progress in all sectors. It isn't possible to win substantive victories on health care, climate change, or anything else if the system is rigged. We have to unrig the system first. Weakening the power of lobbyists, corporations, and wealthy individuals to determine policy will mean that all policies will be less likely to serve their interests. This first step is also hugely popular. Some 70 percent of Americans think the greatest threat today is corruption. People *want* a more representative government.

The second step is to show people that in the unrigged system, government can work for them. This is where portions of the economic democracy agenda—like infrastructure, internet for all, and curbing drug prices—come into play. They deliver immediately tangible benefits to individuals, families, and communities. Simultaneously, leaders and movements should attempt to make these changes in ways that reshape economic power—by combining these household policies with structural reforms like reinvigorating antitrust and geographically minded industrial policy. Reforms that change the structure of the economy will not only help achieve economic democracy but in the process further reduce the power of the wealthy and big corporations to shape politics. The result is a virtuous cycle that can achieve a great democracy.

* * *

"The whole history of the progress of human liberty shows that all concessions . . . have been born of earnest struggle," Frederick Douglass said in 1857. "If there is no struggle there is no progress." The reason progress requires struggle—moral struggle, physical struggle, all-encompassing struggle—is simple. "Power concedes nothing without a demand. It never did and it never will." The path forward will involve struggle, but with hardball and strategic policies, leaders and movements, the battle for a great democracy can be won.[5]

ACKNOWLEDGMENTS

In some ways, I started thinking about this book almost twenty years ago. As a college student in the fall of 2000, I read Stephen Skowronek's *The Politics Presidents Make* just as Al Gore lost the presidency to George W. Bush. I wondered then how it was possible that the vice president, in a time of peace and prosperity, didn't win the election easily. The following summer, after an internship in Washington, DC, I discovered Henry Adams and started reflecting more and more on the cycles of history and the hegemonic dominance of ideologies. It was during this period that I decided I should think about what might happen when the next cycle turned.

From those early years onward, conversations with Pete Buttigieg were invaluable, and this book wouldn't exist without them or without his characteristically thoughtful advice, encouragement, and friendship since. Sabeel Rahman shaped my thinking in critical ways, and he continues to do so in what has now been a fifteen-year set of conversations. Angus Burgin, James Kloppenberg, Michael Sandel, and Roberto Unger deserve special mention for conversations and writings that prompted considerable reflection at formative early moments. Randall Kennedy gave me a chance to organize my earliest thinking along these lines.

For almost fifteen years, I've been variously a student, coauthor, friend, and advisor to Elizabeth Warren. The early years advocating for the Consumer Financial Protection Bureau and confronting the financial crash through the Congressional Oversight Panel pushed me to dig much more deeply into economic policy than I ever had before. Since then, I've been grateful to her for many opportunities to think and act boldly in politics and policy, and I have learned a great deal from Dan Geldon and Jon Donenberg, two of the smartest and most talented people I've ever met.

As I was writing this book, my colleague Morgan Ricks was a constant source of support, encouragement, feedback, and insights. Our near-daily conversations sharpened my views, and I can't imagine this book without them. Vanderbilt Law School provided the perfect home for research and writing, and Dean Chris Guthrie has been encouraging at every turn. Chancellor Nick Zeppos and Provost Susan Wente deserve thanks for support through a Chancellor's Faculty Fellowship. My colleagues Rebecca Allensworth, Tim Meyer, Jim Rossi, Chris Serkin, Daniel Sharfstein, and Kevin Stack were helpful interlocutors, and Quenna Stewart, my terrific assistant, kept me on track.

Chris Hughes, Jeremy Kessler, Bob Kuttner, Jed Purdy, Kate Shaw, and Felicia Wong took up the burden of reading the entire draft and offered extremely helpful comments. I had engaging conversations with or got feedback from Anne Alstott, Kate Andrias, Sasha Baker, Jeremy Bearer-Friend, Rohit Chopra, Lina Khan, Julie Margetta Morgan, Bharat Ramamurti, Mira Rapp-Hooper, Katie Reisner, and Celeste Wallander. My intrepid agent, Chris Parris-Lamb, brought the manuscript to Basic Books and Brian Distelberg, whose edits were thoughtful and perceptive.

Portions of the book have appeared, in many cases in substantially altered form, as "Countering Nationalist Oligarchy," *Democracy: A Journal of Ideas* (Winter 2019); "Regulating Tech Platforms: A Blueprint for Reform," Great Democracy Initiative (May 2018); "Taking Antitrust Away from the Courts," Great Democracy Initiative (Sept. 2018); "A Blueprint for a New American Trade Policy," Great Democracy Initiative (Dec. 2018) (with Tim Meyer); "The Case for Glass-Steagall, the Depression Era Law We Need Today," *Guardian* (June 16, 2018); and "A Simple Plan for Saving the Supreme Court," *Vox* (Sept. 6, 2018) (with Daniel Epps). I thank the editors of these publications for improving those essays and for allowing me to reprint parts of them here.

NOTES

INTRODUCTION: THE EDGE OF A NEW ERA

1. Henry Adams, *The Education of Henry Adams* (1918); Henry Adams, *The Degradation of the Democratic Dogma* (1919); Arthur Schlesinger Jr., *The Cycles of American History* (1986); Arthur M. Schlesinger, *Paths to the Present* (1949).

2. Joseph Schumpeter, *Capitalism, Socialism, and Democracy* (1942); Thomas Kuhn, *The Structure of Scientific Revolutions* (1962).

3. Richard Reeves, *President Nixon: Alone in the White House* 295 (2001).

4. Jefferson Cowie, *Stayin' Alive: The 1970s and the Last Days of the Working Class* (2010).

5. For an overview of the debate over the Heritage Foundation's involvement in developing the idea for health care exchanges, see Timothy Noah, "Author, Author," *Slate.com*, Apr. 19, 2010.

6. My account of these eras is heavily influenced by Stephen Skowronek, *The Politics Presidents Make: Leadership from John Adams to Bill Clinton* (1993), though I focus more on ideas than Skowronek does. For an application of Skowronek's theory to the present, see Jack Balkin, "Obama Hoped to Be a Transformational President. He Failed," *Vox*, Jan. 19, 2017.

7. Matthew Arnold, "Stanzas from the Grand Chartreuse," in *Dover Beach and Other Poems* (Dover Thrift Editions, 1994).

8. Steven Levitsky & Daniel Ziblatt, *How Democracies Die* (2018); Madeleine Albright, *Fascism: A Warning* (2018); Timothy Snyder, *On Tyranny* (2017).

9. Theodore Roosevelt, *The New Nationalism* 43 (1910).

CHAPTER 1: THE ORIGINS AND MEANING OF NEOLIBERALISM

1. *The MacNeil/Lehrer Report*, "Election Fallout: The Parties," Nov. 5, 1980, http://americanarchive.org/catalog/cpb-aacip_507-w37kp7vk13. An account of this program also opens Randall Rothenberg's book *The Neoliberals*

(1984). I have organized the commentators' thoughts by person rather than chronologically in the program.

2.   David Harvey, *A Brief History of Neoliberalism* 2 (2005) ("Neoliberalism is in the first instance a theory of political economic practices that proposes that human well-being can best be advanced by liberating individual entrepreneurial freedoms and skills within an institutional framework characterized by strong private property rights, free markets, and free trade. The role of the state is to create and preserve an institutional framework appropriate to such practices."). David Grewal and Jedediah Purdy describe neoliberalism as the "revival of the doctrines of classical economic liberalism, also called laissez-faire, in politics, ideas, and law," and they note that the key component is "the assertion and defense of particular market imperatives and unequal economic power against political intervention." See David Singh Grewal & Jedediah Purdy, "Law and Neoliberalism," 77 *Law and Contemporary Problems* 1 (Nov. 4, 2014).

3.   On the use of the term *neoliberalism*, see Charles E. Merriam, "Review: The Good Society," 53, no. 1 *Political Science Quarterly* 129 (Mar. 1938); Pierre Dardot & Christian Laval, *The New Way of the World: On Neo-Liberal Society* 52 (trans. Gregory Elliott, 2013); Angus Burgin, *The Great Persuasion: Reinventing Free Markets Since the Depression* 72 (2012). For more on Colloque Lippmann, see Burgin, *Great Persuasion*, 55–56. This account of economic goals is from Dieter Plehwe, "Introduction," in Philip Mirowski & Dieter Plehwe, *The Road from Mont Pèlerin: The Making of the Neoliberal Thought Collective* 14 (2009). On the Chicago School, see Rob van Horn & Philip Mirowski, "The Rise of the Chicago School of Economics and the Birth of Neoliberalism," in Mirowski & Plehwe, *Road from Mont Pèlerin.*

4.   Burgin, *Great Persuasion*, at 88–89, 93.

5.   Burgin, *Great Persuasion*, at 169, 174, 154.

6.   Burgin, *Great Persuasion*, at 174, 181–183; Milton Friedman, "Neo-Liberalism and Its Prospects," *Farmand*, Feb. 17, 1951.

7.   See generally Thomas Ferguson & Joel Rogers, *Right Turn: The Decline of the Democrats and the Future of Politics* 78–79 (1986); Thomas Borstelmann, *The 1970s* 54–56 (2002). On savings and debt, see Bruce J. Schulman, *The Seventies* 135–136 (2001); Jacob S. Hacker, *The Great Risk Shift: The New Economic Insecurity and the Decline of the American Dream* (rev. ed. 2008). On foreign competition and crisis, see Charles Maier, "'Malaise': The Crisis of Capitalism in the 1970s," in *The Shock of the Global* 45 (Niall Ferguson et al. eds., 2010). Bortelsmann, *The 1970s*, 134, discusses manufacturing.

8.   Richard Roberts, *When Britain Went Bust: The 1976 IMF Crisis* (2016); Andrew Marr, *A History of Modern Britain* 366–369, 376 (2007); Simon Jenkins, *Thatcher & Sons* 37 (2006).

9.   Nancy MacLean, *Freedom Is Not Enough: The Opening of the American Workplace* 242–243 (2006).

10.   Jefferson Cowie, *Stayin' Alive: The 1970s and the Last Days of the Working Class* 293–294, 231 (2010).

11. Burgin, *Great Persuasion*, at 155; Ronald Reagan, Inaugural Address, Jan. 20, 1981; William A. Niskanen, Reaganomics, *The Concise Encyclopedia of Economics*, http://www.econlib.org/library/Enc1/Reaganomics.html; see also Ronald Reagan, Address before a Joint Session of Congress on the Program for Economic Recovery, Feb. 18, 1981, http://www.presidency.ucsb.edu/ws/index.php ?pid=43425.

12. On the global context, see Manfred B. Steger & Ravi K. Roy, *Neoliberalism: A Very Short Introduction* 21, 83 (2010). I owe the DLPA framework to Steger & Roy, *Neoliberalism*, at 14, who frame neoliberal policy as focused on deregulation, liberalization, and privatization—to which I have added the austerity component to better capture the fiscal and monetary elements of the neoliberal approach.

13. Sean Wilentz, *The Age of Reagan: A History 1974–2000* 140 (2009); Abner J. Mikva, "Deregulating through the Back Door: The Hard Way to Fight a Revolution," 57 *University of Chicago Law Review* 521, 521 (1990); Niskanen, "Reaganomics."

14. For a discussion, see Wilentz, *Age of Reagan*, at 196–199. On the cost, see Timothy Curry & Lynn Shibut, "The Cost of the Savings and Loan Crisis: Truth and Consequences," 13:2 *FDIC Banking Review* 26–35 (2000).

15. Ferguson & Rogers, *Right Turn*, at 131–132.

16. Jenkins, *Thatcher & Sons*, at 94–96; Marr, *History of Modern Britain*, at 411–416, 391.

17. James T. Patterson, *Restless Giant: The United States from Watergate to Bush v. Gore* 157–158 (2005); H. W. Brands, *Reagan* 309–313 (2005); Harvey, *Brief History*, at 25.

18. Jenkins, *Thatcher & Sons*, at 214–215, 225–226; Marr, *History of Modern Britain*, at 511.

19. John Gerard Ruggie, "International Regimes, Transactions, and Change: Embedded Liberalism in the Postwar Economic Order," 36 *International Organization* 379, 393 (1982); Jeff D. Colgan & Robert O. Keohane, "The Liberal Order Is Rigged," *Foreign Affairs* (May/June 2017).

20. For an interesting reflection on globalization, see Paul Krugman, "Globalization: What Did We Miss?" 4, Mar. 2018, https://www.gc.cuny.edu/CUNY _GC/media/LISCenter/pkrugman/PK_globalization.pdf.

21. Timothy Meyer & Ganesh Sitaraman, "Trade and the Separation of Powers," 107 *California Law Review* (Apr. 2019).

22. Steger & Roy, *Neoliberalism*, at 19–20; Joseph E. Stiglitz, *Globalization and Its Discontents* 13, 53, 47–48 (2002).

23. Jenkins, *Thatcher & Sons*, at 100; Charles Grant & Henry Porter, "Is Tony Blair the Right Man to Be President of Europe?," *The Observer*, Oct. 25, 2009, http://www.cer.eu/in-the-press/tony-blair-right-man-be-president -europe.

24. Marr, *History of Modern Britain*, at 429–431; Jenkins, *Thatcher & Sons*, at 79, 87, 126–128.

25. Michal Laurie Tingle, "Privatization and the Reagan Administration: Ideology and Application," 6 *Yale Law & Policy Review* 229, 230, n. 4 (1988); William E. Schmidt, "West Upset by Reagan Plan to Sell Some Federal Lands," *New York Times*, Apr. 17, 1982; Diane Henry, "Vouchers: Will They Help the Poor?," *New York Times*, Feb. 21, 1982; Ronald Reagan, Statement on the President's Commission on Privatization, Sept. 3, 1987.

26. Rothenberg, *The Neoliberals*, at 125–126.

27. Donald Cohen, "The History of Privatization," *TPM Features*, http://talkingpointsmemo.com/features/privatization/one/; Robert Poole, "Ronald Reagan and the Privatization Revolution," *Reason*, June 8, 2004, https://reason.org/commentary/ronald-reagan-and-the-privatiz/.

28. Jenkins, *Thatcher & Sons*, at 259–260, 263.

29. Jenkins, *Thatcher & Sons*, at 62, 65; Robert Blake, *The Conservative Party from Peel to Major* 339–340 (rev. ed. 1997).

30. Brands, *Reagan*, at 270–273; Ronald Reagan, Address before a Joint Session of Congress on the Program for Economic Recovery, Feb. 18, 1981, http://www.presidency.ucsb.edu/ws/index.php?pid=43425.

31. Wilentz, *Age of Reagan*, at 121; Brands, *Reagan*, at 260.

32. Wilentz, *Age of Reagan*, at 121; William Grieder, "The Education of David Stockman," *The Atlantic*, Dec. 1981, https://www.theatlantic.com/magazine/archive/1981/12/the-education-of-david-stockman/305760/; Brands, *Reagan*, at 308, 263–264.

CHAPTER 2: THE NEOLIBERAL IDEOLOGY

1.   Manfred B. Steger & Ravi K. Roy, *Neoliberalism: A Very Short Introduction* 38–39 (2010); David Harvey, *A Brief History of Neoliberalism* 3 (2005); Pierre Dardot & Christian Laval, *The New Way of the World: On Neoliberal Society* 3 (trans. Gregory Elliott, 2013); Ronald Butt, "Mrs Thatcher: The First Two Years," *Sunday Times*, May 3, 1981, https://www.margaretthatcher.org/document/104475.

2.   "What Isn't for Sale," *The Atlantic*, https://www.theatlantic.com/magazine/archive/2012/04/what-isnt-for-sale/308902/.

3.   Shushannah Walshe, "Romney Camp Continues 'You Didn't Build That' Attacks with Swing State Events," ABC News, July 25, 2012, https://abcnews.go.com/blogs/politics/2012/07/romney-camp-continues-you-didnt-build-that-attacks-with-swing-state-events/; Interview with *Woman's Own*, Sept. 23, 1987, https://www.margaretthatcher.org/document/106689.

4.   Paul Verhaeghe, "Neoliberalism Has Brought Out the Worst in Us," *Guardian*, Sept. 29, 2014, https://www.theguardian.com/commentisfree/2014/sep/29/neoliberalism-economic-system-ethics-personality-psychopathicsthic.

5.   Renae Merle, "Wells Fargo's Scandal Damaged Their Credit Scores. What Does the Bank Owe Them?" *Washington Post*, Aug. 18, 2017. For a broad

historical and philosophical discussion, see Elizabeth Anderson, *Private Government* (2017).

6. "Sens. Bernie Sanders and Ted Cruz Debate Over U.S. Health Care System," *CNN*, Feb. 7, 2017, http://transcripts.cnn.com/TRANSCRIPTS/1702/07/se.01.html.

7. K. Sabeel Rahman, *Democracy against Domination* 84 (2016).

8. Andrew Gamble, *The Free Economy and the Strong State: The Politics of Thatcherism* 35, 32–33 (1988); Simon Jenkins, *Thatcher & Sons*, at 126–128 (2006).

9. Quinn Slobodian, *Globalists: The End of Empire and the Birth of Neoliberalism* 2 (2018).

10. Slobodian, *Globalists*, at 149 (Röpke), 172–178 (Hutt), and 179–180 (Hayek). The phrase is Slobodian's.

11. Karin Fischer, "The Influence of Neoliberals in Chile before, during, and after Pinochet," in Philip Mirowski & Dieter Plehwe, *The Road from Mont Pèlerin* 325, 328 (2009).

12. Ed Kilgore, "Progressives and Liberals," *Democratic Strategist*, Jan. 2, 2007, http://thedemocraticstrategist.org/2007/01/progressives_and_liberals/; Jonathan Chait, "How 'Neoliberalism' Became the Left's Favorite Insult of Liberals," *New York Magazine*, July 16, 2017, http://nymag.com/daily/intelligencer/2017/07/how-neoliberalism-became-the-lefts-favorite-insult.html; Charles Peters, "A Neo-Liberal's Manifesto," *Washington Post*, Sept. 5, 1982, https://www.washingtonpost.com/archive/opinions/1982/09/05/a-neo-liberals-manifesto/21cf41ca-e60e-404e-9a66-124592c9f70d/?utm_term=.b377226a9605.

13. Arthur M. Schlesinger Jr., "The Democratic Party after Ted Kennedy," *Wall Street Journal*, Dec. 7, 1982; Randall Rothenberg, *The Neoliberals* 21 (1984); Robert M. Kaus, "Reaganism with a Human Face," *New Republic*, Nov. 24, 1981.

14. Thomas B. Edsall, "Coelho Mixes Democratic Fund-Raising; Political Matchmaking," *Washington Post*, Dec. 1, 1985; Kenneth S. Baer, *Reinventing Democrats: The Politics of Liberalism from Reagan to Clinton* 179–180 (2000).

15. Al From, *The New Democrats and the Return to Power* 211–212, 215, 216 (2013); Baer, *Reinventing Democrats*, at 222–223. Baer also notes that Will Marshall thought "a dearth of centrist Democrats on the White House staff . . . contributed to the leftward drift" and noted that "Clinton, like us, is outnumbered in his own administration."

16. Robert B. Reich, *The Next American Frontier* (1983); Robert B. Reich, *The Work of Nations: Preparing Ourselves for 21st Century Capitalism* (1991). See generally Rothenberg, *The Neoliberals*.

17. John Greenwald, "Greenspan's Rates of Wrath," *Time*, Nov. 28, 1994; Robert B. Reich, *Locked in the Cabinet* 306 (1997); see also Nelson Lichtenstein, "A Fabulous Failure: Clinton's 1990s and the Origins of Our Times," *American Prospect*, Jan. 29, 2018.

18. Alexander Hertel-Fernandez, Matto Mildenberger & Leah C. Stokes, "Legislative Staff and Representation in Congress," 113 *American Political Science*

Review 1 (2019); Lee Drutman, *The Business of America Is Lobbying: How Corporations Became Politicized and Politics Became More Corporate* (2015).

19. John Lewis Gaddis, *Strategies of Containment* 55 (2d. ed. 2005).

20. James Mann, *Rise of the Vulcans: The History of Bush's War Cabinet* 62–64, 89–90 (2004).

21. Samuel Moyn, *The Last Utopia: Human Rights in History* (2010); Samuel Moyn, *Not Enough: Human Rights in an Unequal World* (2018); Samuel Moyn, "Human Rights Are Not Enough," *Nation*, Apr. 9, 2018.

22. Mann, *Rise of the Vulcans*, at 203, 210.

23. Mann, *Rise of the Vulcans*, at xiv.

24. Mann, *Rise of the Vulcans*, at 214. For one discussion on Kosovo and Iraq, see Richard Falk, "The Iraq War and the Future of International Law," 98 *American Society of International Law Proceedings* 263 (2004).

25. Seth Mandel, "The Cautionary Tale of Samantha Power," *Commentary*, Jan. 2017; Carnegie Endowment for International Peace, C-SPAN Book TV, Feb. 5, 2003, https://www.youtube.com/watch?v=hrRC77QtYcY.

26. Juliet Eilperin, "Hillary Clinton Criticizes President Obama's Foreign Policy in Interview with the *Atlantic*," *Washington Post*, Aug. 11, 2014; Maureen Dowd, "Fight of the Valkyries," *New York Times*, Mar. 22, 2011.

CHAPTER 3: THE LAST DAYS OF NEOLIBERALISM

1. Manfred B. Steger & Ravi K. Roy, *Neoliberalism: A Very Short Introduction* 156 (2010); Edmund L. Andrews, "Greenspan Concedes Error on Regulation," *New York Times*, Oct. 23, 2008, http://www.nytimes.com/2008/10/24/business/economy/24panel.html.

2. Data from Emmanuel Saez, Table A3, col. P99–100, http://eml.berkeley.edu/~saez/TabFig2014prel.xls; Thomas Piketty, *Capital in the Twenty-First Century* 316 (2014); Economic Policy Institute, "The State of Working America," http://www.stateofworkingamerica.org/who-gains/#/start_1979&end-2008.

3. Valerie Wilson & William M. Rodgers III, "Black-White Wage Gaps Expand with Rising Wage Inequality," Economic Policy Institute, Sept. 20, 2016; Laurie Goodman, Jun Zhu & Rolf Pendall, "Are Gains in Black Homeownership History?," Urban Institute, Feb. 14, 2017.

4. FDIC, "Failures and Assistance Transactions of All Institutions by Federal Deposit Insurance Corporation for the United States and Other Areas, 1934–2016," https://fred.stlouisfed.org/series/BKIFDCA641N; FDIC, "Failure and Assistance Transactions of all Institutions for the United States and Other Areas, 1934–2019," https://fred.stlouisfed.org/series/BNKTTLA641N.

5. Joseph E. Stiglitz, *Globalization and Its Discontents* 89, 133–165 (2002).

6. "Too Much of a Good Thing," *Economist*, Mar. 26, 2016, https://www.economist.com/news/briefing/21695385-profits-are-too-high-america-needs-giant-dose-competition-too-much-good-thing; William A. Galston & Clara Hendrickson,

"A Policy at Peace with Itself: Antitrust Remedies for Our Concentrated, Uncompetitive Economy," *Brookings*, Jan. 5, 2018, https://www.brookings.edu/research/a-policy-at-peace-with-itself-antitrust-remedies-for-our-concentrated-uncompetitive-economy/.

7. Martin Gilens, *Affluence and Influence: Economic Inequality and Political Power in America* (2012); Martin Gilens & Benjamin I. Page, "Testing Theories of American Politics: Elites, Interest Groups, and Average Citizens," 12 *American Political Science Review* 564 (2014); Larry Bartels, *Unequal Democracy: The Political Economy of the New Gilded Age* (2d ed. 2016); Kay Lehman Schlozman, Sidney Verba & Henry E. Brady, *The Unheavenly Chorus: Unequal Political Voice and the Broken Promise of American Democracy* (2012); Jeffrey Winters, *Oligarchy* (2011).

8. Bhaskar Sunkara, *The Socialist Manifesto* 235 (2019); Daniel Denvir, "Hillary Clinton's Cynical Race Appeals: The Revenge of Neoliberal Identity Politics," *Salon*, Feb. 19, 2016.

9. On Libya, see Alan J. Kuperman, "Obama's Libya Debacle," *Foreign Affairs* (Mar./Apr. 2015).

10. Kurt M. Campbell & Ely Ratner, "The China Reckoning," *Foreign Affairs* (Mar./Apr. 2018), https://www.foreignaffairs.com/articles/united-states/2018-02-13/china-reckoning; Stiglitz, *Globalization and Its Discontents*.

11. Ryan Lizza, "Inside the Crisis," *New Yorker*, Oct. 12, 2009; Catharine Richert, "Stewart Claims that the Stimulus Bill Is One-Third Tax Cuts," PolitiFact, Feb. 10, 2010, http://www.politifact.com/truth-o-meter/statements/2010/feb/10/jon-stewart/stewart-claims-stimulus-bill-one-third-tax-cuts/; Larry Elliott, "Alistair Darling: We Will Cut Deeper Than Margaret Thatcher," *Guardian*, Mar. 25, 2010, https://www.theguardian.com/politics/2010/mar/25/alistair-darling-cut-deeper-margaret-thatcher.

12. Alexander Bolton, "Lieberman to Vote against Public Option," *Hill*, Oct. 27, 2019; Chris Hayes, "The Perriello Way," *Nation*, Nov. 22, 2010, https://www.thenation.com/article/perriello-way/.

13. Republican Party Platform (2012).

14. For a description and critique of the technocratic approach in Dodd-Frank, see K. Sabeel Rahman, *Democracy against Domination* (2017); Ganesh Sitaraman, "Unbundling Too Big to Fail," Center for American Progress, July 2014.

15. Richard H. Thaler & Cass R. Sunstein, *Nudge: Improving Decisions about Health, Wealth, and Happiness* 1–3, 5 (2008); Maya Shankar, "Designing Federal Programs with the American People in Mind," White House, Sept. 15, 2015, https://obamawhitehouse.archives.gov/blog/2015/09/15/designing-federal-programs-american-people-mind; U.K. Behavioural Insights Team, http://www.behaviouralinsights.co.uk/.

16. Thaler & Sunstein, *Nudge*, at 252–253; Ryan Bubb & Richard H. Pildes, "How Behavioral Economics Trims Its Sails and Why," 127 *Harvard Law Review* 1593 (2014).

17. Cazilia Loibl, Lauren Eden Jones, Emily Haisley & George Loewenstein, "Testing Strategies to Increase Saving and Retention in Individual Development Account Programs," https://papers.ssrn.com/sol3/papers.cfm?abstract_id=2735625.

18. Bubb & Pildes, "How Behavioral Economics Trims Its Sails," at 1610, 1631, 1635.

19. Eduardo Porter, "Nudges Aren't Enough for Problems Like Retirement Savings," *New York Times*, Feb. 23, 2016, http://www.nytimes.com/2016/02/24/business/economy/nudges-arent-enough-to-solve-societys-problems.html?_r=0.

20. Simon Jenkins, *Thatcher & Sons* 164, 78, 51, 88 (2006); Margaret Thatcher, *The Downing Street Years* 306 (1995).

21. William A. Niskanen, Reaganomics, The Concise Encyclopedia of Economics, http://www.econlib.org/library/Enc1/Reaganomics.html; Michael Oppenheimer, "How the IPCC Got Started," EDF, Nov. 1, 2007, http://blogs.edf.org/climate411/2007/11/01/ipcc_beginnings/.

22. Jenkins, *Thatcher & Sons*, at 164, 162.

23. Randall Rothenberg, *The Neoliberals* 27–28 (1984).

CHAPTER 4: AFTER NEOLIBERALISM

1. Brink Lindsey & Steven M. Teles, *The Captured Economy: How the Powerful Enrich Themselves, Slow Down Growth, and Increase Inequality* (2017).

2. Will Wilkinson, "For Trump and the G.O.P., the Welfare State Shouldn't Be the Enemy," *New York Times*, May 27, 2017; Samuel Hammond, "The Free-Market Welfare State: Preserving Dynamism in a Volatile World,' Niskanen Center, May 2018.

3. Alex Tabarrok, "Federal Regulation Is Not the Cause of Declining Dynamism," *Marginal Revolution*, Feb. 5, 2018, https://marginalrevolution.com/marginalrevolution/2018/02/federal-regulation-not-cause-declining-dynamism.html; Rachel Cohen, "The Libertarian Who Accidentally Helped Make the Case for Regulation," *Washington Monthly*, Apr./May/June 2018, https://washingtonmonthly.com/magazine/april-may-june-2018/null-hypothesis/.

4. Brink Lindsey, "Liberaltarians," *New Republic*, Dec. 10, 2006; Jonathan Chait, "Kiss Me, Cato," *New Republic*, Dec. 24, 2006; Steven Teles, "How to Get to Liberaltarianism from the Left," Niskanen Center, June 12, 2017, https://niskanencenter.org/blog/get-liberaltarianism-left/.

5. Writings on a universal basic income are now voluminous but include the following: Andy Stern with Lee Kravitz, *Raising the Floor: How a Universal Basic Income Can Renew Our Economy and Rebuild the American Dream* (2016); Annie Lowrey, *Give People Money: How a Universal Basic Income Would End Poverty, Revolutionize Work, and Remake the World* (2018). A more academic account is Philippe Van Parijs & Yannick Vanderborght, *Basic Income: A Radical Proposal for a Free Society and a Sane Economy* (2017). A slightly

different take, proposing ultimately an increase to the Earned Income Tax Credit, is Chris Hughes, *Fair Shot: Rethinking Inequality and How We Earn* (2018).

6. The Federal Poverty Level in 2018 in the United States, for an individual, was $12,140. Healthcare.gov, "Federal Poverty Level," https://www.healthcare .gov/glossary/federal-poverty-level-fpl/; Luke Martinelli, "Assessing the Case for a Universal Basic Income in the UK, Institute for Policy Research, IPR Policy Brief, Sept. 2017, http://www.bath.ac.uk/publications/assessing-the-case-for-a-universal -basic-income-in-the-uk/attachments/basic_income_policy_brief.pdf; Daniel Zamora, "The Case against a Basic Income," *Jacobin*, Dec. 28, 2017 (trans. Jeff Bate Boerop); Joi Ito, "The Paradox of Universal Basic Income," *Wired*, Mar. 29, 2018.

7. Jacob S. Hacker, "The Institutional Foundations of Middle-Class Democracy," Policy Network (2011).

8. Shoshana Zuboff, *The Age of Surveillance Capitalism: The Fight for a Human Future at the New Frontier of Power* (2019).

9. Zuboff, *Age of Surveillance Capitalism*, at 394.

10. Jan-Werner Müller, *What Is Populism?* (2016).

11. Vishakha Darbha, "6 Times Donald Trump Promised Not to Cut Medicare," *Mother Jones*, Dec. 8, 2017, https://www.motherjones.com/politics/2017/12/donald -trump-paul-ryan-medicare-medicaid/; Dylan Scott, "Trump's Abandoned Promise to Bring Down Drug Prices, Explained," *Vox*, Feb. 2, 2018, https://www.vox.com /policy-and-politics/2018/1/30/16896434/trump-drug-prices-year-one; Heather Long, "Trump Has Done a Big Flip-Flop on Wall Street," CNN Business, Apr. 26, 2017, http://money.cnn.com/2017/04/26/investing/donald-trump-wall-street/index.html.

12. Ryan Grim, "Steve Bannon Pushing for 44 Percent Marginal Tax Rate on the Very Rich," *Intercept*, July 26, 2017, https://theintercept.com/2017/07 /26/steve-bannon-pushing-for-44-percent-marginal-tax-rate-on-the-very-rich/; Louis Nelson, "Steve Bannon Hails Trump's 'Economic Nationalist' Agenda," *Politico*, Nov. 18, 2016, https://www.politico.com/story/2016/11/steve-bannon -trump-hollywood-reporter-interview-231624; Ryan Grim, "Steve Bannon Wants Facebook and Google Regulated Like Utilities," *Intercept*, July 27, 2017, https://theintercept.com/2017/07/27/steve-bannon-wants-facebook-and-google -regulated-like-utilities/; Robert Kuttner, "Steve Bannon, Unrepentant," *American Prospect*, Aug. 16, 2017, http://prospect.org/article/steve-bannon-unrepentant.

13. Steven Bannon, Panel at Conservative Political Action Conference, 2017, https://www.youtube.com/watch?v=kPFpTergAGQ.

14. Lee Drutman, "Political Divisions in 2016 and Beyond: Tensions between and within the Two Parties," Democracy Fund Voter Study Group, June 2017, https://www.voterstudygroup.org/publications/2016-elections/political-divisions -in-2016-and-beyond; Larry M. Bartels, "Partisanship in the Trump Era," at 2, Vanderbilt Center for the Study of Democratic Institutions, Feb. 7, 2018, https:// www.vanderbilt.edu/csdi/includes/Workingpaper2_2108.pdf.

15. Madeleine Albright, *Fascism: A Warning* (2018); Cass R. Sunstein, ed., *Can It Happen Here? Authoritarianism in America* (2018); Timothy Snyder, *On Tyranny* (2017).

16. On norms, see Steven Levitsky & Daniel Zibaltt, *Why Democracies Die* (2018); on illiberal democracy, see Yascha Mounk, *The People vs. Democracy* (2018) and Fareed Zakaria, *The Future of Freedom* (2003). This not to say that these authors ignore economic issues entirely. Mounk, for example, highlights economic breakdowns in some detail. But the emphasis is generally elsewhere. For a critique along these lines, see Jedediah Purdy, "Normcore," *Dissent*, Summer 2018, https://www.dissentmagazine.org/article/normcore-trump-resistance-books -crisis-of-democracy.

17. Jeffrey Winters, *Oligarchy* (2011).

18. See, e.g., Matthew Simonton, *Classical Greek Oligarchy* (2017).

19. Brian D. Taylor, *The Code of Putinism* 52–53, 71 (2018).

20. Taylor, *Code of Putinism*, at 104, 109, 117, 90, 102 (2018).

21. Paul Lendvai, *Orbán: Hungary's Strongman* 94, 85, 99–103, 129–131 (2017); Jan-Werner Müller, "Homo Orbánicus," *New York Review of Books*, Apr. 5, 2018.

22. Lendvai, *Orbán*, at 89, 37, 195, 29; Jan-Werner Jan-Werner Müller, "Homo Orbánicus."

23. Lendvai, *Orbán*, at 92, 138, 181, 151; Müller, "Homo Orbánicus"; Neil Buckley & Andrew Byrne, "Viktor Orban's Oligarchs: A New Elite Emerges in Hungary," *Financial Times*, Dec. 20, 2017, https://www.ft.com/content/ecf6fb4e -d900-11e7-a039-c64b1c09b482.

24. Müller, "Homo Orbánicus."

25. Joshua Kurlantzick, *State Capitalism: How the Return of Statism Is Transforming the World* (2016); Minxin Pei, *China's Crony Capitalism: The Dynamics of Regime Decay* 7 (2016).

26. Pei, *China's Crony Capitalism*, at 16–17, 24, 20–31.

27. Pei, *China's Crony Capitalism* 1–3; David Barboza, "Billions in Hidden Riches for Family of Chinese Leader," *New York Times*, Oct. 25, 2012, https:// www.nytimes.com/2012/10/26/business/global/family-of-wen-jiabao-holds -a-hidden-fortune-in-china.html.

28. Howard W. French, *Everything Under the Heavens: How the Past Helps Shape China's Push for Global Power* 22 (2017); Elizabeth C. Economy, *The Third Revolution: Xi Jinping and the New Chinese State* 42, 38 (2018); Carl Minzner, *End of an Era: How China's Authoritarian Revival Is Undermining Its Rise* 30 (2018). Minzner also calls China's approach populist nationalism and compares it to Venezuela, Russia, Turkey, and Trump; Minzner, *End of an Era*, at 167.

29. Nicholas Kulish, Caitlin Dickerson & Ron Nixon, "Immigration Agents Discover New Freedom to Deport under Trump," *New York Times*, Feb. 25, 2017; Glenn Thrush, "New Outcry as Trump Rebukes Charlottesville Racists 2 Days Later," *New York Times*, Aug. 14, 2017; Michael D. Shear & Maggie Haberman, "Trump Defends Initial Remarks on Charlottesville; Again Blames 'Both Sides,'" *New York Times*, Aug. 15, 2017.

30. Economic Policy Institute, "How Would Repealing the Affordable Care Act Affect Health Care and Jobs in Your State," https://www.epi.org/aca

-obamacare-repeal-impact/; Dylan Scott, "CBO: 13 Million More Uninsured if You Repeal Obamacare's Individual Mandate," *Vox*, Nov. 8, 2017, https://www .vox.com/policy-and-politics/2017/11/8/16623154/cbo-obamacare-individual -mandate-new-baseline.

31. Heather Long, "The Final GOP Tax Bill Is Complete. Here's What Is in It," *Washington Post*, Dec. 15, 2017, https://www.washingtonpost.com/news /wonk/wp/2017/12/15/the-final-gop-tax-bill-is-complete-heres-what-is-in-it/?utm _term=.4eb578027319.

32. Barry Meier & Danielle Ivory, "Under Trump, Worker Protections Are Viewed with New Skepticism," *New York Times*, June 5, 2017; James Hamblin, "A Burdensome Regulation Screening Truck Drivers for a Sleep Disorder," *Atlantic*, Aug. 8, 2007; Shannon van Sant, "Firm Prepares to Mine Land Previously Protected as a National Monument," *NPR*, June 21, 2018; Julia Horowitz, "Trump Kills Rule that Made It Easier for People to Sue Banks," CNN Money, Nov. 1, 2017; Derek Kravitz, Al Shaw & Isaac Arnsdorf, "What We Found in Trump's Drained Swamp: Hundreds of Ex-Lobbyists and D.C. Insiders," *ProPublica*, Mar. 7, 2018, https://www.propublica.org/article/what-we-found-in-trump-administration -drained-swamp-hundreds-of-ex-lobbyists-and-washington-dc-insiders.

33. Rebecca Ballhaus, "Admission to President's Fundraiser Tonight at Trump International Hotel Won't Come Cheap," *Wall Street Journal*, Sept. 12, 2018, https://www.wsj.com/livecoverage/campaign-wire-2018-midterms /card/1536780821; Robert Frank, "Mar-a-Lago Membership Fee Doubles to $200,000," CNBC, Jan. 25, 2017; Ali Dukakis, "Watchdog Group Finds More Spending at Trump Properties by Foreign Governments, Political Groups," *ABC News*, June 27, 2018; Jennifer Epstein, "Mar-a-Lago on $1 Million a Day: Taxpayer Costs for Trump Trips," *Bloomberg*, Feb. 5, 2019.

34. Dylan Scott, "North Carolina Elections Board Orders New House Election after Ballot Tampering Scandal," *Vox*, Feb. 21, 2019; Michael Tackett & Michael Wines, "Trump Disbands Commission on Voter Fraud," *New York Times*, Jan. 3, 2018; Dara Lind, "The Citizenship Question on the 2020 Census, Explained," *Vox*, Mar. 28, 2018; https://www.vox.com/policy-and-politics/2018/3 /28/17168048/census-citizenship-2020-immigrants-count-trump-lawsuit.

35. Angela Caputo, Geoff Hing & Johnny Kauffman, "They Didn't Vote . . . Now They Can't," *APMReports*, Oct. 19, 2018, https://www.apm reports.org/story/2018/10/19/georgia-voter-purge; Richard L. Hasen, "Brian Kemp Just Engaged in a Last-Minute Act of Banana-Republic Level Voter Manipulation in Georgia," *Slate*, Nov. 4, 2018. On Orbán, see David Leonhardt, "'An Appalling Abuse of Power,'" *New York Times*, Nov. 5, 2018; Roxana Hegeman, "New Voters Get Notices Listing Wrong Dodge City Polling Site," *Washington Post*, Oct. 25, 2018; David Leonhardt, "The Corporate Donors Behind a Republican Power Grab," *New York Times*, Dec. 9, 2018.

36. Robert Kuttner & Hildy Zenger, "Saving the Free Press from Private Equity," *American Prospect*, Dec. 27, 2017; http://prospect.org/article/saving-free -press-private-equity.

37. Jacey Fortin & Jonah Engel Bromwich, "Sinclair Made Dozens of Local News Anchors Recite from the Same Script," *New York Times*, Apr. 2, 2018; Alvin Chang, "Sinclair's Takeover of Local News, in One Striking Map," *Vox*, Apr. 6, 2018, https://www.vox.com/2018/4/6/17202824/sinclair-tribune-map.

38. Ezra Klein, "The Doom Loop of Oligarchy," *Vox*, Apr. 11, 2014, https://www.vox.com/2014/4/11/5581272/doom-loop-oligarchy.

39. Kurlantzick, *State Capitalism*, at 20, 74; see also Joshua Kurlantzick, *Democracy in Retreat: The Revolt of the Middle Class and the Worldwide Decline of Representative Government* (2013); Roberto Stefan Foa & Yascha Mounk, "The Democratic Disconnect," 27 *Journal of Democracy* 5, 7, 14 (July 2016), https://www.journalofdemocracy.org/sites/default/files/Foa%26Mounk-27-3.pdf.

CHAPTER 5: TOWARD A GREAT DEMOCRACY

1. See *Federalist* No. 10 (James Madison) (Clinton Rossiter, ed., 1999) ("A republic, by which I mean a government in which the scheme of representation takes place"); *Federalist* No. 14 (James Madison) ("In a democracy, the people meet and exercise the government in person; in a republic, they assemble and administer it by their representatives and agents").

2. Associated Press, "Kim Jong-Un 'Elected' with 100% of the Vote," *USA Today*, Mar. 10, 2014, https://www.usatoday.com/story/news/world/2014/03/10/nkorea-election/6247491/.

3. Aziz Huq & Tom Ginsburg, "How to Lose a Constitutional Democracy," 65 *UCLA Law Review* 78 (2018); Steven Levitsky & Daniel Ziblatt, *How Democracies Die* (2018). Other works in this general genre include the following: David Runciman, *How Democracy Ends* (2018); Alasdair Roberts, *Four Crises of American Democracy: Representation, Mastery, Discipline, Anticipation* (2016) (focusing on "anticipation," including climate change, as the main crisis of today). For an excellent typology of the ways norms break down, see Joshua Chafetz & David E. Pozen, "How Constitutional Norms Break Down," 65 *UCLA Law Review* 1430 (2018).

4. Barak D. Richman, *Stateless Commerce: The Diamond Network and the Persistence of Relational Exchange* (2017); Lisa Bernstein, "Opting Out of the Legal System: Extralegal Contractual Relations in the Diamond Industry," 21 *Journal of Legal Studies* 115 (1992).

5. Andrew Sullivan, "Democracies End When They Are Too Democratic," *New York Magazine*, May 1, 2016.

6. A terrific historical account of the expansion of suffrage is Alexander Keyssar, *The Right to Vote: The Contested History of Democracy in the United States* (2000). An account that places surprisingly little attention on social and economic factors, given its title, is Benjamin Barber, *Strong Democracy: Participatory Politics for a New Age* (1984). Others who expand beyond electoral and

participatory decisions focus on institutions. See, e.g., Daron Acemoglu & James Robinson, *Why Nations Fail: The Origins of Power, Prosperity, and Poverty* (2012). There have been some notable exceptions. Francis Fukuyama is attentive to culture, religion, and other social factors in addition to political and economic factors in *The Origins of Political Order* (2011) and *Political Order and Political Decay* (2014).

7. John Dewey, *The Public and Its Problems* 148 (Swallow Press, 1954).

8. James T. Kloppenberg, *Toward Democracy: The Struggle for Self-Rule in European and American Thought* 4 (2016).

9. Ganesh Sitaraman, *The Crisis of the Middle-Class Constitution: Why Economic Inequality Threatens Our Republic* (2017); Theodore Roosevelt, "Two Noteworthy Books on Democracy," *Outlook*, Nov. 18, 1914, at 650–651.

10. Hanna Fenichel Pitkin, *The Concept of Representation* 60–143 (1967) (distinguishing between representation as "standing for" and "acting for"). For other typologies, see Philip Pettit, "Varieties of Public Representation," in *Political Representation* 61, 65 (Ian Shapiro et al. eds., 2009) (arguing that representation can be indicative, directed, and interpretive); Monica Brito Vieira & David Runciman, *Representation* x (2008) (defining three types of representation: where representatives are told what to do, decide what to do, or copy what to do); Quentin Skinner, "Hobbes on Representation," 13 *European Journal of Philosophy* 155, 156–157, 168–169, 172–174 (2005) (classifying representation as juridical, theatrical, and pictorial). John Adams, Letter to John Penn, Jan. 1776, in *IV The Works of John Adams* 203, 205 (Charles Francis Adams, ed., 1851).

11. Amy Chua, "Tribal World," *Foreign Affairs* (July/Aug. 2018).

12. Sitaraman, *Crisis of the Middle-Class Constitution*, at 52–53; Ganesh Sitaraman, "Economic Inequality and Constitutional Democracy," in *Constitutional Democracy in Crisis?* (Mark A. Graber, Sanford Levinson & Mark Tushnet, eds., 2018).

13. Francis Fukuyama, *Identity* 130 (2018).

CHAPTER 6: UNITED DEMOCRACY

1. An arresting account of the tension between liberalism and democracy is Chantal Mouffe, "Carl Schmitt and the Paradox of Liberal Democracy," 39–40, in *The Challenge of Carl Schmitt* (Chantal Mouffe, ed., 1999), and particularly so given Schmitt's overall corpus.

2. Jacob T. Levy, "Beyond Publius: Montesquieu, Liberal Republicanism, and the Small-Republic Thesis," 27 *History of Political Thought* 50 (Spring 2006); Montesquieu, *The Spirit of the Laws* I.16 (Cambridge University Press, 1989).

3. *Federalist* No. 10 (Madison) (Clinton Rossiter, ed., 1999); Ganesh Sitaraman, *The Crisis of the Middle-Class Constitution* 102–103 (2017).

4. Lilliana Mason, *Uncivil Agreement: How Politics Became Our Identity* 25 (2018).

5. For a critique of the ethics of a liberal procedural republic, see Michael J. Sandel, *Democracy's Discontent: America in Search of a Public Philosophy* (1996).

6. On Bacon's Rebellion, see Edmund S. Morgan, *American Slavery, American Freedom* 328 (2003).

7. C. Vann Woodward, *Tom Watson: Agrarian Rebel* 220, 221, 238–240 (1963) (1938).

8. Martin Luther King Jr., Address at the Conclusion of the Selma to Montgomery, Mar. 25, 1965, https://kinginstitute.stanford.edu/king-papers/documents/address-conclusion-selma-montgomery-march; Woodward, *Tom Watson*, at 370–372, 432.

9. Bob Herbert, "An Empty Apology," *New York Times*, July 18, 2005; Rick Perlstein, "Exclusive: Lee Atwater's Infamous 1981 Interview on the Southern Strategy," *Nation*, Nov. 13, 2012, https://www.thenation.com/article/exclusive-lee-atwaters-infamous-1981-interview-southern-strategy/.

10. Al From, *The New Democrats and the Return to Power* 73–74 (2013).

11. Ta-Nehisi Coates, "Why Precisely Is Bernie Sanders against Reparations?," *Atlantic*, Jan. 19, 2016, https://www.theatlantic.com/politics/archive/2016/01/bernie-sanders-reparations/424602/.

12. David Weigel, "Clinton in Nevada: 'Not Everything Is about an Economic Theory,'" *Washington Post*, Feb. 13, 2016.

13. Asad Haider, *Mistaken Identity: Race and Class in the Age of Trump* 9–10 (2018); Zach Carter, "Clinton Aide: Protestors Don't Want $15 an Hour," *Huffington Post*, https://www.huffingtonpost.com/entry/trump-protesters-15-hour_us_58a1efe1e4b03df370d8db2b.

14. Martin Luther King Jr., "My Pilgrimage to Nonviolence," Sept. 1, 1958, https://kinginstitute.stanford.edu/king-papers/documents/my-pilgrimage-nonviolence.

15. Raina Lipsitz, "Alexandria Ocasio-Cortez Fights the Power," *Nation*, June 22, 2018, https://www.thenation.com/article/alexandria-ocasio-cortez-fights-power/.

16. Haider, *Mistaken Identity*, at 7–9.

17. Yuval Levin, "Taking the Long Way," *First Things*, Oct. 2014, https://www.firstthings.com/article/2014/10/taking-the-long-way; Patrick Deneen, *Why Liberalism Failed* (2018). On soulcraft, see, e.g., Sandel, *Democracy's Discontent*, at 319–321.

18. Yuval Levin, "Blinded by Nostalgia," *First Things*, Oct. 23, 2014, http://www.firstthings.com/web-exclusives/2014/10/blinded-by-nostalgia.

19. Andrew J. Cherlin & Judith A. Seltzer, "Family Complexity, the Family Safety Net, and Public Policy," 654 *Annals of the American Academy of Political and Social Science* 231 (2014); Sara McLanahan, "Family Instability and Complexity after a Nonmarital Birth," at 119, in *Social Class and Changing Families in an Unequal America* (Marcia J. Carlson & Paula England, eds., 2011).

20. Andrew J. Cherlin, "The Real Reason Rich People Marry," *New York Times*, Dec. 6, 2014; Andrew J. Cherlin, "In the Season of Marriage, a Question. Why Bother?" *New York Times*, Apr. 27, 2013; Kathryn Edin & Maria Kefalas, *Promises I Can Keep: Why Poor Women Put Motherhood Before Marriage* (2005).

21. Kara Gotsch, "Families and Mass Incarceration," The Sentencing Project, Apr. 24, 2018, https://www.sentencingproject.org/publications/6148/; Ta-Nehisi Coates, "The Black Family in the Age of Mass Incarceration," *Atlantic* (Oct. 2015).

22. Levin, "Taking the Long Way" (citing Tocqueville on the importance of local institutions and the "habits of freedom"); Robert D. Putnam, *Bowling Alone: The Collapse and Revival of American Community* (2000).

23. Walter Lippmann, *Drift and Mastery: An Attempt to Diagnose the Current Unrest* (centennial ed., 2015) (1914).

24. Justin Fox, "Why German Corporate Boards Include Workers," *Bloomberg*, Aug. 24, 2018; Jan Schwartz & Andreas Cremer, "VW Works Council Says Will Pursue Labor Representation at U.S. Plant," *Reuters*, Feb 16, 2014; Ned Resnikoff, "How Tenn. Politicians Killed Volkswagen Unionization," MSNBC, Apr. 14, 2014. In the American context, the term used was *industrial democracy*. See Sitaraman, *Middle-Class Constitution*, at 179.

25. Levin, "Taking the Long Way."

26. Barry Friedman & Maria Ponomarenko, "Democratic Policing," 90 N.Y.U. *Law Review* 1827, 1829–1830 (2015).

27. Friedman & Ponomarenko, "Democratic Policing," at 1830–31, 1844–1846.

28. Friedman & Ponomarenko, "Democratic Policing," at 1875, and generally.

29. United States Government, Fourth National Climate Assessment (2018), https://nca2018.globalchange.gov/chapter/14/.

30. See, e.g., Rhiana Gunn-Wright & Robert Hockett, "The Green New Deal," New Consensus (Feb. 2019).

31. "If National Service Is So Good, Everyone Should Do It," *Economist*, July 5, 2018.

32. Federal Reserve, Consumer Credit Outstanding, G.19, https://www.federalreserve.gov/releases/g19/HIST/cc_hist_memo_levels.html.

33. Suzanne Mettler, "The Creation of the GI Bill of Rights of 1944: Melding Social and Participatory Citizenship Ideals," 17 *Journal of Policy History* 345, 345 (2005); see also Michael J. Bennett, *When Dreams Came True: The GI Bill and the Making of Modern America* 7–8, 198–199 (1996); Theda Skocpol, "The G.I. Bill and U.S. Social Policy, Past and Future," 14 *Social Philosophy and Policy* 95, 98–99 (1997); Staff of Subcommittee on Education and Health of the Joint Economic Committee, 100th Congress, "A Cost-Benefit Analysis of Government Investment in Post-Secondary Education under the World War II GI Bill" 10 (Comm. Print 1988), reprinted in *The Future of Head Start: Hearing before the*

Subcommittee on Education and Health of the Joint Economic Committee 101st Congress 92–113 (1990).

34. Christopher Zara, "The Most Important Law in Tech Has a Problem," *Wired*, Jan. 3, 2017, https://www.wired.com/2017/01/the-most-important-law-in-tech-has-a-problem/; Derek Khanna, "The Law That Gave Us the Modern Internet—and the Campaign to Kill It," *Atlantic*, Sept. 12, 2013, https://www.theatlantic.com/business/archive/2013/09/the-law-that-gave-us-the-modern-internet-and-the-campaign-to-kill-it/279588/; Danielle Keats Citron & Benjamin Wittes, "The Internet Will Not Break: Denying Bad Samaritans §230 Immunity," 86 *Fordham Law Review* 401, 404–405 (2017).

35. Leonard Downie Jr. & Michael Schudson, "The Reconstruction of American Journalism," *Columbia Journalism Review* (Nov./Dec. 2009); Robert Kuttner & Hildy Zenger, "Saving the Free Press from Private Equity," *American Prospect*, Dec. 27, 2017; Richard Johns, *Spreading the News: The American Postal System from Franklin to Morse* 37 (1998); Geoffrey Cowan & David Westphal, "Public Policy and Funding the News," 1, USC Annenberg Center on Communication Leadership & Policy, Jan. 2010.

36. Some commentators have called for a National Endowment for Journalism, but the terms of their proposal are far different. Bruce Ackerman & Ian Ayres, "A National Endowment for Journalism," *Guardian*, Feb. 13, 2009 ("In contrast to current proposals, we do not rely on public or private do-gooders to dole out money to their favourite journalists. Each national endowment would subsidise investigations on a strict mathematical formula based on the number of citizens who actually read their reports on news sites.").

37. Federal Communications Commission, "Broadcast Incentive Auction and Post-Auction Transition," https://www.fcc.gov/about-fcc/fcc-initiatives/incentive-auctions.

38. Rasmus Kleis Nielsen with Geert Linnebank, "Public Support for the Media: A Six-Country Overview of Direct and Indirect Subsidies" 4, Reuters Institute for the Study of Journalism, Aug. 2011. In dollars, it is $7.6 per capita.

39. Lee C. Bollinger, "Journalism Needs Government Help," *Wall Street Journal*, July 14, 2010.

40. Lucy E. Salyer, *Laws Harsh as Tigers: Chinese Immigrants and the Shaping of Modern Immigration Law* 3 (1995); Hiroshi Motomura, *Americans in Waiting: The Lost Story of Immigration and Citizenship in the United States* 8–9, 191–194 (2006).

41. Motomura, *Americans in Waiting*, at 19–20; Jason Lange & Yeganeh Torbati, "U.S. Foreign-Born Population Swells to Highest in over a Century," *Reuters*, Sept. 13, 2018.

42. Border Security, Economic Opportunity, and Immigration Modernization Act of 2013, S.744; United States Senate, Roll Call Vote, 113th Congress, 1st Session, https://www.senate.gov/legislative/LIS/roll_call_lists/roll_call_vote_cfm.cfm?&congress=113&session=1&vote=00168; Dara Lind, "The Basics of the US

Immigration System: What Was the Immigration Reform Bill the Senate Passed in 2013," *Vox*, Aug. 4, 2015, https://www.vox.com/cards/immigration-immigrants -reform-us/what-is-the-senate-immigration-reform-bill.

43. Government of Canada, "Syrian Refugee Resettlement Initiative— Looking to the Future," https://www.canada.ca/en/immigration-refugees-citizen ship/services/refugees/welcome-syrian-refugees/looking-future.html; Jodi Kantor & Catrin Einhorn, "Canadians Adopted Refugee Families for a Year. Then Came 'Month 13,'" *New York Times*, Mar. 25, 2017.

CHAPTER 7: ECONOMIC DEMOCRACY

1. Ganesh Sitaraman, *The Crisis of the Middle-Class Constitution: Why Economic Inequality Threatens Our Republic* 69, 111–114 (2017).

2. Sitaraman, *Middle-Class Constitution*, at 113.

3. See generally Sitaraman, *Middle-Class Constitution*, at 174–185; K. Sabeel Rahman, *Democracy against Domination* (2016).

4. Sitaraman, *Middle-Class Constitution*, at 137–138, 147–149.

5. Naomi Lamoreaux, *The Great Merger Movement in American Business, 1895–1904* (1985). The case was *Standard Oil Co. of New Jersey v. United States*, 22 U.S. 1 (1911).

6. Jack Nickas, "Airline Consolidation Hits Smaller Cities Hardest," *Wall Street Journal*, Sept. 10, 2015, http://www.wsj.com/articles/airline-consolidation -hits-smaller-cities-hardest-1441912457#:M1ZMKtAVWk5eBA; Nathan Bomey, "Walgreens in $17.2B Deal to Acquire Rite Aid," *USA Today*, Oct. 28, 2015, http://www.usatoday.com/story/money/2015/10/27/walgreens-rite-aid/7468 4642/; Christopher Leonard, "How the Meat Industry Keeps Chicken Prices High," *Slate*, Mar. 3, 2014, http://www.slate.com/articles/life/food/2014/03/meat _racket_excerpt_how_tyson_keeps_chicken_prices_high.html; William A. Gal- ston & Clara Hendrickson, "A Policy at Peace with Itself: Antitrust Remedies for our Concentrated, Uncompetitive Economy," *Brookings*, Jan. 5, 2018, https:// www.brookings.edu/research/a-policy-at-peace-with-itself-antitrust-remedies-for -our-concentrated-uncompetitive-economy/#_edn6; Joseph E. Stiglitz, "Amer- ica Has a Monopoly Problem—and It's Huge," *Nation*, Oct. 23, 2017, https://www .thenation.com/article/america-has-a-monopoly-problem-and-its-huge/; Noah Smith, "Monopolies Are Worse Than We Thought," *Bloomberg*, Feb. 15, 2017, https:// www.bloomberg.com/view/articles/2017-02-15/monopolies-are-worse-than-we -thought; Virgil, "Protecting American Sovereignty against Big Tech's Glo- balist Corporate Power," *Breitbart*, Aug. 24, 2017, http://www.breitbart.com /big-government/2017/08/24/virgil-protecting-american-sovereignty-big-techs -globalist-corporate-power/; *The Economist*, "Too Much of a Good Thing," Mar. 26, 2016, https://www.economist.com/news/briefing/21695385-profits-are-too -high-america-needs-giant-dose-competition-too-much-good-thing.

7. John Kwoka, *Mergers, Merger Control, and Remedies: A Retrospective Analysis of U.S. Policy* (2014); Lina Khan & Sandeep Vaheesan, "Market Power and Inequality: The Antitrust Counterrevolution and Its Discontents," 11 *Harvard Law and Policy Review* 235 (2017); Jose Azar, Ioana Elena Marinescu & Marshall Steinbaum, "Labor Market Concentration," https://papers .ssrn.com/sol3/papers.cfm?abstract_id=3088767; Ian Hathaway & Robert E. Litan, "What's Driving the Decline in the Firm Formation Rate? A Partial Explanation," Economic Studies, *Brookings*, Nov. 20, 2014, https://www.brookings.edu /wp-content/uploads/2016/06/driving_decline_firm_formation_rate_hathaway _litan.pdf.

8. For discussions, see, e.g., Zephyr Teachout & Lina M. Khan, "Market Structure and Political Law: A Taxonomy of Power," 9 *Duke Journal of Constitutional Law and Public Policy* 37 (2014); Sitaraman, *Middle-Class Constitution*.

9. Rebecca Haw, "Amicus Briefs and the Sherman Act: Why Antitrust Needs a New Deal," 89 *Texas Law Review* 1247 (2011).

10. Ganesh Sitaraman & Ariel Dobkin, "The Case against Multimember Commissions," *Administrative Law Review* (forthcoming 2019).

11. Daniel A. Crane, *The Institutional Structure of Antitrust Enforcement* 42–46 (2011).

12. As an example, see Lina Khan, "Amazon's Antitrust Paradox," 126 *Yale Law Journal* 564 (2017).

13. For more along these lines on both the arc of antitrust law and potential reforms to antitrust, see Ganesh Sitaraman, "Taking Antitrust Away from the Courts," Great Democracy Initiative, Sept. 2018. This section is based on this paper.

14. Bloomberg News, "Apple's Tim Cook Calls for More Regulations on Data Privacy," *Bloomberg*, Mar. 23, 2018; Nicholas Thompson, "Mark Zuckerberg Talks to Wired about Facebook's Privacy Problem," *Wired*, Mar. 21, 2018.

15. Khan, "Amazon's Antitrust Paradox," at 780–783.

16. Conor Dougherty, "Yelp's Six-Year Grudge against Google," *New York Times*, July 1, 2017; Mark Scott, "Google Fined Record $2.7 Billion in E.U. Antitrust Hearing," *New York Times*, June 27, 2017; Charles Duhigg, "The Case against Google," *New York Times Magazine*, Feb 20, 2018.

17. This hypothetical is a modification of *United States v. Terminal R.R. Ass'n*, 224 U.S. 383 (1912). For a description of the doctrine, see *MCI v. AT&T*, 708 F.2d 1081, 1132–1133 (7th Cir., 1983). There is some debate over its applicability given the Supreme Court's decision in *Verizon Comm's v. Law Offices of Curtis V. Trinko, LLP*, 540 U.S. 398 (2004).

18. For overviews of this body of law, including the English inheritance, see, e.g., Joseph William Singer, "No Right to Exclude: Public Accommodations and Private Property," 90 *Northwestern University Law Review* 1283 (1996); Alfred Avins, "What Is a Place of 'Public' Accommodation?," 52 *Marquette Law Review* 1, 1–7 (1968).

19. For an overview, see Peter W. Huber et al., *Telecommunications Law* (2d. ed., 1999); Richard A. Epstein, "Common Carriers," *New Palgrave Dictionary of Economics and the Law* (1998).

20. For discussions of the separation principle, see Tim Wu, *The Master Switch* (2010); Lina M. Khan, "The Separation of Platforms and Commerce," *Columbia Law Review* (forthcoming 2019).

21. The FTC's authority under Section 5 is broader than the antitrust laws. *FTC v. Sperry & Hutchinson Trading Stamp Co.*, 405 U.S. 233 (1972).

22. On the kill zone, see Ashley Schechter, "Google and Facebook's 'Kill Zone': 'We've Taken the Focus Off of Rewarding Genius and Innovation to Rewarding Capital and Scale," *ProMarket*, May 25, 2018. This section is based on Ganesh Sitaraman, "Regulating Tech Platforms: A Blueprint for Reform," Great Democracy Initiative, May 2018.

23. David Dayen, "Ban Targeted Advertising," *New Republic*, April 10, 2018.

24. Gautam Mukunda, "The Price of Wall Street's Power," *Harvard Business Review*, June 2014, https://hbr.org/2014/06/the-price-of-wall-streets-power; Thomas Philippon & Ariell Reshef, "Wages and Human Capital in the U.S. Finance Industry, 1909–2006," 127 *Quarterly Journal of Economics* 1551 (2012).

25. This section draws upon Ganesh Sitaraman, "The Case for Glass Steagall Act, the Depression-Era Law We Need Today," *Guardian*, June 16, 2018. For a general discussion of some of these issues, see also Ganesh Sitaraman, "Unbundling 'Too Big to Fail,'" Center for American Progress, July 15, 2014.

26. Morgan Ricks, John Crawford & Lev Menand, "Central Banking for All: A Public Option for Bank Accounts," Great Democracy Initiative, June 2018; Morgan Ricks, John Crawford & Lev Menand, "A Public Option for Bank Accounts (Or Central Banking for All)," https://papers.ssrn.com/sol3/papers.cfm?abstract_id=3192162.

27. Federal Deposit Insurance Corporation, "2017 FDIC National Survey of Unbanked and Underbanked Households," Oct. 2018, www.fdic.gov/householdsurvey/2017/2017report.pdf; John Caskey, *Fringe Banking* (1994).

28. Delaware Division of Corporations, "2016 Annual Report," https://corp.delaware.gov/2016AnnualReport.pdf.

29. Walter Lippmann, *Drift and Mastery* 35 (centennial ed. 2015) (1914).

30. Michael C. Jensen & William H. Meckling, "Theory of the Firm: Managerial Behavior, Agency Costs, and Ownership Structure," 3 *Journal of Financial Economics* 305 (Oct. 1976); Lynn Stout, *The Shareholder Value Myth* (2012).

31. William Lazonick, "Profits without Prosperity," *Harvard Business Review*, Sept. 2014, https://hbr.org/2014/09/profits-without-prosperity; Lawrence Mishel & Jessica Schieder, "CEO Pay Remains High Relative to the Pay of Typical Workers and High-Wage Earners," Economic Policy Institute, July 20, 2017, https://www.epi.org/publication/ceo-pay-remains-high-relative-to-the-pay-of-typical-workers-and-high-wage-earners/; Rob Wile, "The Richest 10% of Americans

Now Own 84% of All Stocks," *Time*, Dec. 19, 2017, http://time.com/money /5054009/stock-ownership-10-percent-richest/.

32. Sitaraman, *Middle-Class Constitution*, at 147–149, 179–180; Louis D. Brandeis, "Testimony before the Commission on Industrial Relations," Jan. 23, 1915, in *Brandeis on Democracy* 99 (Philippa Strum, ed., 1995).

33. Larry Mishel, Elise Gould & Josh Bivens, "Wage Stagnation in Nine Charts," Figure 9, Economic Policy Institute, Jan. 6, 2015.

34. Theodore Roosevelt, Eighth Annual Message, Dec. 8, 1908, in *State Papers as Governor and President, 1899–1909* 495–496 (Hermann Hagedorn, ed., 1925); Office of US senator Elizabeth Warren, press release: "Warren Introduces Accountable Capitalism Act," Aug. 15, 2018.

35. Brishen Rogers & Kate Andrias, "Rebuilding Worker Voice in Today's Economy," at 24–25, Roosevelt Institute, Aug. 9, 2018; Joel Rogers & Wolfgang Streeck, eds., *Works Councils: Consultation, Representation, and Cooperation in Industrial Relations* (1995); 29 U.S.C. 158(a)(2) (2018); Electromation, Inc. 309 N.L.R.B. 990 (1992).

36. Rogers & Andrias, "Rebuilding Worker Voice," at 26–33.

37. For a thorough account of public options, see Ganesh Sitaraman & Anne L. Alstott, *The Public Option: How to Expand Freedom, Increase Opportunity, and Promote Equality* (2019).

38. Federal Communications Commission, "2016 Broadband Progress Report," Jan. 29, 2016, https://www.fcc.gov/reports-research/reports/broadband -progress-reports/2016-broadband-progress-report; Federal Communications Commission, "Internet Access Services: Status as of June 30, 2016," Apr. 2017, http://transition.fcc.gov/Daily_Releases/Daily_Business/2017/db0503/DOC -344499A1.pdf. The data on neighborhoods are for developed census blocks.

39. Executive Office of the President, "Community-Based Broadband Solutions," Jan. 2015, at 14, https://obamawhitehouse.archives.gov/sites /default/files/docs/community-based_broadband_report_by_executive_office_of _the_president.pdf; Electric Power Board, Internet, https://epb.com/home-store /internet (offering 1 Gigabyte download speed internet for $67.99); Electric Power Board, Press Release: EPB Fiber Optics Reaches Milestone of Serving 100,000+ Customers, Oct. 19, 2018; Edward Wyatt, "Fast Internet Is Chattanooga's New Locomotive," *New York Times*, Feb. 3, 2014, https://www.nytimes.com/2014/02 /04/technology/fast-internet-service-speeds-business-development-in-chattanooga .html?mcubz=0; Dominic Rushe, "Chattanooga's Gig: How One City's Super-Fast Internet Is Driving a Tech Boom," *Guardian*, Aug. 30, 2014, https://www .theguardian.com/world/2014/aug/30/chattanooga-gig-high-speed-internet-tech -boom.

40. Alicia H. Munnell, Wenliang Hou & Geoffrey T. Sanzenbacher, "National Retirement Risk Index Shows Modest Improvement in 2016," Center for Retirement Research at Boston College, Jan. 2018; CBS News, "Nearly One-Quarter of Americans Say They'll Never Retire, According to New Poll," July 8, 2019; Stan

Haithcock, "You Just Gave Your Annuity Agent a Great Vacation," *MarketWatch*, Aug. 12, 2014; Council of Economic Advisors, "The Effects of Conflicted Investment Advice on Retirement Savings," White House, Feb. 2015.

41. Steven R. Weisman, *The Great Tax Wars* 3 (2002) (quoting Holmes); Tax Policy Center, "Historical Highest Marginal Income Tax Rates, 1913–2017," https://www.taxpolicycenter.org/statistics/historical-highest-marginal-income-tax-rates.

42. Tax Policy Center, "Historical Capital Gains and Taxes, 1954–2014," https://www.taxpolicycenter.org/statistics/historical-capital-gains-and-taxes. The rate increased in the 1970s from 25 percent to 39.9 percent before dropping ultimately to 15 percent during the George W. Bush administration. During the Obama presidency, the rate increased back to 25 percent; Seth Hanlon & Sarah Ayres Steinberg, "Loopholes in the Estate Tax Show Why Revenue Must Be on the Table," Center for American Progress, Jan. 24, 2013; Tax Policy Center, "Taxable Estate Tax Returns as a Percentage of Adult Deaths, Selected Years of Death, 1934–2011," Nov. 30, 2011; Thomas L. Hungerford, "Corporate Tax Rates and Economic Growth since 1947," Economic Policy Institute, June 4, 2013, https://www.epi.org/publication/ib364-corporate-tax-rates-and-economic-growth/.

43. My mapping here broadly follows Reuven S. Avi-Yonah, "The Three Goals of Taxation," 60 *Tax Law Review* 1 (2007).

44. Reuven S. Avi-Yonah, "Why Tax the Rich? Efficiency, Equity, and Progressive Taxation," 111 *Yale Law Journal* 1391, 1412, 1406 (2002) (reviewing *Does Atlas Shrug? The Economic Consequences of Taxing the Rich* (Joel B. Slemrod, ed., 2000)).

45. Paul Krugman, "The Economics of Soaking the Rich," *New York Times*, Jan. 5, 2019; David Dayen, "Elizabeth Warren Proposes Annual Wealth Tax on Ultra-Millionaires," *Intercept*, Jan. 24, 2019.

46. Jefferson to Adams, Oct. 28, 1813, in *The Adams-Jefferson Letters* 389 (Lester J. Cappon, ed., 1959); Eric Nelson, *The Greek Tradition in Republican Thought* 232 (2004).

47. James Madison, "Parties," *National Gazette*, Jan. 23, 1792, in *James Madison: Writings* 504 (Jack N. Rakove, ed., 1999).

48. Reuven S. Avi-Yonah, "Corporations, Society, and the State: A Defense of the Corporate Tax," 90 *Virginia Law Review* 1193, 1211 1219 (2004).

49. Gabriel Zucman, *The Hidden Wealth of Nations: The Scourge of Tax Havens* (2015). For a discussion of the global issues, see Reuven S. Avi-Yonah, Kimberly A. Clausing & Michael C. Durst, "Allocating Business Profits for Tax Purposes: A Proposal to Adopt a Formulary Profit Split," 9 *Florida Tax Review* 497 (2009).

50. This section draws on Tim Meyer & Ganesh Sitaraman, "A Blueprint for a New American Trade Policy," Great Democracy Initiative, Dec. 2018.

51. David H. Autor, David Dorn & Gordon H. Hanson, "The China Shock: Learning from Labor-Market Adjustments to Large Changes in Trade," 8 *Annual Review of Economics* 205 (2016).

52. Timothy Meyer & Ganesh Sitaraman, "It's Economic Strategy, Stupid: The Case for a Department of Economic Growth and Security," *American Affairs*, Spring 2019.

53. Alisa Chang, "A Trade Deal Read in Secret by Only a Few (or Maybe None), *NPR*, May 14, 2015; Christopher Ingraham, "Interactive: How Companies Wield Off-the-Record Influence on Obama's Trade Policy," *Washington Post*, Feb. 28, 2014.

54. Robert D. Putnam, *Our Kids: The American Dream in Crisis* (2015); Charles Murray, *Coming Apart: The State of White America 1950–2000* (2012); Bill Bishop with Robert G. Cushing, "The Big Sort: Why the Clustering of Like-Minded America Is Tearing Us Apart" (2008).

55. Phillip Longman, "Bloom and Bust," *Washington Monthly*, Nov./Dec. 2015.

56. Peter Ganong & Daniel Shoag, "Why Has Regional Income Convergence in the U.S. Declined?" 2 (Jan. 2015) (unpublished manuscript), http://scholar.harvard.edu/shoag/publications/why-has-regional-income-convergence-usdeclined; Raj Chetty et al., "Where Is the Land of Opportunity? The Geography of Intergenerational Mobility in the United States" 31, 38, 60, National Bureau of Economic Research, Working Paper No. 19, 843, 2014; Anne Case & Angus Deaton, "Mortality and Morbidity in the 21st Century," *Brookings Papers on Economic Activity* (Spring 2017); Paul Krugman, "What's the Matter with Trumpland," *New York Times*, Apr. 2, 2018, https://www.nytimes.com/2018/04/02/opinion/trumpland-economy-polarization.html. Wilson's book was William Julius Wilson, *When Work Disappears* (1996).

57. Enrico Moretti, *The New Geography of Jobs* (2012); David Schleicher, "Stuck! The Law and Economics of Residential Stagnation," 127 *Yale Law Journal* 78 (2017).

58. Benjamin Austin, Edward Glaeser & Lawrence H. Summers, "Saving the Heartland: Place-Based Policies in 21st Century America," *Brookings Papers on Economic Activity*, BPEA Conference Drafts, Mar. 8–9, 2018, at 41.

59. Benjamin Austin, Edward Glaeser & Lawrence H. Summers, "Saving the Heartland: Place-Based Policies in 21st Century America," *Brookings Papers on Economic Activity*, BPEA Conference Drafts, Mar. 8–9, 2018, at 19.

60. The Riegle-Neal Interstate Banking and Branching Efficiency Act of 1994, Pub. L. No. 103-328, 108 Stat. 2338 (1994) opened up the possibility of interstate bank branching, contra the McFadden Act, 4 Stat. 1224, 1228-29 (1927), which had been in place since the 1920s. On the theory behind Robinson-Patman and the broader shift in antitrust ideas, see Matt Stoller, "How Democrats Killed Their Populist Soul," *Atlantic*, Oct. 24, 2016.

61. For a depiction of all the New Deal projects in the country, see The Living New Deal, https://livingnewdeal.org/map/.

62. Andrew R. Goetz & Timothy M. Vowles, "The Good, the Bad, and the Ugly: 30 Years of Airline Deregulation," 17 *Journal of Transport Geography* 251, 253 (2009).

63. Andrew R. Goetz & Christopher J. Sutton, "The Geography of Deregulation in the U.S. Airline Industry," 87 *Annals of the Association of American Geographers* 238–263, 239 (1997); Goetz & Vowles, "The Good, the Bad, and the Ugly," at 251–252.

64. Phillip Longman & Lina Khan, "Terminal Sickness," *Washington Monthly*, Mar./Apr. 2012.

CHAPTER 8: POLITICAL DEMOCRACY

1. Chapman University Survey of American Fears, America's Top Fears 2017, Oct. 11, 2017, https://blogs.chapman.edu/wilkinson/2017/10/11/americas-top-fears-2017/.

2. On gun control, see Steven Shepard, "Gun Control Support Surges in the Polls," *Politico*, Feb. 28, 2018, https://www.politico.com/story/2018/02/28/gun-control-polling-parkland-430099; on Social Security, see Lake Research Partners, "Support for Medicare and Social Security," Feb. 13, 2017, https://www.ncpssm.org/wp-content/uploads/2017/02/voter-summary-22017-1.pdf; on higher taxes, see Matthew Yglesias, "Taxing the Rich Is Extremely Popular," *Vox*, Feb. 4, 2019, https://www.vox.com/2019/2/4/18210370/warren-wealth-tax-poll; on campaign finance reform, Bradley Jones, "Most Americans Want to Limit Campaign Spending, Say Big Donors Have Greater Political Influence," Pew Research, May 8, 2018, http://www.pewresearch.org/fact-tank/2018/05/08/most-americans-want-to-limit-campaign-spending-say-big-donors-have-greater-political-influence/; on climate change, see Yale Program on Climate Change Communication & George Mason University Center for Climate Change Communication, "Climate Change in the American Mind," Dec. 2018, https://climatecommunication.yale.edu/wp-content/uploads/2019/01/Climate-Change-American-Mind-December-2018.pdf.

3. Larry Bartels, *Unequal Democracy: The Political Economy of the New Gilded Age* (2010); Martin Gilens, *Affluence and Influence: Economic Inequality and Political Power in America* 1 (2012); Martin Gilens & Benjamin I. Page, "Testing Theories of American Politics: Elites, Interest Groups, and Average Citizens," 12 *Perspectives on Politics* 564 (2014).

4. Renae Merle, "Mulvaney Discloses 'Hierarchy' for Meeting Lobbyists, Saying Some Would Be Seen Only if They Paid," *Washington Post*, Apr. 25, 2018; Ganesh Sitaraman, *The Crisis of the Middle-Class Constitution: Why Economic Inequality Threatens Our Republic* 242–146, 248 (2017).

5. Kay Lehman Schlozman, Sidney Verba & Henry E. Brady, *The Unheavenly Chorus: Unequal Political Voice and the Broken Promise of American Democracy* 328–331 (2013); OpenSecrets.org, Finance, Insurance & Real Estate, Sector Profile, 2017, Center for Responsive Politics; Ben Brody, "Google, Facebook Set 2018 Lobbying Records as Tech Scrutiny Intensifies," *Bloomberg*, Jan. 22, 2019; Brian Kelleher Richter, Krislert Samphantharak & Jeffrey F. Timmons, "Lobbying and Taxes," 53 *American Journal of Political Science* 893, 907 (2009).

6. Aaron Lorenzo, "GOP Staffers Who Wrote the Tax Bill Cash in with Lobbying Gigs," *Politico*, June 4, 2018. Lee Drutman, *The Business of America Is Lobbying* (2015), insightfully describes how lobbying opportunities push staff to rely more on lobbyists.

7. Robert Rubin went to Citigroup after his time in office; Jack Lew was at Citigroup prior to government service and went into private equity afterward; Larry Summers took a position at D.E. Shaw, a hedge fund; and Tim Geithner went to Warburg Pincus, a private equity firm. On the Trump administration, see Ben Matthis-Lilley, "Swamp-Draining Trump Administration Has Hired 187 Lobbyists, New Report Finds," Mar. 7, 2018, https://slate.com/news-and-politics/2018 /03/trump-administration-has-hired-187-lobbyists-propublic-finds-swamp-much .html; Editorial, "Lobbyists Romp in Trump's Washington," *New York Times*, Jan. 21, 2018, https://www.nytimes.com/2018/01/21/opinion/lobbyists-washington -trump.html.

8. See, e.g., Jason Webb Yackee & Susan Webb Yackee, "A Bias toward Business? Assessing Interest Group Influence on the U.S. Bureaucracy," 68 *Journal of Politics* 128 (2006); Wendy E. Wagner, Katherine Barnes & Lisa Peters, "Rulemaking in the Shade: An Empirical Study of EPA's Air Toxic Emission Standards," 63 *Administrative Law Review* 99 (2011); Susan Webb Yackee, "The Politics of Ex Parte Lobbying: Pre-Proposal Agenda Building and Blocking During Agency Rulemaking," 22 *Journal of Public Administration Research and Theory* 373 (2012); Kimberly Krawiec, "Don't 'Screw Joe the Plummer': The Sausage-Making of Financial Reform," 55 *Arizona Law Review* 53 (2013); Simon F. Haeder & Susan Webb Yackee, "Influence and Administrative Process: Lobbying the U.S. President's Office of Management and Budget," 109 *American Political Science Review* 507 (2015).

9. See Elizabeth Warren, "The Corporate Capture of the Federal Courts," Speech to the American Constitution Society, June 5, 2013; Ellen Eardley & Cyrus Mehri, "Defending Twentieth Century Equal Employment Reforms in the Twenty-First Century," American Constitution Society for Law and Policy, Jan. 2013; Adam Chandler, "Cert-Stage Amicus 'All Stars': Where Are They Now?," *Scotusblog*, Apr. 4, 2013; Lee Epstein, William M. Landes & Richard A. Posner, "How Business Fares in the Supreme Court," 97 *Minnesota Law Review* 1431, 1449–1451 (2013).

10. National Vote at Home Institute, About Us, https://www.voteathome.org /about-us; David Roberts, "The Simple Voting Reform That Works Wherever It Is Tried," *Vox*, May 24, 2018.

11. Alberto Chong & Mauricio Olivera, "Does Compulsory Voting Help Equalize Incomes?," 20 *Economics and Politics* 391 (2008); Anthony Fowler, "Electoral and Policy Consequences of Voter Turnout: Evidence from Compulsory Voting in Australia," 8 *Quarterly Journal of Political Science* 159 (2013).

12. For an overview of proposals on restricting spending and on leveling up through vouchers, see Ganesh Sitaraman, "The Puzzling Absence of Economic

Power in Constitutional Theory," 101 *Cornell Law Review* 1445, 1512–1514, 1524–1526 (2016). On geographic restrictions, see Nicholas O. Stephanopoulos, "Elections and Alignment," 114 *Columbia Law Review* 283 (2014).

13. Christopher Uggen, Ryan Larson & Sarah Shannon, "6 Million Lost Voters: State-Level Estimates of Felony Disenfranchisement," *Sentencing Project*, Oct. 6, 2016, https://www.sentencingproject.org/publications/6-million-lost -voters-state-level-estimates-felony-disenfranchisement-2016/.

14. Bruce Bartlett, "Gingrich and the Destruction of Congressional Expertise," *New York Times*, Nov. 29, 2011.

15. S.3357, The Anti-Corruption and Public Integrity Act, 115th Congress (2017–2018).

16. Rohit Chopra & Julie Margetta Morgan, "Unstacking the Deck: A New Agenda to Tame Corruption in Washington," Great Democracy Initiative, May 2018, https://greatdemocracyinitiative.org/document/unstacking-the-deck-a-new -agenda-to-tame-corruption-in-washington/.

17. Daniel Epps & Ganesh Sitaraman, "How to Save the Supreme Court," *Vox*, Oct. 10, 2018; Daniel Epps & Ganesh Sitaraman, "How to Save the Supreme Court," *Yale Law Journal* (forthcoming 2019); *Janus v. American Federation of State, County, and Municipal Employees, Council 31*, 585 U.S. __, 138 S. Ct. 2448 (2018) (Kagan, J., dissenting).

CHAPTER 9: DEFENDING DEMOCRACY

1. Jeffrey Goldberg, "Hillary Clinton: 'Failure' to Help Syrian Rebels Led to the Rise of ISIS," *Atlantic*, Aug. 10, 2014.

2. Center for American Progress, Election Infrastructure: Vulnerabilities and Solutions 1, Sept. 11, 2017; Danielle Root & Liz Kennedy, "9 Solutions to Secure America's Elections" 1, Center for American Progress, Aug. 16, 2017; Cynthia McFadden, William M. Arkin & Kevin Monahan, "Russians Penetrated U.S. Voter Systems, Top U.S. Official Says," *NBC News*, Feb. 7, 2018.

3. Kim Zetter, "The Myth of the Hacker-Proof Voting Machine," *New York Times Magazine*, Feb. 21, 2018; Lawrence Norden & Andrea Cordova, "Voting Machines at Risk: Where We Stand Today," Brennan Center for Justice, Mar. 5, 2019; Danielle Root, Liz Kennedy, Michael Sozan & Jerry Parshall, "Election Security in All 50 States: Defending America's Elections" 5, Center for American Progress, Feb. 2018; Sue Halpern, "America Continues to Ignore the Risks of Election Hacking," *New Yorker*, Apr. 18, 2018; Fred Kaplan, "America's Voting Systems Are Highly Vulnerable to Hackers," *Slate*, Feb. 22, 2018.

4. Kaplan, "America's Voting Systems"; Root & Kennedy, "9 Solutions," at 1.

5. Taylor Hatmaker, "DHS and FBI Detail How Russia Is Hacking into U.S. Nuclear Facilities and Other Critical Infrastructure," *TechCrunch*, Mar. 15, 2018; Halpern, "American Continues."

6. For a similar argument, but focusing on a new force within the military, see James Stavridis, "Why the Nation Needs a US Cyber Force," *Boston Globe*, Sept. 29, 2013; James Stavridis & David Weinstein, "Time for a U.S. Cyber Force," *Proceedings Magazine* (Jan. 2014).

7. For an overview of "weaponized interdependence," albeit one that focuses more on international networks and Western power, see Henry Farrell & Abraham L. Newman, "Weaponized Interdependence," *International Security* (forthcoming). On the Chinese use of "geoeconomics," Robert D. Blackwill & Jennifer M. Harris, *War by Other Means: Geoeconomics and Statecraft* (2016), is excellent.

8. Kurt M. Campbell & Ely Ratner, "The China Reckoning: How Beijing Defied American Expectations," *Foreign Affairs*, Mar./Apr. 2018.

9. Campbell & Ratner, "The China Reckoning."

10. Aaron Friedberg, "Competing with China," 60 *Survival*, 7–64, at 40 (June/July 2018); Jordan Robertson & Michael Riley, "The Big Hack: How China Used a Tiny Chip to Infiltrate U.S. Companies," *Bloomberg Businessweek*, Oct. 4, 2018, https://www.bloomberg.com/news/features/2018-10-04/the-big-hack -how-china-used-a-tiny-chip-to-infiltrate-america-s-top-companies; Daniel Shane, "How China Gets What It Wants from American Companies," *CNNMoney*, Apr. 5, 2018; Tom Miles, "U.S. and China Clash Over 'Technology Transfer' at WTO," *Reuters*, May 28, 2018.

11. Michael McFaul, "Russia as It Is," *Foreign Affairs*, July/Aug. 2018.

12. Office of the US Trade Representative, "The People's Republic of China: U.S.-China Trade Facts," https://ustr.gov/countries-regions/china-mongolia -taiwan/peoples-republic-china.

13. North Atlantic Treaty Organization, "Origins: NATO Leaders, Lord Ismay," https://www.nato.int/cps/us/natohq/declassified_137930.htm.

14. Celeste A. Wallander, "NATO's Enemies Within," *Foreign Affairs*, July/ Aug. 2018.

15. Wallander, "NATO's Enemies Within;" Celeste A. Wallander, "Russian Transimperialism and Its Implications," *Washington Quarterly* 114 (Spring 2007).

16. Wallander, "NATO's Enemies Within."

17. James M. Lindsay, "The Case for a Concert of Democracies," 23 *Ethics & International Affairs* (Spring 2009); Ivo Daalder & Robert Kagan, "The Next Intervention," *Washington Post*, Aug. 6, 2007; Ivo H. Daalder & James Lindsay, "An Alliance of Democracies: Our Way or the Highway," *Brookings*, Nov. 6, 2004, https://www.brookings.edu/opinions/an-alliance-of-democracies-our-way -or-the-highway/; Ivo H. Daalder & James Lindsay, "An Alliance of Democracies," *Brookings*, May 23, 2004, https://www.brookings.edu/opinions/an-alliance-of -democracies/; Ivo Daalder & James Lindsay, "Democracies of the World, Unite," *American Interest* (Jan./Feb. 2007); Anne-Marie Slaughter & John Ikenberry, "Democracies Must Work in Concert," *Financial Times*, July 10, 2008.

18. Daalder & Lindsay, "Our Way or the Highway."

19. John Stuart Mill, "A Few Words on Non-Intervention" (1859); Michael Walzer, "The Moral Standing of States," 9 *Philosophy and Public Affairs* 209 (Spring 1980).

20. Ganesh Sitaraman, "Progressive Pragmatism," *American Interest*, Apr. 20, 2014.

CONCLUSION: THE POLITICS OF ACHIEVING A GREAT DEMOCRACY

1. Niccolo Machiavelli, *The Prince* 23 (trans. Harvey Mansfield, 2d ed., 1998).

2. Mark Tushnet, "Constitutional Hardball," 37 *John Marshall Law Review* 523 (2004); Joseph Fishkin & David E. Pozen, "Asymmetric Constitutional Hardball," 118 *Columbia Law Review* 915 (2018).

3. Miriam Seifter, "Judging Power-Plays in the American States" (draft on file with the author).

4. Stephen Skowronek, *The Politics Presidents Make* (1993).

5. Frederick Douglass, Speech on West India Emancipation, Canandaigua, New York, Aug. 3, 1857.

INDEX

INDEX

national health care, 50

National Labor Relations Act, 149

nationalism, 71–72

nationalist oligarchy, 6, 70–82, 83;
aggressive economic influence, 198;
definition, 59; great democracy
vs., 207; less representative, 188;
political hardball, 206

nationalist populism, 5, 59, 67–70, 83

negative liberty, 29–30

neoconservatives, 40–42

neoliberalism: austerity, 24–26;
definition, 10–11, 216n2;
democracy vs., 32–33, 87–91;
deregulation, 16–18; deregulation,
liberalization, privatization, and
austerity (DLPA), 16–26, 217n12;
embrace of individualism, 47–48;
foreign policy, 48–49; freedom,
29–33; great democracy vs., 93–94;
Great Recession (2008), 45–46;
identity politics, 48; individualism,
28–29; intellectual origins of,
11–16; liberalization, 18–22;
nudging, 53–55; during Obama
administration, 50–52; oligarchy,
92; post-, 59–60; privatization,
22–24; and Reagan, Ronald,
9–10, 34; rejections of collective
society, 27, 28; stages of, 55–57;
structural domination, 31–32;
technocratic ideology, 51–53; Third
Way, 36–38, 39

neoliberalism era, 3–5, 8

New Deal, 116–117, 172

New Deal Liberalism, 2

New Democrats, 35–36

Niskanen, William, 55

Nixon, Richard, 2, 19

Nobel Peace Prize, 194

norms and institutions, 84–87

North Atlantic Treaty Organization
(NATO), 197, 198–199, 200, 201

North Korea, 83–84

Northen, William, 99

Norway, 75, 194

nudging, 53–55

Obama, Barack: capital gains,
235n42; foreign policy, 43, 189;
individualism, 28; neoliberalism, 4,
50–52; trade policy, 164

Obamacare, 50, 78, 156

Ocasio-Cortez, Alexandria, 92,
103–104, 161, 210

Office of Information and Regulatory
Affairs, 178, 185

oligarchy, 70–82, 92

Orbán, Viktor, 73–75, 80

Patriot Corps, 114–117

Pei, Minxin, 75

Perriello, Tom, 51

Peters, Charles, 63

Pettit, Philip, 227n10

Pildes, Richard, 54

Pinochet, Augusto, 33

Pitkin, Hanna Fenichel, 90, 227n10

place-based policies, 169

Polanyi, Karl, 19

police, 111–113

political change, 1–2

political democracy, 87–88, 175–179;
congressional reforms, 183–184;
defense of, 190, 191; economic
democracy, 89–90; electoral reforms,
179–183; executive branch reforms,
184–185; judicial reforms, 185–188;
lobbying, 177–178

political economy, 70

Ganesh Sitaraman is chancellor faculty fellow, professor of law, and director of the Program in Law and Government at Vanderbilt Law School. Author of *The Crisis of the Middle-Class Constitution*, a 2017 *New York Times* Notable Book, he lives in Nashville, Tennessee.